WHAT PEOPLE ARE

NIGHT OF THE

The *Night of the World* seamlessly weaves through complex philosophical conjunctions and cultural practices in order to articulate a theory of ideology for today's world. Smecker argues that objectivity has become the prevailing ideological form, but he refuses to surrender the terrain of objectivity to ideology. His book is a struggle against this ideological structure in an effort to reclaim a new mode of objectivity that has its basis in the contradictions of subjectivity. It provides a thorough overview of the ways that contemporary ideology penetrates into our being and proffers a political antidote.

**Todd McGowan**, author of *Enjoying What We Don't Have: The Political Project of Psychoanalysis*

With this profound, provocative, difficult, and important book, Frank Smecker delivers a much needed kick in the pants to Western Philosophy. Thank you, Frank, for your courage.

**Derrick Jensen**

An original, truly refreshing endeavour to situate objectivity at the level of ideology. Smecker makes use of Žižek's trademark blend of Hegel and Lacan to delve into, unpack and reconfigure what we regard as "objective" reality. More importantly, he reminds us that any blind acceptance of objectivity today equals serving the interests of capital and feeding the criminal divisions it produces.

**Fabio Vighi**, Co-director of the Žižek Centre for Ideology Critique at Cardiff University, UK

# Night of
# the World

Traversing the Ideology of Objectivity

# Night of the World

Traversing the Ideology of Objectivity

Frank Smecker

Winchester, UK
Washington, USA

First published by Zero Books, 2014
Zero Books is an imprint of John Hunt Publishing Ltd., Laurel House, Station Approach,
Alresford, Hants, SO24 9JH, UK
office1@jhpbooks.net
www.johnhuntpublishing.com
www.zero-books.net

For distributor details and how to order please visit the 'Ordering' section on our website.

Text copyright: Frank Smecker 2013

ISBN: 978 1 78279 180 5

A CIP catalogue record for this book is available from the British Library.

Design: Stuart Davies

Printed in the USA by Edwards Brothers Malloy

We operate a distinctive and ethical publishing philosophy in all areas of our business, from our global network of authors to production and worldwide distribution.

# CONTENTS

Gentlemen! We find ourselves in an important epoch, in a fermentation, in which Spirit has made a leap forward, has gone beyond its previous concrete form and acquired a new one. The whole mass of ideas and concepts that have been current until now, the very bonds of the world, are dissolved and collapsing into themselves like a vision in a dream. A new emergence of Spirit is at hand; philosophy must be the first to hail its appearance and recognize it, while others, resisting impotently, adhere to the past, and the majority unconsciously constitute the matter in which it makes its appearance. But philosophy, in recognizing it as what is eternal, must pay homage to it.

—Hegel, *Lectures at Jena* of 1806, final speech

# Preface:

## In which the premises will eventually come out...

In that minor text of Jack D. Forbes', *Columbus and Other Cannibals*, the author addresses the Cree notion of "Wétiko", a term that denotes the cannibal, or, to be more precise, 'diabolical wickedness or cannibalism.'[1] Forbes extends the application of this term to define a sort of "spiritual sickness"—a "disease," he avers, that has infected much of the West, a disease he equates to civilization itself, one that *drives* the infected toward excess consumption of others, human and nonhuman alike. Does this idea not call forth today's fashionable image of the zombie, that mythical figure representing the obscene horror of the "living dead" which, unable to be satiated, persists according to some sort of blind automatism? What, exactly, is being expressed through such a cadaverous and stygian archetype? As philosopher, cultural theorist and psychoanalyst Slavoj Žižek repeatedly informs us, the answer to this strange enigma is to be found in the Freudian notion of *death-drive*, a too-human dimension of radical negativity, a "blind automatism" of repetition that exceeds self-preservation, that profanely transcends the relationship between humankind and environment, law and order, and so on. One would be mistaken, however, to fully associate the notion of Wétiko with the parasitic nature of reason, *logos*, language, the indestructible insistence of man's libido; that uncanny excess of life characterized by an obtrusive *drive* to repeat past traumas and transgress predefined limits in both nature and society. This drive, that which is more (in)human than the human itself, infects us all until death, to paraphrase the philosopher Hegel; it is what defines the suffering we are often told is endemic to, if not distinctive of, the "human condition" (*frugality is no fun, but excess is misery*). We are thus not only alienated from nature but from ourselves too—our "inner-worlds" are alien, they *insist* beyond just mere bodily existence, to the point of exceeding physical limits: For how is it that, the stuff of mind, thought itself, can elude physical measurement while yet, it controls our physical bodies—especially when anything that is able to budge something physical is itself supposed to be physical, too? No less important, our thoughts are always *about* something other than the empty framework of thought itself, our desires often the desire of (the Other's) Desire.

And what of the occurrence of thought itself—thought *without* any external object, an experience of radical self-withdrawal—subjective alienation; the human reduced solely to the "abyssal point of thinking," a purely formal emptiness as such? According to that medial figure in the development of German Idealism, Friedrich Schelling, before becoming the rational medium of the world the subject is, at its very basis, an "infinite lack of being" *("unendliche Mangel an Sein")*. This interminable, immutable lack of being, a withdrawal from the world itself by which the existence of reality is suspended to mere illusion, describes what is known well in psychoanalysis as "psychotic withdrawal." In his essay "The Three Events of Philosophy," Žižek raises an excellent point: Does this withdrawal-into-self, a *madness* as such, not also bespeak of the human's departure from its natural environment—thereby designating the end of the animal self and thus marking the emergence of "humanization"?[2] In other words, this withdrawal-into-self, this sundering of the link between humanity and its natural environs (*Umwelt*) is proceeded, Žižek asserts, by the establishment of a Symbolic order, which is projected onto the subject's reality 'as a kind of substitute-formation, destined to recompense us for the loss of the immediate, pre-Symbolic real.'[3]

Madness, then, as Žižek puts it, is that inevitable "vanishing mediator," a repressed element that is crucial for the advent of a new, symbolic, framework: can we not suppose, then, that the moment of "madness" is that which designates the middle of the movement from the subject's "animal soul" to its "normal" subjectivity? Before acquiring its subjectivity, the subject must first initiate a profound retreat from immediate (raw) reality. Only then, can the necessary space for reality's symbolic configuration be opened up—a *significant* space, in the most literal sense—in which, through which and by which the subject will acquire his/her subjectivity.[4]

We are ideological beings, each and every one of us estranged from the material reality of our own specious universes.

There is no overcoming of this alienation, no escape from this horrific disjunction, this "original cleft" in nature. There is only acceptance. Ideology is, in a way, the creative result of our immutable attempts at developing this radical imbalance into expressions of how to be in the world. As such, ideology represents to us and for us our unconscious fantasies, which are reflected back to us in our lived realities in the guise of an "objective reality;" reflected in our conscious experiences /perceptions of the world *as such*. Wétiko should therefore be likened not so much to a sickness synonymous with drive, and certainly not something endemic only to Western culture and/or civilization, but rather, it should be likened precisely to the violence that inevitably ensues from a disgust at life, a disgust at *drive at its purest*; thus Wétiko should be likened to the violence that ensues from the attempt to abolish the radical imbalances around which drive incessantly circulates.[5]

Perhaps then, Wétiko should be likened to the socio-ideological metaphor of "garden," for the typical garden that comes to most peoples' minds is the one that, by its very nature, demands for the destructive removal of those "insufferable weeds," ensuring the suppression of their fullest growth and appearance for the sake of the "perfect" garden. Does this tyranny of cultivation, so to speak, an ideology of diabolical wickedness if there ever was one, not arise from the very aspiration to abolish the radical antagonism 'through which man cuts his umbilical cord with nature'?

In other words, there is no organic harmony, no natural balance we must strive to return to; belief in this ecological ideology only follows the same old logic of tyranny—Is it not the case that the world's most horrific atrocities, holocausts and mass murders were carried out in the name of harmonious being and claims to virtue? And what of those exceptions to the harmonious whole, those "intolerable, *excessive* weeds" that just won't *harmonize* with the rest of the "garden" (like the indigenous of North America after the arrival of Europeans, or the Jews in Nazi Germany, or today's slum dwellers around the world)?

In any case, what if this "spiritual sickness," Wétiko, has nothing to do with man's fissure from nature insofar as it has to do with man's vengeful attempts to repress, to abolish this cleft itself?[6] And what if the cure to this disease is to be found not in some ideal return to a sort of prelapsarian origin, not in a return to some kind of balanced state of nature, not in a *particular* ideology, but rather: in a sort of "working-things-out" in ideology itself, *and through its persistent failures?* We are, after all, ideological beings—it is our very nature to be as such: whether you're Abenaki, American, an atheist or a Jew, a pacifist or in the military, the stories you are told about the world shape the way you conceive of and thus perceive the world, and the way you perceive the world shapes how you relate to and thus behave in the world. Or, to put it differently, knowledge—what we know about the world, about reality, and so on—is structured like a dream: *all its content is contained within form, in the form of the concept.* As Poe eloquently put it, 'All that we see or seem is but a dream within a dream.' Knowledge lies in the understanding of a concept; and the nature of the concept is *never* the same as the nature of that which the concept is essentially about. Which is precisely why French psychoanalyst, Jacques Lacan, opined that "understanding" is brought to mind *only as an ideal relation.*

Nonetheless, how we conceive of the world determines how we perceive and thereby behave in the world. And the stories we are told, the stories we tell ourselves, shape and inform how we conceive of the world. Thus our knowledge will always be inherently ideological, as it ever has been.

At a subtextual level, that is what this book is about.

At a more crucial level, however, the central premise of this book drives at something endemic to the substrate of ideology per se—that objectivity is the "constitutive stuff" of ideology, and thus objectivity *is*, in this sense, ideological. And because ideology interpellates the individual, without objectivity there would be no subjectivity. To work this through our previous example: objectivity is the direct result of our "madness," of our withdrawal from the immediate world and retreat into the alien landscape of pure thought itself; it is the result of a primordial "lack-of-being," of subjective alienation. And it is by means of this withdrawal only, in which we come face to face with the immeasurable abyss of our own freedom, that we are able to open up the objective space in which, through which and by which we acquire our subjectivity, in which we can determine freely who it is and, what it is, we want *to be*. The subject is none other than the effect of objectivity as such.

What I'm suggesting is that objectivity is the most elementary ideological operation, for it symbolizes our immediate raw reality, transforming the Real as such into a symbolic totality. Looked at somewhat differently, objective reality can also be viewed as being the result of social (intersubjective) forces—its sole function is to provide and maintain the internal consistency that holds together its subjects' "reality principles," which are always-already ideologically mediated by objectivity, an elemental ideology that reveals itself as empirical fact or necessity.

In any case, this book is, to a large extent, about what we perceive and how we name it. And what a name signifies is not the thing-itself that we perceive; on the contrary: *what is signified is the effect of the signifier—a "meaning effect," an effect that is commensurate with the ideological space (place of enunciation) whence it derives.* That said, what we objectively know about reality, about the world and about ourselves, is founded upon, is propped up by, one thing: *this effect*—the effect of objectivity as defined hereunder, of ideology, of our informed notions, ideas and concepts, of our symbols and so on, which we are all subject to and thus subjects of. To put it bluntly, our subjectivity is constituted, conditioned, and thus determined by objectivity—which is the exception to subjectivity that, as we'll soon see, gives rise in a paradoxical way to subjectivity!

To employ a Žižekian-Lacanian term, the "real-Real," that which denotes the impenetrable "hard bone" of raw reality itself, comminutes[7] itself into an infinite-eternal array of particular effects isolated from any determinable context whatsoever, swirling about inconsistently, unpredictably, in the everlasting flux of life per se. In a way, the (psychological/spiritual/human/etc.) subject is one such dizzying effect, distilled from a myriad of *other* effects, an exception to all other life-effects—for the emergence of the subject gives rise to a uniquely universal notion, the genus of human being. And yet, if we pervert this perspective, that is, if we turn this perspective around on itself, such a universal provides an ideological context in which, through which, and by which the human subject—as an effect of said context—is produced: that is to say, the subject is created, it is determined *retroactively* by the very context it gives rise to: the universal notion of human being. This Lacanian big Other—what it *means* to be human for each and every one of us—produces and informs the human subjects we become. It is therefore the realm of the "non-human"—and we're *not* speaking of the animalistic side of the human being here, but rather—the way in which the human can recognize itself *as human* only in the excessive dimension of the human itself, that is, in the universal sense as such, that makes us "human, all too human." And *that* is how objectivity works.

Let us turn to another example, one that's a bit more abstract and complex. Immanuel Kant held the claim that natural organisms are "mechanically inexplicable": that 'some production of material things is not possible according to merely mechanical laws.'[8] Take a tree for example. As Theodore Greene reminds us in his introduction to Kant's *Religion Within the Limits of Reason Alone*, the tree contains within it both its cause and effect. A particular kind of tree has within itself the creative capability of growth and propagation. And the very *form* of tree—the *genus* "tree"—maintains *itself* by being the source of its own kinds, i.e., particular species. Thus the genus "tree" itself and its subordinate kinds depend on one another mutually. Every part is at the same time an end and a means (e.g., the tree's leaves, roots, and the seed itself, are both a cause and an effect of the (per se) tree's existence). Thus tree is a "self-caused cause"; and its *genus* functions like a Master-Signifier, for its name refers only to itself. Viewed strictly from a blind mechanical point of view, that every part of the tree is both reciprocally an end and a means, is, for the most part, considered impossible—a mechanically causal combination cannot be simultaneously the cause and effect; and yet the tree's internal creative process does not seem to follow blindly, mechanically, in the wake of its own cause. A complete explanation for the existence of the tree, then, forces us to seek out a teleological principal, according to which the tree is explained as having been designed with a purpose, as having a predefined form in which, through which and by which each part, as if *primordially ordained* to play its constitutive role, unfolds. Here we are presented with an antinomy: The *purpose*, the teleological principle behind the tree, its predefined form, is essential to a satisfactory explanation for tree, though this lies in direct opposition to the traditional materialist, mechanistic laws that are often used to explain the existence of all material things. In other words, as Kant put it, that life arises in nature from what is lifeless, that inert matter is able to organize itself into a "self-maintaining purposiveness," developing toward and into its own (what seems like) predefined forms, contradicts reason. Nonetheless, each principle, the teleological one and the mechanical one applies universally; each explanatory principle clashes against the other, each one determined to claim the domain of the natural world. To put it somewhat differently—if one were to explain the tree solely in terms of mechanical laws, one would be left with a sort of explanatory lacuna: for where, exactly, does the universal notion, the genus, the very *form* of "tree" that is both cause and effect (by means of which it is able to organize its own self-maintenance) arise from? What, then, do we make of such a veritable antagonism? The answer: we must look to the contradiction itself! The universal *is* this antagonism, the universal does not coincide with itself, and its particulars are none other than a multitude of attempts to reconcile this inherent antagonism. Reality is thus "constitutively split," split between its material content and its immaterial (*ideal*) form, the figure is always-already separate from its background, seeing is always-already disconnected from the visible... Does this not help support our earlier claim, that there is no original organic harmony, no natural balance one can return to? In any event, it is from within this abyssal though "generative" divide, an irreducible gap situated between form and content, that some *Thing* evokes the thought of the cogitative subject. This is precisely what it means to say that, the ("silent weaving" of the) Spirit of the subject is that which creates the blueprints, so to speak, of the subject's own inscription in the field that it sees: Each visible tree, to keep with our example here, has its invisible double—as Claude Lefort would put it, each 'line becomes a vector, the quality a dimension, the image a category, and the sign a symbol'—and *presto!*—the form, the genus "tree," is produced, or, as Plato would have it, *recollected*. Thus the genus, the universal as such, is none other than that which takes the place of an original void (which is essentially reflexive of the thinking subject... but let's hold this thought for just a moment or two longer).

Obviously, in the material world there is no "one" genus of tree that we can empirically discover, but what this really means is that the universal *form* of tree, the genus *itself*, does not *really* exist (as a physical entity), there exists only a multitude of heterogeneous trees that—*by means of abstracting out their common features*—constitutes the universal genus which, retroactively, circumscribes its particular tree members in all their difference. And yet, it's extremely important to not gloss over the fact that the universal, the genus as such, is itself a particular: it is simply *"not-all"*—for what eludes the universal *is* its particular: Insofar as the universal genus is produced through abstracting the recurrent features of its particular elements, the genus, as something entirely abstract, cannot fully coincide with *any* of its particulars. That is to say, all particular trees are radically different from—either inadequate to, or, in excess of—the universal. The universal and its particulars never seem to accomplish a successful encounter with one another; in every attempt there is always either a remainder (excess) or an empty space left over (deficit); a space that, either way, is occupied by the exceptional 'element which is the set itself in the form of its opposite'—*the universal genus as such*. Which also means that, insofar as it represents the set of trees per se, the genus is the paradoxical element that *is* the absence of itself. Hence this antagonism between universal and particular is "constitutive" of the universal itself: The set of particulars becomes an element of itself, their inherent difference is sublated into the genus "tree." Thus trees are the cause and effect of their own genus, their own form—and the genus is, at the very least, an imaginative element, *re-cognized* by the thinking subject: a successful schematization of the Real as such! Thus, as philosopher Alain Badiou puts it, *'thought is the proper medium of the universal.'* And *that* is how objectivity works.

Here, one should recall Badiou's book, *Being and Event*, in which he addresses the fact that, albeit *beings* exist in plurality, *Being* itself is conceived as being singular, in which all *beings* take part. But where is this enigmatic "One" by which all others attain their respective oneness? To pose the question differently, how do we account for the existence of an exceptional one in an incredibly vast world comprised only of difference and multiplicity? Badiou turns to set theory to unravel this paradox. Just like the structure of language, what discerns a numerical set from another set is a structure of differential relationships. Take for instance the set, "humanity." Counting the elements that belong to this set as a totalized one (as in the "oneness" of humanity), the consistent concept of humanity becomes established through its difference from itself, thereby engendering a concrete and reflexive order of immediate determinacy in which its (human) subjects are able to recognize their actualization as such. What one shouldn't overlook here is that the "oneness" of humanity is a universal ideological notion—as *itself* it does not obtain in the material world other than in an ideational or performative sense. And that's the point, without its particular content, without being predicated of its human subjects, it is pure *nothingness*. As Žižek formulates it in his book *The Parallax View*, this empty universal itself is a *'stand-in* for the radical noncoincidence of the particular to itself.' It is only by filling in the (empty) formal structure itself, that of the universal notion of human being, with real people that real people can, in the very unity of their *human* being, realize themselves *as such!* But the question still remains: How, exactly, does an amorphous set of particular hominids become totalized into an ordered universal, that of humanity, in the first place? How is it that this set positions itself at the same level as its elements? Well, perhaps the answer can be found in a certain kind of negative, radical break in the natural "order" of the animal kingdom itself: Included within the set of all animal particulars there arises an atypical, particular element, which, by dint of its exceptional quality, embodies its universal's structuring principle. And what atypical, exceptional element are we talking about here? None other than desire. Alexandre Kojève explains that

> for the herd to become a society, multiplicity of Desires is not sufficient by itself; in addition, the Desires of each member of the herd must be directed—or potentially directed—toward the Desires of the other members. If the human reality is a social reality, society is human only as a set of Desires mutually desiring one another as Desires. Human Desire produces a free and historical individual, conscious of his individuality, his freedom, his history, and finally, his historicity. Hence, anthropogenic Desire is different from animal Desire [...] in that it is directed, not toward a real, "positive," given object [like a frog being directed toward a fly only when desiring to satiate its appetite],[9] but toward another Desire. Thus, in the relationship between man and woman, for example, Desire is human only if the one desires, not the body, but the Desire of the other; if he wants to "possess" or "to assimilate" the Desire taken as Desire—that is to say, if he wants to be "desired" or "loved," or rather, "recognized" in his human value, in his reality as a human individual [...] All the Desires of an animal are in the final analysis a function of its desire to preserve its life. Human Desire, therefore, must win out over this desire for preservation. In other words, man's humanity "comes to light" only if he risks his (animal) life for the sake of his human Desire.[10]

Therein lies the incongruous logic of exception: There exists for any universal a particular exception to the universal, which gives rise to, and indexes, the universal "as such," while also giving rise to its very own universal, thereby multiplying and facilitating the continuation of exceptions—which embody universality's structuring principle. According to the logic of exception, then, the ideological notion of humanity, its universal oneness, finds its base in the field of desire, insofar as it marks *human* desire as the particular exception to all other animal desires. The result is thus that the particular exception not only indexes what it's an exception to—the set of all animal desires; it also becomes reflexive of its own universal, the ideological notion of humanity. And so, although there does not actually obtain in the world some definitive "one" that embodies the unification of all human subjects, this absence is concealed by an exceptional element: human desire—which is more in-human than the human itself, for it is precisely that which gives rise to the universal notion of humanity.

Here, we should jump tracks to Hegel's analogous example of the monarch, in which an amorphous multitude of particular individuals becomes a rational ordered State only when their federation is embodied by some "non-rational" individual—the monarch—who is excluded from the general body politic and elevated to king for his supposed "Being-a-king." As Karl Marx wrote:

> Such expressions of relations in general, called by Hegel reflex-categories, form a very curious class. For instance, one man is king only because other men stand in the relation of subjects to him. They, on the contrary, imagine that they are subjects because he is king.[11]

The way cultural theorist Joan Copjec explains it: 'the classical master, who was someone everyone—or everyone who counted—was encouraged to "emulate," […] [was] merely the retroactive effect of the general will-of-the-people. The place of this leader [was] thus a point of convergence, a point where the full sense of this unified will [was] located.'[12] What should not get overlooked here is the deployment of the logic of exception: the use of an irrational structuring principle to constitute a rational order. As we can see with Hegel's example of the monarch, the place of the monarch is secured by the will of the people, by the consensus (though irrational) belief that there exists a person, a king, who is inherently, naturally, endowed with a sublime "kingliness." This individual of exceptional regard is therefore exempt from the multitude of all other human particulars—whereby such a logical absurdity, an element of irrationality as such, nonetheless gives rise to a consistent and rational "whole": an ordered society that revolves around a monarch.

In other words, the universal ideological notion of "king" stages for its subjects the very means by which an irrational element is contrived (the monarch: someone who is believed to be naturally endowed with "kingliness") for the sole purpose of taking the place of an original void, whereby a federation, ordered around the monarch who embodies the State as such, takes form and secures its "closure." Like the functioning of a Master-Signifier the monarch "secures" a context, the monarch gives rise to a rational order in which, through which and by which its subjects, the "body politic," are given substance, whereby they are able to recognize their Selves as "present" in a contextual state as such; in this instance, that of subjects of a monarchy. This is what Hegel meant by "reflex category": The outcome of an act of 'totalization through exemption' is a concrete order in which its subjects are able to recognize their own existence, by means of which their "presence" becomes actualized *as subjects*. Though we should not overlook the fact that such a totalization is always-already incomplete, not-whole, ruptured by the void from within—for the monarch only serves to *conceal* the fact that there is an original void of which he takes the place. *And that is how objectivity works.*

In Copjec's essay, "The Subject Defined by Suffrage," she reminds us that modernity started at the advent of (post-Grecian) democracy—specifically, after the monarch was replaced with, as Lefort aptly put it, the 'indetermination that was born from the loss of the substance of the body politic.'[13] In other words, the locus of power that was once embodied by the monarch, upon the advent of modern democracy, 'becomes *an empty place...*'[14] This is why, now that the "throne is empty," so to speak, after democracy usurped its place, modern power is wielded by no one in particular though we are all subject to it, to use a Foucauldian expression. What has insinuated its way into this Throne of Power these days, however, is knowledge—"Big Data." A bricolage of facts assembled by the objective intellects of today's expert specialists and technocrats, et al. This is, to evoke the work of Georg Lukács, the result of capitalism. The problem with this, of course, is that facts are always open to interpretation; and capitalism, to paraphrase Lukács, creates a social structure that both stimulates and endorses the view that "objective" facts are invariable, able to be wrested from their "living context" (without repercussions) and applied to the theories endorsed by the ruling ideology of capitalism (without repercussions)—an ideology that promotes the view that objective phenomena can be inspected in isolation, a view which fails to see how these "objective" facts are founded on the protean 'historical character' of the very social structure upon which they are based.[15] But already, I may be jumping ahead of myself here.

What I'm getting at is this: Reality itself is constitutively split; the difference that inheres throughout all of reality is inherent to reality itself: as a proper Hegelian might put it, this pure difference is none other than the fact that reality does not, cannot, coincide with itself. There persists in nature, in reality, an innermost, irreconcilable antagonism between materiality (matter) and immateriality (form), between flesh and spirit, mind and body—*essence* and *appearance*; all that is immediate in reality *is* appearance, and the difference between essence and appearance is internal to appearance, insofar as there is a play of inner forces *within* all that appears. And so the gap between essence and appearance, a void as such, marks the place of the subject's inscription, and thus the emergence of objectivity—*the place from which the subject seeks to understand the essence of reality as it appears to the subject and for the subject.* No less important, objectivity, as such, is the "constitutive stuff" of ideology—like a Higgs particle, it is the most elementary ideological element: it gives mass to our ideologies, those explanatory structures that help organize our understanding of the world. Thus objectivity's sole function is to attempt to suture this intrinsic rip that separates the "world in here" from the "world out there," thereby providing a (deceptive, though convincing) sense of wholeness to our forms of life, to the ruling ideologies in which, through which and by which, we, as subjects, acquire our subjectivity.

Even so, objectivity does not help us find our place in the world; on the contrary, objectivity has already found our place for us, for it is that which creates *for us* the very "world" we live in. Objectivity may serve to represent reality in symbolic form, but the only reality we know is that which is symbolically mediated. To put it simply, to emphatically believe that objectivity delivers us to pure truth, to believe that it successfully closes the gap between what is symbolic and what is real, is, psychoanalytically speaking, psychotic. And that's the problem with capitalism.

What I mean is precisely this: Ideology is, *in nuce*, the prohibition of impossibility. However, the Freudian notion of death-drive tells us that the impossible *is* attainable—hence our enjoyment, it comes from a moment of pure excession, transgression, the challenging of the ideological "closure." But in capitalism, things work a bit differently. Here, in the ideological space of capital, individuals seek their enjoyment in commodities, in objects that are interned *within* the very ideological system that produces them. Therefore one's enjoyment remains rigidly confined within the very thing one should be attempting to transgress. Or rather, one's enjoyment is rigidly confined in an extremely polymeric ideology: Capitalism gains strength, its interpellative agency becomes more potent, its very structure bends and swells and thrives with every transgression! Why: Because with capitalism, in capitalism, everything is reduced to brutal economic reality (including science itself; the latter's discoveries end up serving only the networks of capital), and in such a space capital's objectivism becomes our only reality, and thus literally *everything*, prohibited or not, becomes absorbed into the world of capital. That is to say, the logic of pure capitalism overlaps with the logic of pure objectivism, a Logic of the Object that results in a psychotic fantasy in which subjectivity is nowhere to be found—here, the gap between what is symbolic and real closes in on itself. As Paul Ricouer put it so well in his essay, "Consciousness and the Unconscious," in capitalism man *lives* this ideology of 'economic objectivity as a [...] modality of subjectivity,' which gives rise, in an autopoietic way, to its very own representations, instincts, affects and effects, and so on.[16] And being at the very heart of this logic is not the same as *being-in-the-world*.[17]

So, if ambition, intrigue, submission and responsibility are, as Ricoeur put it, the apposite 'human feelings that are organized around' the object that is "power," then capitalism's appropriation of objectivity as such confers upon itself a seemingly insurmountable control over its subjects. To wit, let us not forget that human subjectivity is that which is constantly attempting to overcome a lack—*that is why capitalism exists in the first place*: it sinisterly dons the visage that it completes this lack, despite never really doing so, so we continue to buy the commodities we produce and fetishize, 24/7/365. This is precisely why capitalism is self-engendering, we allow commodities to supplement our lacks, and *this covers up our lacks.* Or rather: commodity fetishism covers up the fact that we're covering up the lack.

As the great playwright Bertolt Brecht once put it: "Nothing should seem impossible to change." What we are in need of in these times, it seems to me, is a new Master-Signifier. Either an ideology or representative thereof that will be in the business of restructuring the symbolic coordinates of the current social arrangements in which, through which and by which we experience the world—thereby influencing a radical shift in the way we "objectively" see our environment, enabling a fresh outlook on the physical world itself. Facilitating a complete break, once and for all, from capitalism. Only then will we be able to relate to the world in a novel way. But there's a caveat to this: we must be careful not to repeat the role of the hysteric. As Lacan once responded to the students who were uprising in May of 1968—'As hysterics, you want a new master. You will get one.' And to follow that up with Georges Bataille's words: 'the idea of a revolution is intoxicating, but what happens afterwards? The world will remake itself and remedy what oppresses us today to take some other form tomorrow.' So how do we do this whole revolution thing successfully? How do we usher in a new Master-Signifier, while at the same time, putting to permanent rest the need for an external master? This is the predominant question of our time. How do we revolt without being, from a psychoanalytical standpoint, hysterical?

I can't give a direct answer to this. But I do believe the clue to the first step is to be found by looking deep within our own selves, by confronting the horrific abyss that is none other than our own freedom and self-responsibility. We must go "mad" to become "mature," for one who needs a master remains mired in foolish immaturity, anaclitic to a detrimental fault. We must, because we can, define our own limitations once again, while this time discarding the need for a master altogether. Only then, will we have a fair shot at freeing ourselves of the manacles of capitalism—restraints, let me remind you, that we've put upon ourselves. And if that doesn't work... we shall repeat the failure again, only better!

That said, here are the main premises of this book; no bullshit, no slipping my premises by you. They are laid out below in no particular order, which, like an *I Spy* book, I leave them to you, the dependable reader, to detect in the main body of this text. Do not, however, expect all these premises to be touched upon explicitly. Carry them with you in thought, allowing them to serve as the very background against all that you pore over. And of course, I leave open the necessary space for an exception: that there may indeed be other postulates embedded in this work that I have not accounted for in the following premises.

**Premise One:** There are three ways in which we can talk about objectivity: (1) objectivity as it's situated at the level of the Real— reality in its most raw and ambiguous state: phenomena that is *appearance only*, that is, appearance as appearance. Real objectivity belongs to the world of entities and their respective domains that persist outside of human meaning. What is objective, at the level of the Real, is elusive to symbolization; so here, even what may be empirical, that is, observable, cannot be discussed in everyday terms, cannot be properly characterized, and so on. This level of objectivity ruins most, if not all, consistent structures of meaning, interpretation, and so on. As such, it is a vortex of unfathomable depth, which exists separate from—*though situated at the core of*—the following two structures of objectivity: (2) Objectivity as it is situated at the level of the Imaginary; appearance as *something*, appearance as it is directly, initially experienced. A relational mode of Being that directly refers to the subject's immediate experience of, and relation to, the external world—in which, by which, and through which the subject forms an imaginary, "narcissistic identification" with a part of external reality (the object-Other), which reflects back to the subject its own (awareness of) "Self." Here, appearance passes through the "mortifying mediation" of thought, which is always accompanied, for the most part simultaneously, by a Symbolic intervention. This refers to the way in which one characterizes what one "sees", how one's reality *becomes/is* one's "objective" reality, which indexes the not the minimal difference between the Real and reality in so far as it refers to the subject's ideologico-Symbolic situation he is inscribed in. Which brings us to (3): objectivity as it is situated at the level of the Symbolic: Here objectivity performs the ideological function of representing, for its subject, raw reality in its symbolic-objective form. This tripartite structure of objectivity therefore describes how, by means of objectification, we assimilate images from external reality into our consistent "inner worlds". In other words, one should grasp objectivity as the unity of its three dimensions as such.

**Premise Two:** Ideology (and thus today's ideology of "intellectual objectivity") serves to supplement an immutable lack in our network of knowledge of the world and of our Selves.

**Premise Three:** Despite objectivity's "illusory" quality, that, like the Lacanian big Other, objectivity *doesn't really exist*—that it is primarily a function of and for the (psychological) subject, which aims to ensure the guarantee of consistency in lieu of the fact that, in reality, there is no such external guarantee—it is virtually impossible to exist in the world as a subject without objectivity, that, objectivity, as such, has its basis in the contradictions of subjectivity. In other words, objectivity, *as arising from this innermost contradiction*, is that which provides the subject its subjectivity.

**Premise Four:** What matters most in the world, what is *real* in every register of experience (Symbolic, Imaginary, Real), is effect: the results of our words (language), symbols (*logos*), ideas and concepts (reason), which sculpt how we objectively see/relate to (perceive/behave in) the world. If our effect on and in the physical world is damaging to the world and its inhabitants (which no doubt it is today, the culture of industrialized civilization, couched in capitalism, is committing what we might as well call "omnicide"—evidenced by catastrophes such as climate change, the tainting of fresh waters with carcinogenic materials, the acidification of the world's oceans, unprecedented species extinction rates, the accelerated loss of the world's tapestry of forests through large-scale logging operations, the corporate theft of communally held land, the loss of diverse cultures and languages, endless war as a means for profit, and so on *ad nauseam*), then it's time that we develop a praxis that aims at reconfiguring how we perceive the world and our place therein.

**Premise Five:** Perception is objective which *becomes* purely subjective: How we assimilate images from external reality into our consistent "inner worlds" is by means of objectification: a dialectical process that initially takes place in the subject's imaginative world "within," but requires a Symbolic intervention from "outside." For example, by the time I see a car, I already preconsciously know what I see to be a car. That is to say, before I'm fully conscious of the car, before I can even say, "I see a car," the image of the car has been unconsciously indexed to its registered symbol (sound-image), "car." There has been a Symbolic intervention, one which has unconsciously interposed itself into my direct experience in order to integrate this direct experience with the inner consistency of my subjective world. And that is how, following my perception of the car, I am able to enunciate in language that it is a "car" I am seeing. This process serves to reinforce my sense of oneness in and with the world at large, my sense of Self (*being-in-world*) as such.

**Premise Six:** As singer, songwriter and harpist Joanna Newsom puts it: 'while the signifieds butt heads with the signifiers / we all fall down slack-jaw to marvel at words / while across the sky shoot the impossible birds / in their steady illiterate movement homewards' — That is to say, the signifier "bird" does not *really* directly correspond to the thing signified, to the bird itself. This is why Lacan claimed that words "murder" the thing itself; why I could, for example, point to a particular bird and say, "There is a bird," and not ever fully mean that particular bird itself. Signifiers correspond to the *meaning effect* that the sound-image, i.e., symbol, (e.g., "bird") invokes, rather than the thing itself.

**Premise Seven:** One of philosophy's primary aims should be to undermine our immersion in ideology. To approach this point somewhat obliquely, what I mean is precisely this: Rather than arguing that science is just another "explanatory narrative" that serves to articulate the desires of the culture from which it has emerged, I support the claim that science is a mode of knowledge creation based on the detection of emerging, (empirical, or not) facts; that science, at its purest, deals with reality at its rawest, with the "unschematized Real." Though let us not forget that facts — and this is the caveat — are ultimately interpretational, for they are plucked from a larger web of relationships, they have histories and other entanglements; they are not, in reality, ever isolated. Therefore, how we *understand* facts is essentially, *structurally*, idealistic. I don't intend to scrutinize science all that much in this book, (only a little); rather, my aim herein is directed toward something that is, for the most part, "preknowledge" based. To wit, facts can be understood only through the concepts we form around them. And our concepts are, for the most part, shaped and informed by ideology, how we are taught/told to objectively view the world. In other words, ideology specializes in quietly whispering into our ears the presuppositions that shape and inform our perceptions, interpretations, explanations, and understandings of facts. For that reason, the concepts we form around (empirical, or not) facts are whim to the very protean nature of the historico-ideologico-cultural context from which these concepts arise, from which we *think*; which is ultimately the result of social forces, *and*, our personal, subjective relations to the social network from whence these forces derive—*which, in toto, is always undergoing the process of historical change*. Therefore our knowledge, too, will only ever be fluid and dynamic, never static. And our concepts will always be in need of revision. A little tweak here, a little tweak there... And thus the truth of our knowledge will always be something that is in motion. The philosopher's main role in the world should therefore be an ethical one—to help us understand *how* we are seeing/thinking *what* we are seeing/thinking, to shine light on alternative ways by means of which we can relate to the world, and to elucidate all the new problems that crop up with the advent of new knowledge. Sure, through science's involvement with/in the "infinite" nature of reality itself, discovery of new facts about the world and the universe will continue to happen; so long as we recognize that, as Lacan put it, the scientific *logic* behind how we gather these facts, not its *empiricism*, is science's real mechanism; but what we make of these facts, what we *do* with these facts, is ultimately determined not so much by a precise logic but rather, by how we are taught to conceive of and relate to the world, which is essentially a function of the dynamic interplay between human need and desire, which accords to its own exceptional logics. It is against such a background that philosophy should be employed; thus it should be political and theoretical in its application: it should seek to provide sufficient reason as to why or why not we should or should not appropriate certain scientific facts for the satisfaction of our needs and desires.

**Premise Eight:** We do not need to change our material realities, we simply need to change the way we perceive and relate to them. The subject's consciousness *is* (driven, charged, informed by) ideology, which "secures" the subject into a certain relation with the world. Consciousness, as such, is what impedes (and, *mutatis mutandis*, what entrusts) the subject's capability for achieving the autonomy necessary for radically altering his or her perception of and thus relation to the world. In other words, if ideological narratives shape the way we conceive of and perceive the world, and if the way we perceive the world influences our behavior in the world, and if our behavior in the world is to the world's, or the subject's, or another's detriment, then these narratives are either radically flawed or have become rotten, or, both, and therefore require comprehensive reformation. To effectuate such a reformation begins with a *renascence* of consciousness itself, which requires, first, a rupture in the subject's consciousness, a disengagement from the very ideology that has shaped and informed the subject's presuppositions of the world, whereby one will then be capable of establishing a new consciousness in the world, of the world. This cannot occur without sufficient action.

**Premise Nine:** We are creatures without any knowable essence, determining our essence. The subject, the human individual, as Hegel formulated it in the *Phenomenology*, is not from the start a consciousness that is in full possession of its thoughts; the subject is a "place of unrest" (*Unruhe*), unable to understand itself and thus strives to "get back to him/herself" in order to understand oneself, to re-appropriate one's Self within its place of inscription. Thus one's (sense of) "Self" is an "objectal correlate" of one's subjecthood: In the Kierkegaardian sense, the Self is a relation that relates the subject to itself, constituted and maintained by the socio-Symbolic lifeworld in which the subject dwells. In other words, the subject is an effect of its Self as such.

**Premise Ten:** Hegel's figure of "Spirit" exists. Spirit belongs to that level of being in us, the unconscious of the subject, from which we are invariably excluded. As such, Spirit serves the intention to unify all moments of the subject's experiences in the structure of consciousness. And consciousness, the pure Ego, is nonetheless produced by the creative enterprises of Spirit's involvement of its subjects with the Symbolic. As we'll read later on, Spirit is the activity that creates, for its subjects (individually or collectively), objective reality, in its return to itself. In other words, Spirit creates the very place to which it returns (for example: Self-consciousness is subjective Spirit objectified). To put it somewhat differently, as Hegel posited, if the subjective field of experience is to be determined in any way, if it is to be qualified as such, if it is *named*, its determinate character becomes *object to it*. What is comprehended is therefore objective: Spirit comprehends.

**Premise Eleven:** Here we have another strictly Hegelian premise: What is subjective is activity; and what is objective is the activity itself: the activity once it's realized in the very act of its "return to itself."

**Premise Twelve:** Engaging with ideological shadows is our ultimate reality—as Marx put it, these ideological shadows are cast by the movement of our material bodies. Though, to enable a return to Hegel, each shadow cast is merely the specular image of subjective Spirit, that infinite, immaterial, non-mortal essence within us all, invigorating and bringing to life inert matter, which thereby animates the "bodily causes" behind the activity of our (ideological) shadows. Our shadows are thus the specular images of Spirit.

**Premise Thirteen:** Reality is "constitutively split," split as such between materiality and immateriality, between materialism qua physicality and the invisible realm of Spirit, idealism (the latter pertaining to the realm of forms, ideas, concepts, etc)—and the subject too is constitutively split, split between mind and body (*res cogitans* and *res extensa*). Further, unlike Plato's belief— that the only thing real in this world is beyond human sense— that the universal forms are more real than that which appears in them, through them and by them—the argument I support is the one that posits the claim that, the very *tension* between these two elements, between form and content, between materiality and immateriality, mind and body, is constitutive. Such antagonistic suspense provides the impetus behind dialectical development, the very movement that accounts for the animation of life.

**Premise Fourteen:** The subject's reality is structured for him/her in the sublime act of "belief." But it's not that simple: the subject's reality is not structured around just per se belief, but on account of the Real *in* belief itself—the "real effects" of belief: Belief, as a performative, impacts the materiality of the world— *it changes its "object."* Belief, like intention, is thus a force capable of influencing real change in and upon the material universe. For example, if one is taught to see mountains as dollar bills, instructed to believe that mountains are retainers of resources to be exploited, blown to bits and razed for access to strata of coal, then one will see and treat mountains this way; if one is taught to believe that mountains are a dynamic landbase, essential to the lives of many beings, then one will see and treat mountains another way. (For this premise, I am indebted to the words of philosopher and environmental activist, Derrick Jensen.)

**Premise Fifteen:** In terms of defining our existential background, the "natural" world, the "universe," or whatever you want to call it, the dialectic between a holistic organic unity and a collection of atomized particulars each experiencing and expressing the world in their own unique and inconsistent ways, finds its reconciliation in the Hegelian Absolute qua radical loss—a "generative void": a non-realizable dimension of incon- sistency and radical contingency, endlessly drawing in and discharging a multiform flux of life-effects and expressions.

**Premise Sixteen:** Necessity is the only sufficient means for guaranteeing all the presuppositions that compose the "objective certainty" of the subject's lived reality.

**Premise Seventeen:** Necessity arises from radical contingency. For example, my existence is certain though not necessary; it was founded entirely on radically contingent circumstances; and how my life will unfold is entirely contingent just as well.[18] It is necessary, however, that I drink water if I wish to continue to exist, and that is objectively certain. Hence necessity arises from radical contingency.

**Premise Eighteen:** To establish yet another Žižekian ally: To not only introduce, help restore, and situate within the context of today's dominant culture and its symptoms the fundamental concepts of Lacan's work, but to also accomplish a sort of "return to Hegel"—to rectify today's misleading image of Hegel as being some "monadic totalist," and to join in with the Žižekian choir that is revealing Hegel's negative dialectic as being more of a sort of "black hole" around which everything passes through.

**Premise Nineteen:** The subject is not complete, but bears an immutable lack. We are radically alienated from ourselves and from the world into which we are born: we do not know what sort of beings we are in the Real. And despite all that we do know, the very nature of reality remains absurdly unknown to us. The role of objectivity serves to efface this lack, despite its emergence from this lack.

**Premise Twenty:** An object-Other can never be fully revealed in its representation. The subject (which, as German philosopher Arthur Schopenhauer once put it, is presupposed by dint of an object's presence) seeks to conceal this representational lacuna precisely by placing a part of him/herself (i.e., the subject's notion of the object-Other) within such a void. The dialectical reversal of this is thus that, what eludes the object-Other's full-dress representation *is the subject's very inscription in the object-Other*: The lack of an accurate representation of an object is reflexive of the void at the core of the subject, a void that has been trans-positioned into the object being represented. That is to say, the subject's lack is displaced into the object, which thereby opens a space in the object in which the subject then inscribes him/herself, from which the subject then (unconsciously) sees (him/herself seeing) the object; viz., the subject thinks through the object precisely by letting the object think through the subject in its notion as such! This object thereby becomes what is called an *objet petit a*, a Lacanian term denoting a "stand-in" for an immutable void at the core of the subject. As Žižek puts it: '*objet a* is the strange object which is nothing but the inscription of the subject itself into the field of objects, in the guise of a stain which acquires form only when part of this field is anamorphically distorted by the subject's desire.'[19]

By means of situating objectivity at the level of ideology, while placing it within a dynamic, experimental and, at times, unorthodox interplay with Hegelian and Lacanian philosophy, *Night of the World* offers a unique and radical re-thinking of objectivity. And through the deployment of Žižek's philosophy, we will speculate over both objectivity and ideology, evoking methods of thought not so prevalent since German Idealism was all the rage. That said, it's crucial one does not make the mistake of conflating vocabulary with concepts. This is not a "psychoanalytic" work, and this is not your classic treatise on transcendental idealism. To put it paradoxically, by remaining inveterately faithful to Hegelian dialectics, I will not sanction the "invariability" of any particular theory. This text is, in the spirit of Kierkegaard, the result of an imaginative hypothesis, pieced together by concepts and speculations only.

# Prologue:

# Identifying the symptom

*What constitutes the basis of life, in effect, is that for everything having to do with the relations between men and women, what is called collectivity, it's not working out (ça ne va pas). It's not working out, and the whole world talks about it, and a large part of our activity is taken up with saying so.*

—Jacques Lacan

## *The fourth estate and its symptom*

In March 2007 Karl Rove, the Senior Advisor and Deputy Chief of Staff to former American President, George W. Bush, took to the stage to "bust a move" at the Radio and Television Correspondents' Dinner in Washington, DC. This rather distasteful performance—Rove staggering about on stage, his buffoonish histrionics comprising a blend of what appeared to be pantomimed karate chops, some arm-crossing, and the occasional finger pointing, all of which was punctuated with him growling obnoxiously into the microphone, 'I'm MC Rove'—attracted the attention of major news media. NBC covered it, CSPAN aired it, FOX News was all over it... And why not? After all, the purpose of this event was to celebrate the front-line of America's "honest" reporting. Even so, this bread and circus coincided with what was perhaps the deadliest year to date in Iraq, one which followed four anguished years of what many independent journalists and alternative media condemned as an illegal occupation (as of July 2006, the US invasion and subsequent occupation of Iraq had taken the lives of 655,000 Iraqis).[20]

For many, this first-rate media event signaled the logical, yet inglorious culmination of a recurrent trend in journalism:

objective news reporting, with its underlying idea that neutrality and nonpartisanship are integral characteristics of newsgathering and reporting.

Such an idealized blend of journalism and objectivity purports to deliver a robust balance of viewpoints and facts from a *fourth estate*, an institution presumed to exist apart from government and large interest groups. Though in many respects, this couldn't be any further from the actual state of things. That a small number of large corporations control the major US media leads many to reasonably contend that this "objective" mode of journalism is of a purely tactical nature: although it sounds good, the push to remain neutral and nonpartisan serves merely to boost the commercialization of journalism as such.[21] Further, considering today's media corporations are among some of the largest beneficiaries of the global capitalist economy, using trade organizations and the free market as a means to increase profits, the injunction to remain objective plays a key role in suppressing conscionable dissent directed at the capitalist economy that would otherwise encumber profitable revenue. As Robert W. McChesney puts it, 'there has been a kind of "Eleventh Commandment" in the commercial news media: Thou Shalt Not Cover Big Local Companies and Billionaires Critically. This makes very good economic sense, as the local powers are often major advertisers.'[22]

This injunction to remain objective, which in these times, as we'll soon see, is often coupled with the injunction to remain loyal to the ruling class, is structured somewhat like the paradox of the Freudian superego: the more you obey, the more you are guilty; or in the Marxist sense of surplus-value: the more you profit, the more you want; or in the Lacanian sense of the sublime object: the closer you get to the object cause of your desire, the more this object eludes your grasp.[23] In this particular case: the more you tell the ("objective") truth, the more the truth itself slips away from you.

Conversely, any attempt to bypass objectivity as such, in effect, frames one as dishonest—dishonest precisely in the sense of disloyalty: when the subject finds itself in a position whereby the basis, strength, scope, legitimacy and attitude of his/her loyalty to authority conflicts with loyalty to a higher order.[24] That is to say, today's injunction to be "objective" is, itself, not actually a promise of any sorts to deliver us to any real truth but rather, like any ideology, its universality serves to conceal its own absurd, perverted truths, for example: Justice is not exacted on the rich and powerful who commit crimes against humanity when justice is administered to protect the rich and powerful from those who seek to reveal their crimes against humanity. And there is no shortage of examples for such "recusant" agents who sought to expose such perversions of power—from Socrates, who was condemned to death for "corrupting" the youth, to Sophie and Hans Scholl, the core members of White Rose (a nonviolent resistance group opposing Nazi Germany) who were beheaded for disseminating brochures, from Isaak Babel to Pavel Kohout to Julian Assange, Chelsea Manning and Edward Snowden, the annals of history, up to and including today's epoch, have for us a canon's worth of subversive (heroic) behavior, of blatant opposition against the status quo and the latter's predominant forms of knowledge(-creation), as well as the aftermath of such dissenting provocations.

And so, in the similar sense that one is not encouraged in their youth to criticize and undermine parental authority, we are given fair warning not to be too critical of the ruling ideology and its supportive institutions.[25]

What we have here can be likened to a good old comical "Žižekian trilemma": of three features—honesty, sincere support of the status quo, and intelligence—it is possible to combine only two, and not all three. For if one is both honest and sincerely supportive of the status quo, one is not very intelligent; if one is intelligent and sincerely supportive of the status quo, well, one is not being completely honest; and if one is honest and intelligent... one is clearly an enemy of the state, a subversive as such! In other words, once you challenge the status quo for the sake of a higher code, you suddenly find yourself placed in the position of being unfaithful to the ruling order. In this case, once one calls into question the very article of faith that presupposes the validity behind (even the notion of) an invariant "objective" truth, one is often regarded by the masses as foolish, absurd, irrational—an agent of blasphemy who not only bites the hand that feeds, but also, in the very act of bearing one's teeth, humiliates that which often demands of all of us nonnegotiable respect. For, at the very least, is it not the case that one who attacks, doubts, questions and/or criticizes today's doctrine of intellectual objectivity—and this is key—is often reproached as being superstitious, delusional, perhaps crazy, maybe even "primitive," childish, or just plain stupid? By these lights, today's doctrine of unyielding intellectual objectivity is just as strict, just as self-referential, and just as self-defining, self-confirming, and intolerant of alternatives as any other doctrine of belief and/or ruling ideology.

Viewed from this angle, it's as if we're compelled to step back and bear witness to something much larger in scope here, something within which "intellectual objectivity" *itself* is inscribed. It is, *as if*, all this time, we've been too close to our object in one way or another (in this case, that object being objectivity per se), precisely in the sense that we have been attuned to viewing the world through this very object we seek to analyze— to the extent that, as if we were peering through a telescope to gaze upon celestial objects, the instrument through which we have been focusing our gaze (this "instrument" being, metaphorically speaking, none other than "intellectual objectivity" itself), has, in a certain sense, been occluding a much different view of the universe altogether: In a crucial way, by being too close to our object (that is, by being "intellectually objective"), we are not only missing completely *the way in which the telescope itself ("intellectual objectivity") enframes, for us (the observer), the universe that is being observed*, but also, we are failing to recognize *the way in which both ourselves (as observer), and the telescope (again, today's intellectual objectivity), are inscribed together in what is being observed*. And so, by substituting "intellectual objectivity" for "telescope" here—do we not, from such an angle, catch sight of a unique "frame-within-a-frame" construction, a conflation of injunctions as such, a sort of nesting doll, as it were, in which the dictate to remain loyal to existing structures of power is encapsulated within, *enframed by*, the injunction to remain intellectually objective?

Which brings us to a couple of the premises of this book. Aside from expounding the ways in which objectivity is virtually identical to ideology, another primary task herein, let us call this the *ethical* aim, is to demystify and explain for the relationship that exists between today's injunction to be "objective" and the abstract-real regime of power/authority from whence it derives: a system comprised of dominating urges and desires, one that exerts its power universally—capitalism. For the injunction to remain intellectually objective in today's dynamic world of capital is none other than a function of the universal of capital itself. Capitalist society has become so dynamic, so fragile, and so uncertain, that if you are completely absorbed in the world of capital then the world begins to take on such an unbalanced form; the world begins to appear as chaotic, as "too much to handle." Therefore, remaining "objective" is the perfect supplement to tolerate such an unstable world while carrying it forward. Thus the more objective one is, the more absorbed in the world of capital one becomes. And like the proverbial case of Hegel's monarch, or a totalitarian system of governance, this ruling ideology, like a Master-Signifier, serves to conceal its own absurd truth: that its "necessity" (e.g., the stupid conviction that "there is no alternative" to capitalism) arose from traumatic contingency, from historical conditions, and that therefore it can and probably will end in traumatic contingency just the same, for there are indeed real alternatives to capitalism—there exist a number of other historical possibilities—and this truth can only come to light through a direct critique of capital's universal status and those institutions whose sole function are to reinforce its universality.

Many deeply sense that today's "objective" attitude is problematic.[26] And in many ways it is—in terms of journalism alone, the injunction to remain objective has helped accelerate the suspension and firing of journalists and columnists dedicated to reporting on and writing about white-collar crimes and institutional corruption, *creating a divisive rift within the fourth estate itself.*[27]

And so sticking with the topic of journalism for the moment, with regard to the "gone but not forgotten" war in Iraq, as independent investigative journalist Dahr Jamail once explained to me—'the mainstream media [under the guise of being objective] was really misleading the American public, spewing out propaganda, cutting and pasting info for articles like, for example, Judith Miller of *The New York Times* and her ilk who had a penchant for putting out unverified facts if not blatant lies about what was happening [in Iraq].'[28, 29]

The predominant criticism among independent journalists today is that the propagation of objectivity as such throughout schools of journalism—with all its verbiage about profession-alism, and the latter's venerated marriage to a detached and no less specious "open-mindedness," which we can only hope ends in annulment soon—combined with an overwhelming corporate influence and control over the media, has dealt a crushing blow to honest reporting while allowing for the dominant culture, especially its ruling class, to manipulate information and fabricate narratives that ultimately serve to dissimulate the truth of its misconduct. That NBC decided to air Karl Rove and his cohorts dancing on stage back in July of 2007—airing the celebration of what still carries with it to this day in many circles of discourse the musty odor of scandal—rather than run a story on, say, the illegal conduct of Blackwater military contractors (and called *that* journalism) suggests that this accusation is anything but irrational. Though of course this should come as no surprise considering NBC is owned by GE (General Electric), that GE specializes in weapons manufacturing, has ties with the military, Big Oil, etc. Taking into account the nature of their business, it surely wouldn't behoove GE should NBC overtly portray war as an illegal and brutal occupation. Therefore, it seems very likely, if not apparently so, that these large media corporations and their political sponsors not only encourage, but also make use of, objective news reporting as a tactic to advance their own agendas.

So there goes objectivity.

And as Jamail professes, 'as journalists, we give a damn about what we're reporting—we care about the people and the places we are reporting about, or at least we should, and that makes for honest reporting. And so, there goes objectivity.'[30]

## *Unpacking objectivity*

And there we have it. A roaring debate over the use of objectivity in the newsroom, and yet no one is actually being objective. Owing mostly to this contradiction—one that is no doubt obscured by the infighting over divergent ideas of objectivity; an antagonism, might I add, that cuts across a single realm of discourse (journalism)—one would thus seem hard pressed in their determination to seek out an intelligible, single definition of objectivity, seeing that all this dispute over one little term, and yet no concrete example of it, will surely leave one harried and confounded. But here we should make the proper Hegelian move: we should allow for this innermost antagonism to put into motion the very dialectic that will guide our analysis of what it means to even be objective. Chances are, the notion of objectivity most have in mind is either radically flawed, or, a semblance of something far more complex than the hackneyed and naïve notion of it being something in opposition to "subjectivity."

This of course brings us to the essential enigma at play here: what exactly is objectivity? And for that matter, what is it about today's notion of objectivity that provokes such anxiety among those who renounce it? In the case of journalism, does it simply call for journalistic *passion*—that which invariably drives and inspires a story—to be replaced by a radically misconstrued Pyrrhonian skepticism: a botched understanding of the purely neutral stance that "Nothing can be known" through the senses, thereby (that is to say, resulting from the very misconception of *"Nothingness"*) demanding the total suspension of judgment? And, as such, does this style of news reporting compel one to be, in every respect, indifferent to the events taking place in the world—if that is even possible?—thus compromising the integrity of a journalism that would—*should*—otherwise monitor the Establishment for better or worse? If so, can we not also make the claim that today's general sense of objectivity imparts a similar blasé attitude across the board? Does objectivity, as it's conceived in these times, engender a sort of numbing indifference to a rather complex and inconsistent, though animate and sensuous world?

But what if the problem is not with objectivity per se? Rather, what if it's the case that our current understanding of objectivity is completely wrong? From a typical, though heavily watered down and bastardized Kantian-Hegelian perspective, objectivity refers to an element embodying universality and necessity. In other words, objectivity can designate that which is often ascribed to any "thought-product" (the result of logical thinking) that is valid for all, which embodies a category everyone must use. For example, when a theory, idea, proposition, etc. is inter-subjectively verifiable, when it passes the "test of general veracity"—as in the case of being thoroughly worked out and confirmed by ardent and rigorous experimental tests, to then be fully accepted by a community of scientists or other "experts," and so on—this assures its objectivity, and thus its universal *truth* as such.

We can flesh this out with a simple illustration. Imagine you're asked to go to the grocery store to buy fruit. Surely, regarding such a task, you wouldn't return with a head of lettuce, some asparagus, a package or two of sliced ham and a roll of toilet paper. What I mean is, when used in the sense exemplified above, the term "fruit" is a universal category everybody can use. It's requested of you to go buy some fruit, and you know exactly what to do, you go buy some fruit—not vegetables, not audio equipment, not soda or comic books, but fruit; you return from the store with perhaps some apples, bananas, some oranges—whatever items they may be, you "truthfully" return with *fruit*. And the same kind of helpful classificatory schema can be admin-istered through the use of categories denoting non-physical entities too, e.g., the categories of "good" and "evil" or "ethics" or "comedy," and so on down the list.

And although the logic of the universal entails a far more sophisticated account (as was explained in the preface of this work[31]), for now, to put it in a somewhat homespun way, we can liken a universal category to that of a (universal) genus comprising a multitude of species (particulars).

Bearing all this in mind, one could reasonably argue, at least from a speculative standpoint, that the values upheld by today's independent investigative journalists and alternative media (e.g., compassion, a code of ethics, honesty, dedication to one's position, etc.) are particular values which can indeed be regarded as logical, as well as sensible "thought-products" that either embody, or are features of, valid categories that all journalists should emphatically endorse when conducting their reporting.

Have we not, then, from this angle, arrived at an entirely different understanding of what it could mean to be an "objective" news reporter? If journalism were to suddenly accept the abovementioned formulation of objectivity, it would thereby make our opponents of objective journalism unwittingly in favor of objective journalism, despite their strong resentment towards it. And so to resolve this ugly contradiction, lest one runs into confusions, one may be inclined to take the easy way out: back up immediately and discard the Kantian/Hegelian formulation of objectivity altogether, a formulation of objectivity that many today would, without question, claim is not applicable *in any way whatsoever* to, and that it varies diametrically from, the sense of objectivity apropos objective news reporting. For it's often claimed that journalistic objectivity differs from Kantian/ Hegelian objectivity in that it (journalistic objectivity) is to be understood, as mentioned earlier, as being synonymous with neutrality and nonpartisanship; whereas the Kantian/ Hegelian mode of objectivity, that of the sciences and philosophy, is often linked to mind-independent facts that hold true despite any feelings, beliefs and/or judgments. (It should be pointed out that such variation of objective sense also testifies to the various modalities of objectivity itself. For objectivity's multivalence, its propensity to give rise to a variety of modes in which its form can be experienced and expressed, is an inherent feature of objectivity that often gives rise to much confusion.)

Conversely, as convincing as it may seem, rather than throw away the Kantian/Hegelian formulation so to resolve the contradiction it engenders, one could do the revolutionary thing: push forward and accept the Kantian-Hegelian formulation, subvert the order to which this formulation is currently bound, and elevate those journalistic values such as honesty, compassion, dedication—values shared and propounded by many non-careerist journalists and alternative media groups—to the level of Kantian/Hegelian objectivity, sanctioning such things as honesty, compassion and so on, as principles one *ought* to follow when conducting journalism. With regard to Levi-Strauss' quote cited in endnote 31, doing this would be just as consistent and reasonable as if all of a sudden the grouping of onions, garlic, turnips, radishes and mustard, even though botany separates liliaceae and crucifers, were to fall under a new single category called "sulfurs"!

In any event, for some, the above argument may seem somewhat flimsily crafted; something may not sit quite right. Perhaps, then, we should approach the issue of objectivity from an entirely different angle... for it could be the case that we're missing something else entirely, something with a far greater extent of import, something that has only been alluded to till now... So let's go ahead and take our analysis over to the "other side" of things. Perhaps those who trenchantly oppose the use of objectivity, both in and out of the newsroom, are telling us something far more radical than what is laid out above, something that they themselves may not be fully aware of, something which they may in fact be disclosing through a certain kind of silence of their own. Maybe this growing disapprobation, a *resistance* if there ever was one, held towards objectivity, is, in the psychoanalytic sense, a *symptom* of our times—what Lacan attributed to the silence of the speaking subject. For it is not the spoken word that stands out against the background of silence, but rather: What is said makes 'the silence emerge as silence.' That is to say, what is candidly enunciated often accentuates that which is not: a trove of disavowed secrets, desires we keep hidden even from ourselves; that which we have "forgotten" we have known all along. What I'm suggesting here can be best articulated in the Hegelian sense of the "Beautiful Soul"—that is to say, *what if it is the case that many, though not all, who condemn the use of objectivity literally need this oppositional figure for the sake of their own subjective consistency?* Without this Big Culprit, "intellectual objectivity," those who decry it would perhaps lose the very external point of reference that is none other than the precondition of their "rebellious" character; which is to also say: One's experience of denouncing objectivity may in fact serve to define their sense of Self. In this instance, does one's unabating vilification of objectivity not mark one's subordination to objectivity? Thus the performative authority behind today's intellectual objectivity may not actually thwart one's self-realization, as many critics of intellectual objectivity often claim, but rather, it may give substance to and thus serve to fulfill one's personality. Therefore the incessant discontent held towards objectivity may actually serve to sustain such objectivity! *And what if this is precisely how ideology functions today?* In this "Beautiful soul" behavior—through such a behavior, by such a behavior—today's ideology is able to fully disclose itself, revealing all the intimate details and secrets behind the way it functions, while continuing to function. And so what if it is the case that, on the one hand, ideology not only gains its support by those who, like today's objective journalists, unquestioningly obey its universal injunctions; but on the other hand, what if ideology also receives a sort of "negative" reinforcement—precisely through those who (disavowedly) depend on it as a means to lament over its "cruel conditions"?

Which invokes another slew of questions. At a much deeper, structural level, what if it is the case that ideology is unable to manage without objectivity, a more extensive objectivity that guarantees the necessity of all that is empirical? What if a firm reliance on objectivity is the very means by which ideology is able to prop itself up and attain its position as an "externalized" (objective) point of reference in which, through which and by which, in a strictly Althusserian sense, its subjects receive and sustain their subjective consistency? And so it's my belief that we can make sense of the tenacious nature of this antagonism only by situating objectivity at the level of ideology.

Although the subject with which we are dealing at this precise moment is specific to journalism, in the case of the overall work before you, its subject matter is none other than that of both objectivity and ideology, and everything else subtended by these universals. And in these times, as a consequence of the mere folly of postmodernism, ideology is again and again referred to as "culture" — yet, to cite Terry Eagleton, it often goes unnoticed that culture, conceived as such, has become 'a new form of absolutism and foundationalism, one quite as virulent as any more political creed.'[32] For the sake of better understanding the material herein, the term "ideology" is to be interchangeable with culture's "big Other," the latter being that which embodies and supports a culture's narratives, beliefs, and lived fantasies.

And because I've chosen to "line the ducks up" in just the way that I have, I feel strongly that we should finish drawing forth this material, here and now, by analyzing what our journalists precisely (do not) have in mind when discussing and disputing objectivity — something of which I firmly believe is not entirely about journalism at all. To repeat an emphasis from earlier, it is conceivably the case that our journalists are conveying something whose scope extends far beyond their own respective sphere of discourse: something inextricably linked to the nature of the dominant culture itself, something linked to the authority of "objective certainty," the authority of the big Other (ruling ideology) that anchors and sustains this culture's narratives, beliefs, and lived fantasies. For, if we were to focus only on journalism *per se*, and not on the universal to which it is appended, it would be as if we were trying to understand the function of a *particular* part of the body, without any knowledge of the body *for which* it functions. A hand lifts an apple, not to lift an apple, but to feed into the mouth that which provides sustenance for the body.

It is against this background that we should begin by asking the following question: What is the larger body for which objectivity serves? Therefore we should question whether or not the notion of objectivity that journalists, philosophers, scientists, et al. have in mind entails something that is beyond their own respective understandings of objectivity, something that these individuals, dare I say it just one more time, are not fully aware of. To provide an answer to such a question we simply need to explore the very disposition of objectivity itself; though rather than digging deep into its inherent qualities, all we need concern ourselves with is appearance. We must be thoroughly watchful for "perplexing first impressions." This is, so I've read, the basic starting point of the psychoanalytic procedure, which shall aid us in discovering those paradoxical moments in which the wholeness of objectivity per se is ruptured by an opposing element that is, nonetheless, *contained within the very field of objectivity.*

## A not-so enlightening Enlightenment

Because it is the nature of my thought to not think in linear fashion—something I should have disclaimed right off the bat—this book, too, will emulate the temperament of my thought; hence the explanatory endnotes embedded in the text for the reader's engagement, and the meandering of sentences that seem to venture up and down the crests of paragraphs before finally arriving at their destination. And so here I wish to introduce another digression, for two reasons: (1) To briefly expound on what I meant, moments ago, when I stated that the purpose of incorporating psychoanalytic theory into this work is to help us "discover those paradoxical moments in which the wholeness of objectivity per se is ruptured by an opposing element that is, nonetheless, *contained within the very field of objectivity*"; and (2) to bring to the reader's attention some sense of a source of today's common notion of objectivity: the Enlightenment. We'll start with the latter.

The Enlightenment began with an intellectual commitment to achieving a universal concordance between peace and justice, a struggle toward intellectual and spiritual freedom. As Jürgen Habermas reminds us, according to the Baron d'Holbach (the emblematic figure of the Enlightenment), 'man is unhappy because he has an erroneous view of nature.' Accordingly, d'Holbach and his followers felt it important, if not imperative, to attain an understanding of reality through a rigorously detached, objective perspective of things in the world.[33] Hence the conviction of the Enlightenment, the source of today's injunction to be objective—the belief that objective knowledge of the laws of nature will reveal to us essential truths, specifically those truths concerning how we ought to live.

It's interesting to reflect on and bear witness to how this ideology gave rise to its own contradiction, how this promotion of objectivity—*contains within its own field an opposing element which ruptures its consistency*. For what was, at its inception, scientific objectivity's vision of delivering peace, justice and happiness as a means to overcome the more insular, parochial perspectives that supported earlier misapprehensions of the world, soon became entrenched in its own insularity of sorts: the mechanistic, materialistic, rationalistic view that broke the world down into a container of objects, bereft of their own volition, a world impoverished of Spirit, an aggregate of senseless and meaningless things secured within an inflexible cause-and-effect relationship, "present-at-hand" for their manipulation by the morally superior objective specialists. In the words of Charles Guignon, 'if nothing exists except inherently valueless material objects in push-pull causal interactions, it becomes plausible to suppose that values are not part of the furniture of the world,' that the Enlightenment stance 'of detached, moral superiority tends to cut us off from the sources of compassion and selfless love that make genuine benevolence possible in the first place.'[34] And to push these charges to the brink of a sobering extreme, one should consider the percipient observation that, by dint of such a prevailing materialistic, mechanistic, instrumentalist, objective view of the world, civil society, in its state of ((post-)industrial) modernity, has become, and continues to be, increasingly organized like a concentration camp; it is tailored almost exclusively around production, overly rationalized, and virtually heedless of the concerns of the individual, having no encouraging consideration for its "exceptions," and thus driven to slowly but surely eradicate all that exceeds the whole for the sake of attaining Utopia.[35] For that reason alone, I find it ethically necessary to expose the ways in which objectivity is, and has been, radically and egregiously misconceived for a very long time. My intention, however, is not to straightforwardly attack objectivity per se; rather my criticism will be executed in a more drawn-out fashion, the ultimate aim being to retain a certain, enduring integrity of objectivity proper.

But what we should focus all our attention on *right now* is this "God's-eye view" of the world, the "view from nowhere" that the Enlightenment dreamed up. This way of seeing things *sub specie aeternitatis*, a perspective believed to be located, fixed, outside the parameters of subjectivism, outside the deadlock of relativism, does not refer to any mastery, *but to an alienation.* And that is both the crux and focus of our analysis: the unwitting construction of a big Other, in which all "knowledge wanders about" in the field of the Other, the Other supposed to know: God, the big Other as such. Those secular humanists, those idealists of the Enlightenment, they had no idea that, unbeknownst to them, they had reintroduced the presence of God in the guise of objectivity!

And to speak gratuitously, I should add that this is not some "metaphorical game," though no doubt there are certain ambiguities that just won't go away. That's expected. Nevertheless, the aim herein is to discover that truth which lies in the work of perspicacious thinkers of the past and present. What I shall put forth is therefore to be neither demanding nor absurd, though no doubt it will at times turn confusing and, owing to its polemical nature here and there, occasionally contentious. And so in the words of J.L. Austin, 'the only merit I should like to claim [...] is that of being true, at least in parts...'[36] For if the truth of a subject—and we will be analyzing many subjects throughout—does not reside in itself but rather in an *object* that is, as Lacan once put it, 'of its nature, concealed,' it is then none other than the efforts of analysis that are to shine light on the object's *fundamentum*, which often hides under its own shadow.

That is to say, in order to fully grasp the nature of objectivity, to properly interpret and understand its given purpose, we are on the lookout for its symptoms—or perhaps what it itself is a symptom of... In any case, the way in which we shall proceed from this moment forth is identical to the way in which Žižek begins his critique of ideology in *The Sublime Object of Ideology*— in the theoretical manner by which Freud insisted the analyst interpret the analysand's dreams: We should not attempt to penetrate the (manifest) form of thought in order to analyze some hidden, "latent content"; rather, we should only ask why the subject's unconscious desires are articulated in the forms of thought that they are. Hued by this light, we would be inevitably ineffective if we were to invest boundless energy into "figuring out" what the content of objectivity, should there even be any, is and/or means. Such a theoretical incursion will prove to be fruitless, inefficacious. Instead, our answers wait for us in the following question: *Why does today's predominant ideal of objectivity assume the form that it does?*

This should not go without addressing, however, that the task here is *not* to seek an immediate answer to such a question. On the contrary, our task is to interpose our own inquisition into the question itself, to perform a sort of lateral intervention into the very essence of the question, and to follow, with patience, wherever that essence may lead us. To paraphrase Hegel: the only way we can learn the truth about the Spirit of our own epoch is to gain access into the Spirits of the past. This shall engender the art of culling the logical conclusion of an original misunderstanding.

# The Long Awaited Introduction

The basic understanding of objectivity, as elaborated by Hegel, demonstrates that objectivity has a *threefold* significance:

- 'The significance of what is externally present, as distinct from what is *only* subjective, meant, dreamed, etc.'
- 'The significance, established by Kant, of what is universal and necessary as distinct from the contingent, particular and subjective that we find in our sensation.'
- 'The significance of what is there, the significance of the *In-itself* as thought-product,' viz., what exists separate from *what* we think about, but that which is also distinct 'from the matter *in-itself*.'[37, 38]

Here it is crucial to notice the definite homology between Hegel's threefold significance of objectivity and the dimensions of the Lacanian triad, *RSI* (Real, Symbolic, Imaginary). This triad, Lacan explained, constitutes the three realms that encompass the subject's psychological activity, which functions to place both subjectivity and psychic phenomena within a specified framework of perception of, and dialogue with, the external world. In his 1991 book, simply titled *Lacan*, Malcolm Bowie alternatively refers to this "(un)holy trinity" as Fraud, Absence and Impossibility.[39] And this is precisely how we will parse objectivity—by equating Hegel's three significances of objectivity with the Lacanian trinity as it is conceived as: Fraud (Imaginary), Absence (Symbolic) and Impossibility (Real).

The importance of relating these two systems to each other (Hegel's threefold significance of objectivity and Lacan's *RSI*) is to provide a unique, step-by-step explanation of the constitution of the object, or, just the same, objectivity. And to fully comprehend each of the three dimensions of Lacan's triad, as they correspond to Hegel's three significances of objectivity, will require, to some degree, a tortuous explication of the *ISR* trinity itself, in which we will situate, at each step of the way, objectivity, its genesis, and its various modes of expression, up to and including its ideological nature.

It is therefore my ambition to explain for the very process behind object creation, i.e., *objectification*—and, without a doubt, we'll come to find that such a process is exceedingly complex; for not only does objectivity advance *from* the subject, proceeding towards its culmination in the universal of objectivity per se, but, all things being equal, in a paradoxical, temporal-loop way, objectivity doesn't entirely originate in the subject—*it also arrives to the subject from the ideological universe from whence it derives.* In other words: objective reality is the "result of the social productive process," much like that of Althusser's theory of ideology: that ideology (in this instance, objectivity) "interpellates" individuals as subjects, i.e., objectivity determines the subject's subjectivity—the subject is an "imaginary construct" fabricated through the process of objectification.

In order to explain how such a procedure is possible, to untangle this aporia, we must first proceed from the abstract base of what we will call the "eternal absence of a first cause": that is to say, our point of departure is that of a nothing that counts for something; which see...

# Part I: Fraud: The Imaginary

## §1. On Alienation and Separation

'Our bodies,' once wrote Yamamoto Tsunetomo, a samurai of the feudal domain of Saga in Hizen Provence, Japan, 'are given life from the midst of nothingness.' To exist where there is nothing, Yamamoto tells us, is the meaning of the phrase, "form is emptiness." 'That all things are provided for by nothingness is the meaning of the phrase, "Emptiness is form." One should not think that these are two separate things.' In many ways, what we're about to discuss is best encapsulated by these opening lines, which present us with a perplexing fact—the sheer emptiness of pure form. It is this void at the core of structure itself, an "absent center" as such, that, like the *élan vital* that explodes from the core of Brecht's first play *Baal*, as a result of the play's inner tension between the irreducible elements of *matter* and *idea*, expels Spirit (i.e., *mind itself*, purposive activity) into the world, whose caroming movement is an entangled, creative interplay within one's reality between the appearance (the "*imag-ination*") of reality, and how appearance proceeds from imagi-nation to its symbolization, whereby one's objective reality is thereby fashioned. It is a process by which the subject is retroac-tively produced as an effect of objectification as such. Thus the emptiness of form, a void that the subject takes the place of, the place of the subject's inscription, plays an indispensable role in objectification, for it possesses a remarkably constitutive nature, one that is always at work in the very *process* of objectification, a process through which some *other* thing gets transformed in the mind of the cognitive subject, reified, from a *thing-in-itself* to a *thing-for-us*. Or, as Hegel would have it, objectification is the dialectical process in which, by which and through which something "immediate-abstract" becomes, for the subject, something "objective-concrete"; a transformation as such that produces an effect that not only instantiates the subject's existence, but *is* the subject.

What we are essentially dealing with here—this effect qua subject—is borne from a "locus of alienation." The subject *is* the effect of its attempts at reconciling an inner antagonism—the subject is the knot of contradiction that is none other than the sum of its own enunciations and cogitations; a clash between outward social mask and inward face; which is to also say that, the subject is the result of the dialectic of the virtual Other of language itself, which seizes the subject by means of the subject's inner, self-moving Spirit that "speaks" through him/her. The subject, then, as such, is both sides of a contradiction; alienated from itself in its own difference from itself.

It is essential to grasp what we mean by this alienation. It is always the case that, for the subject, that which is externally present is always-already separate from the subject, though at the same time this "separateness" is cunningly misleading: *subject and object are united by, and in, this alienation;* "united" not in the standard understanding of the term, but united in the sense that the irreducible gap between these two contradictory terms holds these terms "together" along its edges, sustaining the antagonism as such. The subject also appears outwardly to that which is externally present to itself; thus the separateness between subject and object-Other is none other than a redoubling of the subject's own alienation from itself: "How do I appear to others; what sort of object am I to others?"[40]

This alienation is a feature of the Lacanian Imaginary (Imaginary because we are dealing with a perceptive order), a dimension in which the subject encounters the *'mirror stage as an identification,'* the latter resulting in the 'transformation that takes place in the subject when he assumes an image.' It is by means of this transformation that the subject's ego, the subject's notion of Self, is produced.[41] We'd be mistaken, however, to think that the mirror stage is a single moment in the individual's life. In fact, it never leaves the individual—it's a permanent structure of subjectivity, a stage that traverses the subject's Being throughout his/her entire life. As such, it is a stage that gives rise and/or strength to the relation between imaginary ego and its constitutive image(s)—or, if I may nudge things outside of their orthodox bounds, if only so slightly, this is a stage that gives rise and/or strength to the relation between imaginary ego and, its constitutive *notion* which induces the subject's apperception (the notion, too, as we'll see, is dependent upon its very own constitutive image).

## §2. The mirror in the notion

All notions are conditioned, shaped, and informed by a socio-Symbolic (ideologico-objective) order, propped up and sustained by an intersubjective network into which the subject is inscribed. That said, the notion is that which undergoes a "formal metamorphosis"; its 'incarnation,' Stephen Ross writes, is 'never quite adequate to its fantastic precursor [...] [A]s soon as [the notion] is articulated, elevated into consciousness, it is subject to the structuring imperative of the Symbolic order.'[42] To wit: the stories we are told about the world (ideologies) are always at work, shaping and informing the ways in which we think about and perceive both the world and our place therein...

The main point here is to illustrate the Hegelian concept that, when followed to its logical conclusion, one's self-alienation inevitably results in objectification, which begins with, and in, the formative process of ego-formation, the creation of the subject's "objectal correlate," the *Self*. Thus the subject's self-alienation is, in all respects, what summons/produces objectivity, the latter being the very mode in which, by which and through which the subject, by means of "structurally coupling" itself with and in the field of the object-Other, realizes its *Self* in the historicotemporal process it is caught up in. That is to say, objectivity is a perceptual mode, one that is both established and engaged with by the Spirit of the subject, *for* the subject, as a means to attempt to overcome its self-alienation, as a means to deliver the subject away from the immediate-abstraction of the world in order to arrive at both a concrete meaning of the world and the role(s) the subject will come to assume therein. Put more concisely: through the creation qua summoning of objectivity there arises perception of both Self and one's world—a frame of mind (and, in a sense, a reference) by which one is able to "retroactively posit" the concrete-objective (pre)conditions that one comes to *believe* provide sufficient, reasonable, explanations for his or her present reality and place therein.

To fully understand this idea of radical subjective alienation, and the "constitutive" function it provides in the dialectical process of objectification, it's crucial that we acknowledge the chiasmic-like process involved in the subject's attempt at freeing him/herself of their self-alienation in the following way: The subject's alienation is realized in the reflection of (this alienation) *itself*, a reflection that is both produced by, and given from, the objective significance first conceived by the subject in the form of a *notion* that is abstracted from, then imputed on, what is externally present-at-hand *to the subject* and *for the subject*. And to say that a subject's alienation becomes realized in the wake of receiving a notion of what is external to it, is just the same as saying that what is external to the subject is, properly speaking, imputing itself as a pure "thing-of-thought," as something *Other* that is given *to the subject*, and *for the subject*, in its notion. And the notion is a peculiar *thing*, it's essentially a sort of formal structure lacking any substantiality in and of itself—for although the notion is, as Hegel put it, an "*existent*" that is for the subject and, at once *the subject's* notion, a notion can only be *about* something other—i.e., the notion's *substance*, its content, can only be acquired through and by something *other* than itself.[43] The implication here is that the act of cognition—the forming of a notion *about* something other—presupposes a direct, yet asymmetrical relation between subject and object, between perceiver and perceived. Asymmetrical because the perceived object-Other is constitutive of the perceiver's ideational content, but the perceiver's ideational content does not, in any way, constitute the "inner integrity" of the object-Other's Beingness.

How is it, then, that alienation and relation co-exist so intimately with each other?

## §3. Loss of a loss

When Rodolphe Gasche claimed in his book *The Tain of the Mirror* that 'any entity is what it is only by being divided by the Other to which it refers in order to constitute itself,'[44] he was making a direct (Hegelian) reference to the subject's locus of alienation and its unique "causal" nature in the world. One way we can apprehend this is by looking to the basic thrust behind Hegel's *Phenomenology*: that the subject's initial, mindful awareness of something other coincides with an initial lack of knowledge and thus a lack of understanding of this other thing; and this initial *lack* of understanding then begets its own subsequent loss in order to create the necessary space for the arrival of the subject's notion (of the object-Other). Let's say that I seek to understand something, something of which, initially, I lack a complete understanding. In such a case, this initial lack of understanding (of this thing I aim to understand) must also be given up to a loss—so that a *notion* of the very thing I seek to understand may replace the initial lack of understanding of this thing. To put it very simply: for something to come, something must go; for a notion of something to arrive in thought, the initial lack of understanding of this something must go. It is through this process, via a "loss of a loss" as such (hereafter, "second-order loss"), that something unique occurs to the subject, in the subject, and for the subject: the manifestation of a notion, which in effect changes what is initially external to and thus separate from the subject into an *object*, thereby bringing the subject at "union" with the object, a union marked by the subject's very gaze (act of perception) upon the object as such. What ultimately takes place *with*in, through, and by this "notional structure"—a structure that is engendered not only by difference (i.e., subject and other), but also, at a more elementary level, by this "second-order loss"—is the determinate moment when the subject's notion of *Self* emerges, when the subject first appears for itself in the guise of the notion of *Self*: what we will call an "objectal correlate" of the pure subject itself.

In other words, the proper way to understand what's just been said is to invert it: The subject's initial lack of knowledge and understanding of an other thing is none other than the inverted appearance of the subject's original lack of knowledge and understanding of the nature of its own self: *What appears as reality "out there" is none other than the inversion of an ontological void inherent to the subject itself.* Nothing better exemplifies this than the Cartesian formulation: "I have a notion of whether or not there exists this other thing, therefore I am thinking, therefore "I" exist." The notion of the object-Other is unfailingly suggestive of the notion of Self: which is to say, the notion of the object-Other is *reflexive* of the thinking subject, or rather, the notion of the object-Other *retroactively* confers on the cognitive subject its notion of Self. The "I" that thinks about the object-Other thus serves to supplement the radical lack of this "I" as such.

In other words, we must not lose sight of that, which, for Monsieur Descartes, was in shadow: the fact that the notion itself, *in-itself* and *of-itself*, is devoid of any substance. Its pure form, before ever being about something other than itself, is essentially empty: which is to say, what precedes the notion, what precedes even thought itself—that which marks the place of the subject itself—is a radical loss, a void as such. Thus the notion itself, whether it's about one's Self, or something other than one's Self, arises from, is constituted *because of*, this fundamental lack, a lack that is not only situated at the core of the subject—*but one that precedes the subject*. This lack is a nub of "fecund" nothingness, a pre-ontological void swirling at the core of the subject and its reality, a lack that is "generative," or rather "constitutive" of the subject and its reality—for it is this void from which all notions arise, and around which all notions circulate, ultimately constituting for the subject its (protean) notion of Self, an objectal correlate of the subject as such.

## §4. Self as the object of the subject

Does it not seem, then, as if the notion itself is a vital aspect of object creation (objectification)? In the subject's notion of something external, this something *other* radically changes: it assumes its *objective* image; it changes from a *thing-in-itself* to an *object-for-us* in its notion; from a *thing* that is presented from "out there," to an *object* of representation persisting in the subject's mind, which, by dint of the subject's cognitive activity, is reflexive of the thinking subject. Thus the notion of something external *retroactively* presents to the subject its own notional, objectal correlate: its *Self*. Which is to say: the object-Other is always-already an "externalization" of the subject's inner core.

That said, we should now turn to what Lacan has written about Descartes' discovery of the cogito (this "discovery" being none other than the result of a radical misconstruction of "certainty," and thereby the inadvertent construction of, in the Lacanian sense, an "Other"): it is his knowledge of *something* certain—that he exists as that "I" which is discerned as that which is thinking, and to not 'make of the *I think* a mere point of fading'—that Descartes has done something quite uncanny: 'He puts the field of this knowledge at the level of the vaster subject, the subject [qua Other] who is supposed to know.'[45] That is to say, it is arguably the case that Descartes' discovery marks the very moment when the unconscious, the field of the Other, was formally introduced into our history. Descartes' cogito provides, unwittingly, a unique though inexplicit illustration of the Self as something separate from the (pure) subject itself, though nonetheless a representation thereof: It's as if the notion of Self is the product of a self-engenderment of the pure subject itself; as if the Spirit of the subject has extended beyond the place of the subject in the purposive act of thinking *about* something other — it is, *as if*, subjective Spirit has moved beyond the negative space of the subject to create for the subject an *objective* point of "external" reference of itself and for itself, as a means to retroject upon the subject its own positive notion of Self.

Therein we are able to detect the subject's radical alienation from itself, marked by the gap between the "transcendental," apperceptive "*I*" (the Kantian "*thing* that thinks," the essentially insubstantial structure of thought which, according to Lacan, is not actually transcendental at all but rather the "object-libido" based at the very core of the subject) and the "*I*" of empirical experience (the Other of the "*I*" that thinks: the Self). Thus the subject can apprehend itself only *after* encountering the notion of its Self — the latter being the subject's *objectal correlate* — which is reflected back to the subject only in, and thus by, the object-Other (in its notion) — *which ultimately "coincides" with the subject.*

What has been said can also be expressed by saying that, in order for the subject to attain its notion of Self, this notion must receive its substantial content by and through the experience of alterity, through difference as it appears outwardly, i.e., externally, to the subject. We arrive at knowledge of "who" or "what" we are by and through our engagement with something *other*, something perceived as different than us. Though it should be recognized, as stated above, that the *perceived* external world, in all its *otherness*, is inextricably connected to our subjectivity through our objective relation with it: The object-Other is nonetheless something to which the subject has "lost" a part of itself: what is essentially always-already lost is the subject's "unified identity." And through the subject's unavailing endeavors to regain this original loss as such, a part of itself must pass over to the side of the object-Other—that being none other than the subject's *notion* itself, which has left its subjective place of "origin," has passed over to the Other side, the side of objects; in the words of Alenka Zupančič,

> the subject finds itself on the opposite side of objects or things (seeing them, exploring them, learning about them) only insofar as there is a "thing from the subject" [notion] that dwells among these objects or things, a fragmentary remainder of subjectivity dissolved into the "stuff of the world" through the occurrence of a primordial severance.[46]

This primordial severance marks the starting point of a cut in reality that *is* the place of the subject's (Symbolic) inscription, a fissure, so to speak, that marks the moment when, to use a familiar Nietzschean expression, "One becomes Two": when a part of the subject, its *notion*, passes over and into the object-Other. What this means is that the subject, at its most fundamental level, is a *"lost object,"* fragmented as such, and thus not a complete entity unto itself—the subject requires something *other* to constitute (the notion of) its Self; the subject finds its Self in the other, through the other, and by the other in its notion. Can we not paraphrase crabby ol' Schopenhauer here? The object-Other presupposes the subject; what is other always-already represents a subject. And by the same token, the claim that the subject has lost a part of itself calls attention to the fact that this "lost" part directly corresponds to the void that is *internal* to the subject—*insofar as this void is transposed into the place of the Other, appearing in the guise of the object-Other that assumes the place of this void.* Thus the subject is the other in its notion; the void at the core of the subject appears in the mode of its opposite: *as the external object-Other that takes the place of the void as such.*

As we can see, the associative link between subject and object-Other—that the subject acquires its Self by and through the other as such—bears an immutable lack, a void at the core of the subject itself, indicated by the "second-order loss" mentioned previously. The subject endeavors to fulfill this lack with the object-Other by identifying, one way or another, with the object-Other precisely in its notion, and this process both creates and takes place in the subject's ego. The ego is thus a nexus of all notions of the object-Other, which are, like the gaze itself, redirected back to the subject whereby they become integrated into a (deceptive) "unity" of Self.

Here, it's crucial to point out that this unification is anything but a closed totality (which will be explained further on). And what's more, this specious unification of Self is not founded on the "real object," not on the *real* entity as it exists separate from the subject, but rather: The ego and its unification is founded on, this process occurs through, the subject's representations, notions, concepts and ideas, etc. that are aimed at and about object-Others—which are none other than (mis)constructions of the real things they are about. This is why, in my opinion, object-oriented ontology misses its own crucial point: Though it would seem that an object-oriented ontology can always collapse back into a subject-oriented ontology (simply because an object presupposes the subject by virtue of the fact that the determination of an object always entails the use of the notion, which, *eo ipso*, presupposes the subject) the case is rather that, object-oriented ontology should prop its legitimacy upon the very fact that *the field of object-Others itself, the world of objects, is precisely what creates (the illusion of) an ontological closure for the subject.* In other words, the field of objectivity serves to provide us with a dependable sense of ontological consistency. But we should take this a step further even. We should take seriously the dialectic between a subject-oriented ontology versus an object-oriented ontology in order to arrive at its Absolute understanding: that the only *true* ontology here is one that is equivalent to "non-being"; for the *pure* subject posits its Self in and through the field of the object-Other precisely because the subject, as such, is essentially a void, an empty form lacking the very Self it posits in and through the object-Other.[47] As such, the pure subject is essentially a-substantial and irreflexive. And thus, at least on the side of the subject, from which we deal in metaphysical matters, there is not complete ontology.

## §5. The generative void

The postulate here is that the subject's Self-identity has its origin in a *constitutive lack*, a "lack" because the subject, without its notion of Self, does not exist. This primordial, empty "inner-space" is none other than the place of the subject's inscription. In other words, there first exists, in the subject, only pure difference, the difference between the subject and its empty place of inscription, the "disparity between existence with itself": the minimal difference between the negative, empty framework of thought itself, bereft of any substance, and the Self-determination of subjective Spirit, which seeks out, in its activity, the substance that becomes subject. The subject's notion of Self arises not when this Self is posited in its difference from itself, but when this pure difference as such is displaced into the field of the object-Other — as it appears in its difference reflected by the otherness inherent to the multitude of which the subject is itself an estranged particular. That is to say, the subject's difference from itself is (de)posited in(to) its difference from the Other. This is precisely what it means to posit the paradoxical claim that the Self materializes out of the animate manifold which *appears* as external to the subject, while at the same time, the Self emerges from the pure difference from itself: Though the subject is nonetheless a *part* of, inherent to, the reality it sees, it also exists *apart* from this reality. The subject is thus the empty space that remains when the rest of its world is removed. Is this not the basic starting point of one's radical freedom? "I am what the rest of the world is not, a negative space, a silhouette of my own form that stands against all else, ready to be filled with whatever substance I so choose." This "productive nullity" is the very basis of the subject. The pure subject *is* this negative space from which subjective Spirit emanates, from which Spirit begins its quest in the field of the object-Other in order to gather therefrom, for the subject, the subject's objectal correlate; a process *as such*, in which, by which, and through which the subject acquires its sense of Self. Without Self-identity, without any substance, there is only a *nothing* at the core of the subject—that is to say, the subject's Self(-identity) is *not inborn*, it is only ever acquired from the side of the object-Other into which this "nothing" is displaced; that being so, the very nature of Spirit is to *relate* to the world from which it is otherwise alienated. This is the basic import of Hegel's *Phenomenology*: one's sense of Self, Self-consciousness, hijacks— to make as its own limit and ontological "source"—what a "pre-conscious" life, that of an absorption into the rawness of the Real, would have been had it been immersed in a world without *Spirit* and cognition proper. As Maurice Merleau-Ponty writes in his chapter "Hegel's Existentialism" from his book *Sense and Nonsense*, if the subject were to remain in this "pre-conscious" mode of existence, it would perhaps be under the governance of a 'force which disperses itself wherever it acts, a "dying and becoming" which would not even be aware of itself. Thus in order for there to be consciousness, in order for one to have a sense of Self, the subject must forego its state of "pre-consciousness" and become

59

total and aware of itself—which is in principle impossible for life. An absence of being would have to come into the world, a nothingness from which being would be visible, such that consciousness of life, taken radically, is consciousness of death.

But what if we think of this primordial void, a lack of an integral, unified Self, as *"generative"*? As mentioned above, this absence, a void as such, is precisely that which sets in motion the "seeking-out" activity behind the dialectic of identification, which is responsible for the subject's notion of Self, a notion that is arrived at—and acquires its substantial content—only by and through something external, something other in which the subject "externalizes" something internal of its own—its *lack!* And there we have it, the subject's lack thus appears in the guise of its opposite, as some *thing* other than itself, as an object-Other, which holds the place of, "gives body to," the subject's lack, thereby furnishing, for the subject, an external point of reference that serves to provide the subject as such with a sense of subjective consistency.

The subject is thus split, split between its notion of substantial Self (which corresponds with something other that is *for* the subject's lack)[48] and a fundamental lack in the subject itself that bears an immutable absence of this Self, which, paradoxically, precipitates the notion of Self as a supplement to this original lack. This notion of Self then advances upon the world, striving to encompass all of its differences, differences that are, in their immediacy, marked by the apparent split between the subject and the object-Other, which is none other than the "outward" appearance of the fissure intrinsic to the subject itself—the subject's inner-disparity between its own Being and nonexistence—as it's inverted in its opposite. The subject's Self, however, *cannot* encompass all of its differences precisely because, as Derrida alluded to in much of his work, *the subject is the very embodiment of this opposition between presence and absence.* Thus the Self-qua-notion undergoes a long and slow process of object creation, a process entailing the (mis)construction of its surroundings into objects in the *attempt* to "unify" the subject's identity in all of its differences. This "unification" is doomed to fail from the start, however, simply because there is no *real* object involved in this process of unification, there is only a thought-product that supervenes, that is placed on, a *real* entity; and thus the Self, too, is none other than an identity construct as such, an "objectal morsel," so to speak, that has crumbled off from a larger aggregate of objective elements known as the socio-Symbolic order.

What I mean by this is that, the entire process of objectification *seems* to begin with the subject's conscious perception of an external entity, whereby the subject's conscious perception of the entity in effect changes the entity into an object of the subject's gaze. This process of objectification, however, does not actually begin solely from, or occur isolated in, the Imaginary order of "conscious" perception; it's much more complex than that, for, albeit perception is first staged in the Imaginary order, it is always followed by a Symbolic intervention.

The Self is therefore an illusion, a sort of cognitive simulation, one that always appears to the subject, for the subject, against the background of its own original loss, that loss being the original lack constitutive of the subject's Self. Thus the Self emerges from an internal rupture as such—and that is precisely why it serves to encompass all differences in and of the subject in its oneness (of Self) *as such*; it serves as a means to retroactively confer on the subject some sense of objective self-understanding—a *history*—that serves to supplement the original lack of Self.

This innate split, between being and knowing, between the subject's place of inscription and its Self, between subject and object-Other—between zero-qua-nothingness and oneness, one could even say—is not only deeply woven into the constitutive fabric of the subject, it also serves as the impetus behind the development of the subject's worldview. This void as such is the innermost constituent of reality itself, for it is none other than the void-qua-subject-qua-existent that introduces this very cut into reality.[49]

In any event, we can now see that objectivity refers to some "object-Thing" that is more in the object than the object itself. It is none other than a piece of the subject that is externalized into the object: it is precisely the way in which the subject inscribes itself in the object-Other in its notion, a notion that emerges from the generative void at the core of the subject itself. But is the subject really aware of all this? No. Despite the fact that the subject is simply "seeing" its Self in the notion of the object-Other, the subject does not actually realize that he or she is doing so.

## §6. The concept, in which all knowledge wanders

What this means is that, objective knowledge never fully arrives at its proper place, for it is not so much a knowledge that coincides perfectly with the object-Other, insofar as it is a knowledge that is reflexive of the subject's own Symbolic condition: the place from which the subject thinks, the subject's own socio-Symbolic context (whether we're talking about a position of Marxist objectivism, Cartesian objectivism, Bentham-utilitarian objectivism, Ayn-Randian objectivism, or whatever). This ideological (objective) domain is what shapes and informs both the manner in which the subject thinks and, ultimately, the bulk of concepts that emerge from within such a space.

In terms of sussing out truth, *good ol' objective truth*, this throws a bit of a monkey wrench into the whole scheme of things. Most people these days often want "objective" explanations, not stories. But what most people often forget, what they keep secret from themselves even, what they disavow, is that all explanations are (embedded in larger) "stories," so to speak, in which they themselves are inscribed. And just like stories, explanations may contain an element of truth or two—but it's like saying Mitt Romney and Newt Gingrich are great dads. Just because something may be true doesn't mean it tells the whole story.

Let me be perfectly clear, the only way we *can* know anything true about an object is by knowing what it *is not*: viz., starting from one's complete lack of knowledge about an object, one devises first a notion that then develops into a *concept* for the object, which serves as a sort of stand-in for the object. One then further develops the concept by learning what the object is not in its concept. And the "truth" of the concept unfolds through its own errors, insofar as the concept is followed to its logical end. Can we not see, then, that since the concept is merely a stand-in for its object, the concept itself is a signifier that doesn't refer directly to its object inasmuch as it refers back to the act of subjective cognition (an act of cognition, nonetheless, that is shaped and informed by the subject's Symbolic situation), the very place whence the concept derives—the base of the subject's desire?

As Judith Butler writes, such an 'imaginary relation, the one constituted through narcissistic identification,' (constituted by, in, and through the subject), 'is always tenuous because it is an external object that is determined to be [a moment of] oneself [in its concept]; this failure to close the distance between the ego [and its object of thought] haunts that identification as its constitutive discord and failure.'[50] And so it follows that it is the social pact, the subject's inscription in the Symbolic, that 'overrides the tenuousness of [the antagonism inherent to] imaginary identification and confers on it a social durability and legitimacy.'[51] As such, the object at its zero-point, as a real entity, exists as that unfathomable, ambiguous external thing that is the impetus behind the notion given by the object in the first place—*the very notion that initially compels one to consider the object 'in the deter-*

*minacy that is posited by its concept.'*

In other words, the object *is* the "external core" of the subject, the object that the subject thinks through. That is to say, in concept, subject and object are inextricably one: 'what appears as a property of the "object" is actually a property of our own interpretative procedure of the object.'[52] And objective thought—that which carries out an interpretative procedure—is shaped and informed by the larger Symbolic order in which the subject is inscribed.

Thus all that knowledge *"is"* is the understanding of a concept. And all a concept *"is"* is an evolving notion of anything and everything *other* than us. And because we can never place ourselves in the position of an *other*, because we can never know an other's pure, inner integrity, it is, accordingly, impossible to truly know an other. Therefore, "objective" knowledge is, in this sense, merely pretension: that is, we pretend to know, and we believe in *that*. Thus our lived reality is structured according to our beliefs, moreso than what we know. And our beliefs are always hooked onto some ideological field in which a Master-Signifier determines for us the paradigmatic context which this field takes on. To put it in Lacanian terms, the "university discourse" (a social-link that designates a specific kind of discourse, the business of which is the "systematizating mortification" of thought itself, which, as such, seeks to intellectualize all projects of imagination and artistic creativity) is that which elaborates the network of knowledge; and a given network of knowledge is not only sustained, but also shaped and informed, by the Master-Signifier that presides over it. Take as an example President George W. Bush's education-reform bill that was signed into law on 8 January 2002, the "No Child Left Behind" Act of 2001. Under this act, assessment of childhood education in public schools became based exclusively on quantitative data, specifically, standardized testing, thereby excluding any qualitative influence on, and assessment of, student development in the public schools system.

In any case, "truth is that which chases after itself"; it changes according to the way in which knowledge, as it is gathered in concept, changes. And a change in the network of knowledge is always pursuant to a change in the Master-Signifier.

Another way we can formulate the nature of the concept is by drawing attention, once again, to the fact that, when we consider the notion of an object-Other *in-itself*, what we are essentially dealing with is more than just the standard Kantian Thing-in-itself (*Ding an sich*)—the idea that every thing is, in itself, an "infinite recess," unknowable and inaccessible by any other thing. Rather, to be meticulously astute about the matter, there is a deeper issue afoot here, one that is much different than the suspicion that we can never know a thing in its "pure integrity"—*the way in which we, as subjects, are inscribed in the world of things we observe*. Our desire to know things-in-themselves presents a "split," a "cut," in the very fabric of Beingness in which we lodge ourselves. Lacan writes to this effect:

What is at issue here is not the philosophical problem of representation. From that point of view, when I am presented with a representation, I assure myself that I know quite a lot about it, I assure myself as a consciousness that knows that it is only representation, and that there is, beyond, the thing itself. Behind the phenomenon, there is the noumenon, for example. I may not be able to do anything about it, because my *transcendental categories*, as Kant would say, do just as they please and force me to take the thing in their way ... In my opinion, it is not in this dialectic between the surface and that which is beyond that things are suspended. For my part, I set out from the fact that there is something that establishes a fracture, a bi-partition, a splitting of the being to which the being accommodates itself, even in the natural world.[53]

Thus, as Hegel claimed, the gap that is *within* oneself, which makes its appearance outwardly in the form of the antithesis between subject and object, is filled in by the thought of the (desiring) subject. The subject's desire to know—effectuated by the subject's act of apprehending its separateness from the world "out there"—presents a splitting in the very fabric of Being, a distortion representative of a "wound of/in nature" as such. And this distortion nonetheless becomes the constitutive element of the subject's reality; the subject's initial notion unfolds into a developing concept in which, by which and through which the subject's reality becomes mediated: That is to say, the *concept* of an object overturns this original distortion; the object-Other, as it exists first in its notion and then in its concept, diminishes this lacunal distortion—it fills this gap, so to speak.

The antithesis between subject and object, between the subject's object of desire and the subject itself, is thus "overcome" by the *concept* of the object, *in the concept itself,* in a mode of objectivity as such: The subject's concept of the object-Other, which emerges from the very division that cuts across the subject and the object-Other (which, again, originates from *within* the subject), unites the subject *with* the object-Other in the "oneness" of the concept—i.e., subject and object-Other become inextricably "one" as such. Through the concept the subject transcends its bodily restrictiveness; in the concept, the finite extends beyond its own immediate finitude—subjective Spirit moves beyond material beingness, the subject's thought extends beyond its bodily restrictiveness—moving toward that which limits it. And the subject's thought, perforce, *arrives* at that which limits the subject: the subject arrives at the unknowability of the object-Other through the processable activity propelling the development of the concept as such.

Thought therefore paradoxically creates the locus of the Other *by means of entering into the field of the Other.* The subject's thought is *about* some other *real* thing, and is thus invariably directed outward, toward this something-*other*, something other than the subject, something that, through difference per se, both limits the subject's Self while, at the same time, retroactively creating and giving substance to the subject's Self.

It is through the ordering of thought, and in said order of thought, that the subject arrives at the side of the object-Other in its notion; should this notion continue to develop into an emerging concept, the subject will begin to inscribe both him/herself and the other into what becomes the developing-concept. This agency of knowledge creation, that of contemplation, or, imagination even, is the very means by which subjective Spirit carries itself beyond its subject's finitude, making its way toward the side of the object-Other (the dimension of the Other) before curving back toward its place *in situ.*

Is this not a simple question of economics really? A means to organize thought products into a consistent and totalized reality, *for the very subject that is none other than an effect of such a process of organization?*

## §7. *Rebecca*, a model for dialectical materialism

A decent enough way to explain how the subject presents a cut in reality can be found through interrogating today's doctrine of scientific materialism: the belief in the central assumption that everything is, in essence, insensate material governed by constant physical mechanical laws—including the phenomenon of mind itself, mind being that which enables our awareness of the world around us and our experiences therein. According to this view, all matter is essentially non-conscious, there is no "inner life"; subjectivity is, merely, as philosopher Daniel Dennett puts it, illusion; something to the effect of "puffs of steam," as it were—the fugacious side effect of mechanical non-conscious operations. In other words, human consciousness, in the opinion of today's diehard cognitivists, is an illusion, the mere byproduct of matter and its material activities, like steam billowing out of the smoke stack of a locomotive. I can agree up to a point that consciousness is an "illusion" of sorts, a kind of "magic trick" that is the result of just that—tricks played by simple... well... actually, tricks which are played by very complex operations. But what, exactly, is coordinating this elaborate trick? Can we not find another way to look at this issue without engendering a mystified Idealism-obscurantism? Can there not be another way to think, to *imagine*, materialism? The answer, of course, is: yes.

It is simply impossible, all abstractions aside, to actually remove subjectivity from the world altogether when observing something or conducting an experiment—to return to Schopenhauer's claim, "the object presupposes the subject." The meaning of the latter proposition can be best understood if we think of the object in the same way as Deleuze himself considered objects: as things existing, experienced, and expressed in three incommensurate modalities at once: (i) "objects as isolated positive entities occupying a particular location in abstract geometric space" (as Liebniz reminds us in his *Metaphysics*, the *concept* of the extension of a body in "abstract geometric space" is, in a sense, *imaginary*: viz., though in fact an object, regardless of the presence or not of an external witness, has as an intrinsic property of a specific extension in geometric space, for this to be realized *in concept*, there requires a subject to *think* this, and therefore the concept *itself* presupposes the subject); (ii) "as objects of contemplative representation" (the act of contemplation also presupposes a subject); and (iii) "as objects perceived through the standpoint of the subject's existential engagement, reduced to their potential use within the horizon of the subject's interests, projects, desires, and so on" (which is also... you guessed it: subjective—for the *use* of some thing, of an object (which is not the same as Graham Harman's formulation of "tool-being"; the latter being the "unseen efficacy" of a given entity, the non-disclosure of a being's total potential activity, which is concealed precisely by what is revealed through the being's salient activity only—by its "functionality": those actions which lead to an explicit end-point, while all excess potential activity withdraws back into concealment), is often reflexive of an original *want*, a desire propped up by a motivating idea prior to the use of the (desired) object. As for the nature of consciousness being like that of discharged steam from a locomotive, well, even if this were true, a locomotive doesn't produce itself; its existence requires, to a certain extent, someone to *think* of the idea itself, and then an engineer, laborers, etc., to fabricate the thing itself; it also requires someone, if not an entire team, to operate it. In other words, albeit the existence of a locomotive involves its necessary material components, before these components can ever be arranged, organized into the proper order that constitutes the locomotive, the idea as such must exist beforehand.[54] And in terms of consciousness being an illusion, a sort of magic trick, as it were—what is "It" that is *performing* the thaumaturgical act?).[55, 56] These three modes of objectivity, then, are, *simultaneously*, mutually interdependent for their respective definitions and, wholly incommensurable with one another. Does this not parallel well with how Hegel viewed objectivity: that it has *three* significances as such?

The significance of drawing a cogent parallel between these three modes of objectivity, and Lacan's *RSI* triad is to show that consciousness, subjective experience, the nature of notions, ideas and concepts, and so on, cannot be entirely explained for in the traditional terms of mechanical, vulgar-materialist processes; there is a lacuna in the materialist explanation of things precisely because this lacuna is part of the fabric of reality, part of the material universe itself. And this "hole" *is* the subject. For there always remains a void—like a stain that will not go away—one that the subject takes the place of, or rather: *The subject is essentially this void, a nothingness that counts for something.*

This is precisely what today's materialists should acknowledge, and then proceed to admit the following: that, as Hegel surmised, *'there Is only Nothing*, and all processes take place "from Nothing through Nothing to Nothing."'[57]

But what if this Nothing is really a "Nothing that counts for Something"... much like a black hole? For when an object collapses under its own gravity, inverting itself so radically, in such a way that it creates a rip in the fabric of space itself, one can think of the black hole as 'a kind of self-sustaining gravitational field.' That is to say, despite the full collapse of something into nothing, *this "nothing" still counts for something.* Despite the absence of a preexisting thing, this absence nonetheless exerts a palpable force. As Žižek paraphrases Roger Penrose: In physics one reasonably 'considers the possibility that a field generated by a material object could persist in the object's absence.'[58]

What better way to exemplify this than with the character Rebecca, from Daphne du Maurier's novel, *Rebecca*? Which was later adapted for the silver screen and directed by Alfred Hitchcock. Rebecca, the titular character of the novel, as someone who exerts a presence *all the time*, does not really exist—*she's deceased*. Though despite her death, despite her absence, *she exists everywhere*, there is some *thing* that was always-already in her other than her herself, that persists; and characters nonetheless dwell in this *thing's* (*her*) world. After all, it is *her* book! That is to say, Rebecca's very absence exerts a palpable force, as a "Nothing that counts for Something." Do we not find here a remarkable illustration of the subject's Spirit, an individual *Thing-in-itself* that, despite its seeming "a-substantiality," somehow coincides with an extension of force? In other words, something takes the place of nothing.

Can we not surmise, then, that the place of the subject's

inscription is like that of a black hole: a rip in space within space, a void *within* the "wholeness" of the universe that exerts a force; a vortex that pulls into its center what it is not as a means to determine and acquire a sense of what it is, and through that an understanding of this sense of what it is? As Liebniz posited, the subject is an expression of the whole universe in its own manner, from its own empty place of inscription—or, one could also say that the (pure) subject is an "empty container" in which its acquired identifications accrue.

So perhaps today's vulgar materialists should consider incorporating a little German Idealism in their doctrine: that our objective situation in material reality *is* our subjective situation; as such it is a gaping hole within reality itself, always-already "open" insofar as we are engaged in this reality. And that, furthermore, the whole of material reality is *not* a closed order determined solely by universal laws, but is rather something that contains within it an "empty space," that which is "not-All," a negative space around which the "All" of everything circulates in nomic or law-like fashion.[59]

## §8. The logic of the signifier

The committed Lacanian reader will notice how all this distinctly parallels Lacan's formula for the signifier; he writes:

a signifier is what represents the subject to another signifier. This latter signifier is therefore the signifier to which all the other signifiers represent the subject—which means that if this signifier is missing, all the other signifiers represent nothing. For something is only represented to. [I.e., something is only represented for something else].[60]

What is meant by this, is that within a matrix of differentiality, within a system of varying signifiers, the opposite of the *presence* of one signifier is not another signifier in its immediacy, but rather the *absence* of itself: its *lack*: the initial, constitutive void that marks the place of, *coincides with*, its place of inscription. In structuralist jargon, the presence of a term is equivalent to the absence of its opposite term, and this absence of the opposite term, a void as such, is nonetheless contained *within the presence of the initial term*. And the presence of the other (signifier), the opposite, "fills out" the void of the first signifier's absence. Namely, the presence of a signifier corresponds with the absence of its opposite, i.e., it "holds the place of" its opposite, containing the void within itself as such.

In other words, a term, a signifier—the subject's *Self* for example, always appears against the background of its own possible absence. And its appearance materializes in the presence of its opposite, in the presence of something other, another signifier:

> Thus is marked the first split that makes the subject as such distinguish himself from the sign in relation to which, at first, he has been able to constitute himself as subject.[61]

Lacan designates this absence with the matheme $, the "barred" signifier, which is also the Lacanian matheme for the *pure subject* (hereafter, "subject-proper"). And so it follows that a signifier, S1 (the "Master-Signifier," the subject's *Self*), represents for another signifier, S2 (the chain of signifiers, which includes the subject, its Self, and everything the subject is (and is not) predicated of), S1's lack—this lack being S1's place of inscription: $—the latter corresponding to the subject-proper, which always appears in the guise of its Self-representation (S1) for another signifier (S2) as such. Moreover, within the signifier's dyad, there is never a direct correspondence between a signifier and its opposite, rather: the opposite, the other as such (S2, the object-identification), helps give rise to, gives "substance" to, the first signifier (S1, the subject's Self), which coincides with its own possible absence, its place of inscription. As such, S1 serves to conceal the lack, the constitutive void ($) from which it—i.e., S1, the subject's Self as such—emerges, and around which all other signifiers persist. That is to say—and here is where things get more complicated, so one should read this slowly and perhaps a few times through—the signifier is that which represents the subject-proper for another signifier; and hence 'there results that, at the level of the other signifier, the subject fades away,'[62] which is to also say: the first subject-proper's *Self* (S1) represents for another subject-proper's *Self* (S2), the first subject-proper: *a void* ($), and vice versa—so that S2 (appearing for/to S1) is also, itself, a void ($) representing to another subject-proper's *Self* (S2), its *Self* (S1). Thus S1 coincides with the difference between/within both subjects, operating as a paradoxical element that *is* the absence itself. And thus the subject(-proper) fades away as its Self (its signifier) holds the subject-proper's place in its representation for another Self (another subject's signifier). And through this process of relation—by means of difference as such—the subject's signifier, its *Self*, accrues its formation by means of supplementary identifications found in its difference, in that which is *other*.

Can we not see, then, how, in this instance, as a *representation* of the subject-proper, the signifier itself (e.g., the Self), too, is none other than an objectal correlate of the subject-proper? Perhaps, then, we should consider the logic of the signifier as another example of objectification. For the very purpose behind the signifying chain and its paradoxical logic, an act of objectification as such, is to create Self-meaning for the subject from, and in, a world that is otherwise alien and thus essentially "meaningless." The logic of the signifier is thus a means to not only understand such a world but to *relate* to it as well, to find one's *place* in it. Let's go further…

Lacan referred to the signifier as being both the "metonymy

of the object" and the "metaphor of the subject." To wit, the signifier, the notion of Self, the objectal correlate as such, holds a "metonymic" relationship with the very object-Other that gives rise to it, another signifier; and it holds a "metaphoric" relationship towards the a-substantial void that is the subject-proper. Here, we should bear in mind that, in the latter sense, that of metaphor, the signifier is a sort of "one" that stands in for a zero, *a nothing that counts for something*: the difference between the subject proper and its place of inscription, thus marking the very movement from "zero to one." Therefore zero is not entirely a pure nothing—or rather, scratch that: As pure nothingness, the "zero" nonetheless accounts for *nothing in the form of its opposite: as something: One.* This is what it means to say that the void *is* the subject-proper who attains an identity, a sense of Self—a *nothing that counts for something as such.*

The common doxa on signifiers is that they attain their positive meaning via a self-negation within a relational matrix of differences (e.g., the all-too-familiar structuralist example owing to the work of Ferdinand de Saussure: A word means what it does only in relation to what it doesn't mean). On the contrary, however, signifiers enter into this relationship of difference by dint of what Lacan claimed to be a "third" term: the void of their possible absence ($). Now, this void is the crucial element around which the entire battery of signifiers operates. In other words, the operative difference within the signifying chain, i.e., the very difference which confers meaning onto signifiers, does not actually reside in the difference between signifiers, as Saussure had posited, but rather: *Meaning derives from the difference between the ordered space of the signifying chain and that which is "outside" the signifying chain: a nothing, a void, which is contained within the entire system.* Thus the system itself accounts for the very difference between that which consists within it, and, its outside: a Nothing. That is to say, for the subject, there is literally *nothing* that exists outside of language, and this void, the difference between the system's interior and "exterior" is accounted for *within* the system itself: the void as such is contained *within* the "whole" system of language. And the act of concealing this (constitutive) void, which gives rise to the illusion of the system's "wholeness," is effectuated by what is often referred to as an "empty" signifier, a signifier that refers only to itself, otherwise known as a "Master-Signifier". The Master-Signifier's sole function is thus to "suture" this "proto-ontological" void shut by an "act of concealment"; which is to say, this act of concealment occurs by placing a signifier that only refers to itself in the place of the void as such. E.g., the very word *"meaning"* serves to conceal the inherent *lack* of meaning inscribed in the "whole" language system that is the signifying chain—remove the signifier "meaning" and all that is left is the very nothingness, the void of *non-meaning*, that it conceals, a void of non-meaning from which all meaning blossoms. In effect, this act of "suturing," as such, gives rise to an ordered space, it "frames" a context in which all other signifiers are able to attain their respective meanings (identities) in a differential matrix, and thus attain Self-realization, recognizing themselves in the Other as such. It is by dint of the Master-Signifier that all the other signifiers are secured in their place within such a context, one in which their slippage of meaning (identity) is preempted against.

Here it is crucial to take note of the twofold function of the Master-Signifier as it consists of those two terms mentioned above, "metonymy" and "metaphor": (1) as an exception to all the other signifiers—that the Master-Signifier is a signifier that refers only to itself and not to another signifier—it has what can be considered a *metonymic* relationship with the universal whole: the Master-Signifier plays the role of "metonymic substitute" for the entire signifying chain, as in Hegel's example of the monarch, whereby the monarch itself, as a term, simultaneously stands for the entire social domain it gives rise to; or, to be a little more modern here, we can substitute *Nation* or the *Market* for monarch. And (2) the Master-Signifier obtains a *metaphoric* relationship with the void in the signifying chain: the Master-Signifier qua exception "fills out" the void internal to the whole system of language.[63] This is what it means to "think of the void only through that which assumes its place." (It's not unlike the very way ideology itself functions, as Žižek illustrates in *The Sublime Object of Ideology*.) That is to say, the Master-Signifier, a name that refers only to itself, takes the place of, and thereby conceals, the innermost (constitutive) void of the whole network of language, thus simultaneously creating and sustaining an ordered space in which signifiers can attain their meaning within a differential matrix as such. And as Claude Levis-Strauss discovered, this paradoxical logic can be extrapolated beyond the system of language, applied to the very way in which societies organize themselves, especially ideologically. This is not all that dissimilar from the way in which today's sense of objectivity, functioning as a Master-Signifier, holds in place the paradigmatic network in which its subjects are influenced to perceive other entities as objects, to perceive events "objectively," and so on.

## §9. The zero and the One

It should be said: the logic of the signifier can also be explained through number. Thanks to philosopher Alain Badiou. Though before remarking on Badiou's philosophy, before illuminating the obvious homology shared between the logic of the signifier and that of the number, let's briefly direct our attention to Frege who, in 1884, provided us with his definition of number. Until Frege came onto the scene, every definition of the number that had been put forth fell victim to "elementary logical blunders." As Bertrand Russell wrote, before Frege it was accepted that "number" was identical with "plurality." But this of course created much confusion—for example: 3, as in the instance of the *number* "3," is a particular number; and the instance of 3, as in "3 *things,"* is a distinct triad.[64]

> The triad is a plurality, but the class of all triads—which Frege
> identified with the number 3—is a plurality of pluralities, and
> number in general, of which 3 is an instance, is a plurality of
> plurality of pluralities.[65]

Essentially, on one level, what we're dealing with here *is* multiplicity. The reason for this is simple: If there exist distinctions, if
there is *difference* in the world, only then can we count. That is to
say—if there exists no distinction, then there is no *concept* of
number whatsoever. Why? Because number derives from
counting—and there can be no counting of anything if there is no
distinction. So where, exactly, does the concept of "one" derive;
how is it that thought can arrive at the concept of "one" despite
the radical absence of any pure "one" when all there is "*is*"
multiplicity? And by what means, on what account, does the
subject's thought alight upon a particular object amidst a
multitude of particular objects, so to determine that that *one*
particular object will be first, thus constituting the "count-as-
one" *as such*, thereby commencing the very act of counting? To
put it differently, how do we explain for thought's arrival at the
concept of per se oneness, when all that seems to really exist is
the multiple itself? If oneness were to precede multiplicity, then
distinction never would have taken place (and by that account no
acknowledgement of multiplicity either). Without distinction
there is no counting, no "count-as-one," thus no number—no
"*one*"; and therefore, no such thing as oneness per se. Hence
there seems to exist only the multiple. However, if we were to
pervert this perspective, if we were to turn this perspective
around on itself—if oneness were to precede multiplicity, all
there ever would be is a static oneness; there would be no
otherness, no difference, just an invariable oneness as such. This
oneness would essentially be self-reflexive. Its number would be

its number! Like that of a Master-Signifier, its name would refer only to itself, taking the place of, and thereby concealing, its innermost (constitutive) void. And that's the point. To think of one, to think oneness per se, *is to think of the void only through that which assumes its place*; one always appears against the background of its own absence. The one is thus split in its own sameness as such, between its place of inscription, zero, and its "self-standing unity": one. And so if there exists some particular, some "*that*" (i.e., some *thing*) which assumes the place of the void, well clearly there exists an exception to the void. And there we have it—the one differs from itself, in itself: as such it *is* the zero that gives rise to its opposite qua exception: the one! And as a result we have distinction, distinction between the void and that which assumes its place: its exception as such. And that is how we arrive at the "count-as-one," by which we are able to count particulars belonging to a multitude as such—all of this preceded by a constitutive void, *a nothing that counts for something*. That is the dialectic of number, the very base of the Onto-Logic, the place from which the paradoxical logic of concrete universality and its constitutive exception derives.

Here is what one should take away from all this: Frege wanted to exclude the role of the subject in order to construct a completely logical, scientific theory of the system of numbers.[66] But without the subject there is no *performance* of the numbers, math doesn't happen, the numbers just sort of heap up amorphously, thus limiting the very efficiency of the system of numbers. When it comes to *counting* the numerical elements that comprise something, if we exclude the subject altogether, the system fails to include its empty concept, the "supernumerary," the "*X-factor*"—the subject that operationalizes the network of numbers—and thus the system doesn't close. Therefore the subject *is* this X-factor, this impossible "one" which seems to always elude the multiple, for if you include the cognitive subject here, then the numbers *perform*, they move, they can be *counted, manipulated, and so on.* That is to say, thought arrives at the concept of "one" precisely as a means to apply the notion of "count-as-one" in order to count the elements comprising the multiple—*for any other object that is counted is also reflective of the subject doing the counting.*

For thought to grasp the unit of some object, to go from the pure multiple to a definitive "count-as-one," there first requires the transformation of a thing-in-itself into a thing-for-us. That is, as discussed earlier, some *other*-thing must present itself as a *thing*-of-thought to the cognitive subject, which is merely the appearance of the cognitive subject in its opposite. In other words, the presence of an object, a *thing-of-thought*, includes within it its own possible absence, which is reflexive of the subject's own possible absence, and the place of this void is filled by the cognitive subject in the form of its notion; thus the external entity and the subject are bound together in the object as such, *in its notion*. Or, to put it more simply, the object presupposes the presence of the thinking subject. What this implies is that, essentially, the initial object that is decided to constitute the "count-as-one" *is none other than the subject itself (though without the subject realizing this); thereby creating the illusion of subject-object difference despite this subject-object difference existing as subject-object sameness as a means to positive the void inherent to the subject as such.*

That said, the process by which we arrive at the *unit* of the object involves a Symbolic intervention: the *concept* of number, of unit, which is applied to the object as such. As Jacques Alain Miller puts it, we should not overlook that Frege's system begins with the obligatory framework comprising the three concepts of the concept itself (Frege defined number as being a "trait of the concept"): 'the object and the number, and two relations, that of the concept to the object, which is called subsumption and that of the concept to the number which [Miller calls] assignation [...]

[i.e.,] number is assigned to a concept which subsumes objects.'[67] That is to say, all concepts exist, and are defined, only as "subsumers" that are in direct relation towards that which it subsumes: an object. And an object, as just discussed, is any external thing that has changed from an in-itself to a for-us, only in so far as the external entity falls under, and becomes "one" with, the subject's range of perception. Once a thing-qua-object is subsumed under its concept, the concept assumes the place of the entity, thereby serving as a "stand in" for the *real* entity; and for the subject, the entity becomes more real in its symbol than in itself. This is what constitutes the entity's objectification qua unit, as *"one."* (The ethical implications involved in this are no doubt grave, for it's much easier for someone to manipulate an "object" than it is to manipulate a living entity; and no less important, not only is it easy to manipulate something you believe to be an insensate object, it's much easier to manipulate something you perceive to be a number...)

There is another way of getting at this same point: When Lacan stated that "one" cannot be one at all, but that it's rather a zero, he means that the zero *is* the concept under which no object really falls: The concept, unto itself, as an empty formal structure, nonetheless counts for something: it's a *nothing* that counts for *something*—the *objet a*. To unpack what this means we should back up a few steps. For any entity to arrive at its assigned number, at its unit, what comes first is the subject's lack of absolute knowledge of the given entity itself, i.e., the absence of any knowledge of the *thing-in-itself* (which precipitates the process of object creation). And why is there an initial, absolute lack of knowledge of the *thing-in-itself?* The answer: Because *for us*, the *thing-in-itself* does not exist. To talk about some *thing* always requires reference to something else, and thus the thing is limited by that something else: in so far as you have a multitude of different particulars, an assertion about one particular, as it turns out, in fact, involves many other particulars. And that's the limiting factor. The idea that there is a *thing-in-itself*, a *being-for-itself*, ultimately breaks down, because (1) it is always in relation to some other thing, and (2) at the level of perception, it is also always a thing *for-us*, for consciousness. If I identify a thing with properties, then the *thing-in-itself*, the thing *being-in-itself*, is thought of as differentiated from everything else, except that as soon as I use the word "differentiation" I have to compare this thing to everything else: E.g., there exists this *thing*, it has properties, but I can abstract out its properties and say, "Oh... well, it has this property and not that property, and this property is in contradiction to that property, and that thing over there has all these other properties, and it's not *this thing here*..." and so on. Thus the idea that there is some *thing-in-itself* that I'm discerning with perception breaks down, and I have to acknowledge the vast array of "The Also": the thing's relationship to *other* things. What this means, and this goes all the way back prior to Plato even, is that perhaps there is no "one," but only a multiplicity, and every multiple is none other than a multiple of multiples. The "one" is an illusion; as such it is the intervention of consciousness, deployed to simplify the complexity of the multiple. Or to put it differently, the multiple is none other than the explosion of the inner disunity of the one; the multiple exists as a series of attempts to fill in the gap inherent to the one as such. As Plato remarked, this multitude of difference, the not-one, can only be understood as such in its heterogeneity: 'The others are Other.' And it is through this notion of "Other" (which stands for the multiplicity of all the others, and which presupposes the subject)—that is posited in and by the one of consciousness—that the subject arrives at the (self-reflexive) simplified *concept* of the oneness of the multitude.[68] Therefore, it's from the *concept* (of oneness, a self-reflective extension of the subject) that we begin our counting: thus the concept itself really counts as a zero—since it emerges from the empty framework of thought itself—to which we can then add integers. In other words, to paraphrase Badiou, for a concept of some *thing*, for some entity to be thinkable, thought itself must 'suppose a structure' in which the very thing in its pure multiplicity is presented as 'consistent and numerable' (e.g., an amorphous multitude of particular others constituting the universal notion of Otherness per se). That is to say, before the intervention of the concept of one can take place, the pure multiple is *ungraspable in the subject's thought*: 'there is no form of object for thought which is capable of gathering together the pure multiple.'[69] To grasp the multiple, then, thought requires the structuring of the concept of the one in and through difference: 'without the one, it is impossible to have an opinion of the "many."'[70] It is precisely in this sense that the one (which doesn't really exist) is none other than the zero: the very *concept (of one)*—borne in upon, and thus reflexive of, the subject itself!—under which no object actually falls. That is to say, the entity, the *thing-in-itself*, as wholly other, which is radically indeterminate because of its underlying void-qua-multiplicity (the correlate of something is always something-else), is *not* identical with its concept, and the concept of something is never identical with itself (because the concept *in-itself* is empty, and thus never in accordance with that which the concept is *about*). For that reason, the entity as such is not *really* subsumed under its concept, this relation exists only *for the subject* as a means to supplement the subject's initial lack of knowledge of the given entity's being-in-a-state-of-pure-multiplicity: which is to say, the concept subsumes no external *thing-in-itself*, as well as being alienated from itself, and therefore the concept coincides moreso with the subject than with the external *thing-in-itself*. This is what it means to say that the concept, as that which subsumes an object, is a zero that counts for something, as the primary "count-as-one." In other words, it is the passage from the initial and absolute lack of concept (Nothing) to the form of a concept (zero) which acquires its substantial content by being about some other object, which constitutes the "*count-as-*

*one"*; which ultimately coincides with the mentation of the subject.

In a sense, we can say that the one is the result of the self-engendering of a pre-ontological void. That is to say, we can equate the first "one" with the empty signifier, to the extent that, like a Master-Signifier, or like the subject's *Self* for that matter, the metaphorical function of the one is to conceal the constitutive void from which it arises, to the effect that, by doing so, it creates an ordered context, a logical system of operational numbers.

The very function of the concept then, that it is formed around a designated (unknown) entity-qua-object, serves to show that, despite thought's inability to fully grasp the entity-qua-object's radical multiplicity, this object nonetheless still *exists in its concept* as a (reflexive) means to substantiate the subject's presence. That is to say, the concept itself, separate from the object it subsumes, counts for something in and of itself: it counts for the place of its inscription, the subject-proper! And the very inscription of this concept constitutes the passage of the zero-qua-one of subjective quality to the one of objective quantity: The void (\$) is a zero, which counts as — it is represented by — "one" (S1). And just as we saw with the example of the signifying chain, this "one," like a Master-Signifier, represents in metonymic fashion the void for all the other "signifiers" (numbers). Does the following not instantiate this?

Let us take a number. The number three. It will serve to constitute the concept[:] *member of the series of natural numbers ending with three.* We find that the number assigned to this concept is four [...] Where does it come from? Assigned to its redoubled concept, the number 3 functions as the unifying name of a set: as reserve [...] In the order of the real, the 3 subsumes 3 objects. In the order of number [...] it is numbers which are counted: before the 3, there are 3 numbers — it is therefore the fourth.[71]

Why: Because the *concept* of 3 must count for something *itself*, which should nonetheless be included with the three numbers.

Just like the notion of Self and, just like the signifier, the concept of number too, seems to serve as an *objective* supplement to an original void from which it arises. These objective supplements serve to give meaning to what essentially lacks any meaning, designating the movement from zero to one. And as we'll soon see, what we are witnessing by this passage from non-meaning to meaning (from zero to one) is the intervention of the Symbolic order: when the ideal unity of something is embodied and externalized in its signifier, in its concept, in its symbol—*in its objectification*.

## §10. From objectivity to the subject

Returning now to the subject's notion of Self, it's important to stress, yet again, that the notion, virtually identical to the concept, though premature in its initial stages of development, is a "dead" and "purely formal structure" that lacks any substantial content in-itself; for it must correspond with something else, an other, to receive its content. And because it is such that, *for the subject*, the other exists in its notion moreso than it does in-itself, of-itself, a precise accordance of the other with its notion is impossible (for the simple reason that one can never really know another's mind, for one can never see directly into it, or, if the other is some thing without a mind, the same can be said about its "inner integrity"). And the same holds for the subject's notion of Self: we are excluded from directly accessing the unconscious activity behind the creation of Self. Therefore, to posit the claim that a subject's alienation becomes realized in the wake of receiving a notion of what is external to it, is also to say that the subject's *Actuality* does not exist *in-itself*: this actuality can only be established within the structure of the cogito, the empty place of inscription of the notion of Self, which again, is essentially an empty formal structure that lacks any substantial content in-itself, of-itself—and thus it requires something *other* for its substance. Can we not, then, posit the claim that objectivity, the *givenness* of the world the subject perceives all around, serves to conceal an inner void, one that marks what the subject lacks in self-actuality? That it is only through objectivity as such that the subject can externalize this immutable lack into an object, whereby the object, in turn, gives body to the subject's lack as such, thereby producing the subject's subjectivity? What this implies is that the subject is none other than the subject of (its own) objectivity, a subject of its own conditioned perception, a "looking-backwards," so to speak, as such. Thus to do away completely with objectivity is to lose one's subjectivity altogether.

By dint of this immutable lack, the subject is always-already obstructed, obstructed *from within*, from bringing itself to any sort of real positive fulfillment, since all attempts at fulfillment always involve something other than the subject. What this suggests is that the very existence of the subject as such—or better yet, even the *notion* of the subject itself—indicates a radical displacement of the subject, through which and by which the subject is to search for its Self in *Otherness*, to search for its performative role in the very "lifeworld" he or she is inscribed into. That is to say, it is from outside of the subject, from an "objective" viewpoint (i.e., from within the larger objective, socio-Symbolic field in which the subject is inscribed, from which his or her own perception is furnished), that the subject acquires its sense of Self.

It is this antagonism between the "inner" and "outer" worlds, between subject and object-Other, between being and knowing—an antagonism that nonetheless resides *within* the subject—that sets in motion the subject's dialectical development of Self. And it is precisely this process that results in the subject's attempt to incorporate all differences within a unary oneness as such. Such an undertaking, however, is ultimately imaginary, illusory—fraudulent even. For example, I may be many things at once: a male whose name is Frank, a writer, as well as someone who loves noodling jazz riffs across the fretboard of his guitar, and a fan of the band Converge... I'm also a factor in many relationships: a lover, a son, a brother, a friend, an enemy, and so on... I also have vices and virtues. All these things are, in themselves, different from me and different from one another, though they are nonetheless "united" together, there is a "meshing without mushing"; they become aspects of a unified identity by and through the notion of Self. This notion of Self attempts to encompass all these differences within a Oneness—but there's a catch: this movement to "encompass all differences" breaks down, it's cursed, so to speak, by an "inherent impediment"—the Self, as a universal in which all its differences are "accounted" for cannot account for its own initial loss: the primordial void which ruptures the universality of Self from within. For the notion of Self itself is inaugurated by its own original loss: viz., it is always something other, something on the side of objects, that gives rise to the subject's sense of Self. Thus the Self is, as such, none other than an objectal correlate *of* the subject, which gives body *to* the subject, allowing for the subject qua Self to take the place of the void situated at the core of the subject. The subject's Self therefore represents and thus conceals the place of this void, which is none other than the subject proper, the subject's very place of inscription.

The Self (a universal as such) cannot account for its own lack, and therefore it cannot *really* account for *all* differences. And this is precisely what obstructs the subject, from within, from ever "becoming itself."[72] To put it literally—*the subject can never fully become its Self.* Or, in other words, the subject can never fully become its object: the sole point of the object, of objectivity, is to conceal the void at the core of the subject. Objectivity is thus a perceptual dimension in which, through which and by which subjective Spirit manifests, for the subject, the notion of "Self," thereby allowing for the subject to recognize itself in its notion as such. What this means is that: *objectivity is what gives to us our subjectivity*. Without objectivity we are reduced to our basic a-substantiality, to our primary "nothingness," our non-actuality.

## §11. The parental role of consciousness, and the emergence of the fantastic desire

In light of all this, the subject's consciousness is that which serves to "positivize" the subject's empty notions; to secure the empty framework of thought with its substantial content, content that is derived from that which corresponds to what the subject's thought products are directed toward, or rather, *what the subject's notions are about*. To put it simply, consciousness serves to simplify the complexity, the radical inconsistency of the world; as such it serves to help create and sustain a sense of wholeness and stability to the subject's lived reality.

The subject's consciousness is that which helps organize and manage, over the duration of the subject's social existence, the vast collection of items of knowledge, of education, of norms, etc., products of socialization as such—i.e., normatively-conditioned presuppositions of "positivized" things in the world; a collection of data that is both given to the subject in advance from, and taught by, the apparatuses of the larger Symbolic order. Like the paternal role of the Father, consciousness helps one master the "disruptive emergence" of their *desire* to be free of their subjective alienation, thereby effectuating a sense of stability in the world. In other words, the paternal role of consciousness assures for each of us that, despite the ineradicable truth of our own self-alienation, everything and everyone has a precise and meaningful place in the world. This creates for the subject a stable foundation to which the subject is anchored. That is to say, consciousness is none other than the subject's "private" piece of the larger socio-Symbolic, ideological order in which he/she is inscribed. It helps erect and maintain, for the subject, the illusion of being "set free" from the base of subjective-alienation, while also ensuring for the subject that there is a secure place in the larger intersubjective network in which the subject is placed. This paternal function operates in the same manner as the Master-Signifier: it serves to anchor a symbolic structure, providing a context in which, through which and by which, meaning is created. As regards the maternal side of consciousness, this serves to represent the world to the subject, for the subject, in the image of wholeness. As Todd McGowan writes, the 'maternal image of wholeness provides the ideological assurance that underlying the apparent openness of the social order, the signifying system is actually closed. Beneath the antagonisms that manifest themselves throughout society, this form of ideology discovers connections that trump every division.'[73]

And to put it very abstractly, what eludes this "wholeness" of consciousness, however, is a another term, one that's embedded *within* the maternal figure itself, and thus *within* the "closed order" of parental economy—"Woman": the female as not just the maternal figure, as not just the paternal supplement, but rather: the maternal figure as a "sexed" subject with her own desires too, desires that ex-sist outside the domain of the masculine register; the maternal figure whom, despite being responsible for maternal "wholeness," nonetheless ruptures this wholeness by the very fact that "she," too, has a *jouissance* all her own, one that can very well be separate from phallic jouissance altogether. Woman, too, is "sexually charged"—she does not have it all, and thus wants it all, which contradicts the universality of the "parental economy" in which she is inscribed as its guarantor of wholeness. This is why Lacan made the (in)famous claim that "Woman does not exist." It's not that he was attributing, affirming, and propounding some subaltern status on/regarding women but rather, that "Woman," 'as an all-encompassing idea (a Platonic form) is an illusion,' that, as such, "Woman," with a capital *W*, as another "Name of the Father" (i.e., as a function of the male economy of desire) is the exception to *man*kind that gives rise to the universal of mankind. That is to say, as a phallic signifier, Woman completes man—as an idea *as such*, an idea that arises from within the masculine register, Woman sets in motion the entire phallic economy of male desire. In other words, Man *has* phallus, and Woman *is* phallus: viz., Man *has* desire, and Woman *is* that desire: the signifier (ideal form) "Woman" gives body to the utter lack of phallus from which the entire economy of (male) desire arises. This impossibility of woman having phallus sustains the male desire as such—it sustains the phallic function that promotes, *literally*, an *infinite* perpetuation: Precisely as such, this formula of sexuation invites man to deposit his seed in woman, from which their offspring will emerge, flower, and follow suit, in perpetuity. Thus the "vaginal" is the "generative void," it is excessive in its promotion of the infinite as such. But here, one should avoid making a crucial mistake: This "fertilization myth," a male fantasy *par excellence*, is none other than the phallogocentrizing of the "generative void" itself. Rather, what makes the void "generative" is its essential negativity: it is literally a "non-All," a "nothing that counts for something," it is the *pure* subject as such—*the empty place of inscription*. This is why Lacan posited that the pure subject is Feminine. In other words, there is always a particular place from which one can say *No!* to the promotion of male desire, *No!* to (masculine) universality. In other words, there is always a particular that can resist inscription into the dialectic of male desire as such—a particular exception that has no exception to itself, one that, unlike the particulars involved in male desire, does not attempt to circumscribe difference within its oneness, one that does not attempt to enclose all that there is within the sameness of its universality. The Feminine, *as such*, is "*not-All*": there is no exception here that gives rise to a universal order like there is on the side of the Masculine. The Feminine is that which resists, that which says *No!* to Symbolic authority — which is to be referred to as the abyss of one's radical freedom, the part of consciousness that ensures us our subjective autonomy.

The lesson here is simple: Despite the "parental economy" that ensures wholeness and stability for the subject, there is, always-already, lying in wait, a third element: that which is "not-whole," that which will disrupt the Symbolic efficiency of any image of wholeness; there is the subject's consciousness, and then, within that, there is the subject's radical autonomy, the power of conscious choice, which can disrupt the "wholeness" of consciousness itself. The other point here is that no two elements can be coupled or contrasted without a mediating, though incommensurable, third (viz., Father, Mother [which together account for the Masculine], and that which resists full inscription altogether: Feminine).

In any event, consciousness, as Hegel wrote in *Phenomenology*, is that which 'takes the shape merely of pure Ego': as pure stability and wholeness, as *certainty* of one's Self. As such, consciousness is the subject qua "self-standing" object, it is the 'abstractest and the poorest kind of *truth*. It merely says regarding what it knows: it *is*.' In other words, the subject's consciousness is not something that *thinks*; as Hegel put it, 'the I does not contain or imply a manifold of ideas'; on the contrary, consciousness provides and sustains, for the subject, the *objective* certainty of Self as a means to conceal the utter lack of Self. It is as if the subject's *desire* to move beyond its self-alienation, to move beyond its own original lack of Self (-understanding), externalizes itself in the field of the object-Other at each (failed) attempt to attain and satisfy itself. Is this not unlike Lacan's paradoxical formula for the *objet petit a?* The fetishized object (of knowledge, of desire, of...) fills in the gap of castration, the gap separating the subject from its empty place of inscription, thereby constituting the very fantasmatic screen in which, through which and by which the *objet a* is sustained. It is not unlike Empedocles' view that the soul, upon birth, falls into a condition from which it must free itself, and whereby it posits its substance in, by and through the worldview it creates. That is to say, it is, *as if,* to conceal the subject's fundamental lack, this lack qua void generates the subject's desire to be free of its immanent self-alienation. And this desire thereby moves beyond the bodily restrictiveness of the subject, (re)appearing in the subject's reality to its consciousness, *in its consciousness,* for its consciousness, in the guise of an external entity — appearing on the side of objects — in the guise of something *other,* in the very thing(s) which the subject desires, thus "distorting" reality as such. As Hegel wrote at the beginning of his chapter on consciousness in the *Phenomenology*:

> in sense experience pure being at once breaks into two "thises" [...] one this as I, and one as object. When *we* reflect on this distinction, it is seen that [...] I have the certainty through the other, viz. through the actual fact; and this, again, exists in that certainty through an other, viz. through the I.

In our search for "support in some finite positivity," we extract something (an image) from the external reality "out there" in order to fill the empty, inner space "in here." What follows is such that, under the guidance of the parental-like economy of consciousness (as it is conditioned by the larger ideological field in which the subject is inscribed), we begin to further abstract our thought; we make an effort to correspond our thought-products with what is external, only *after* what is external presents itself to us as a thing-of-thought in the formal structure of the notion, which evokes in the subject its notion of Self.

And so the subject's abstraction of thought is none other than the erecting of a "fantasmatic screen," so to speak, upon which the subject's desires are staged; which is to say, it is upon such a "screen" that the subject views its *Self* performing an endless series of (failed) *attempts* to put in precise correspondence what is external with its notion. To put it in simpler terms, the subject's "inner space" is whence this "fantasy screen" derives. As Žižek puts it in *The Pervert's Guide to Cinema*, 'While reality is "out" there in all its raw form, our perception "elevates" this reality to the "magic level": the subject's perception is the erection of a fantasmatic screen onto which the subject's dreams are projected.'[75] It is precisely this process in which, by which and through which the subject stages its attempts to overcome an original estrangement that, no matter what, no matter how many times the subject tries to free itself of its subjective alienation, this estrangement always-already separates, *prescinds*, the subject from what appears to be an objective reality enduring outside his or her subjective experience; *and this separation is inscribed in the whole of reality itself*: that is, separation, this split as such, is part of reality.

Therein we have an illustration of what Hegel referred to as "self-relating negativity": The subject realizes itself as an "I" through 'knowledge of what is purely negative of itself,' through knowledge of "sense things": the subject posits that it *is*, its Being is realized by and through what it is not, and what it is not is initially presented to the alienated subject via external images, which are then redoubled, mediated, by and through the subject's consciousness. Of course, however, the Imaginary dimension incorporates more than just the subject's alienation as such. In the words of Alexandre Kojève: 'the more [the subject] is conscious of the *thing*, the less he is conscious of *himself*. He may perhaps talk about the thing, but he will never talk about himself; in his discourse, the word "I" will not occur.'[76] In other words, contemplation *simpliciter* reveals only *Being* per se. In order for the reflexive awareness of one's *Self* to be realized, for the word "I" to occur—the *being* subsumed under *Being*—something other than just mere contemplation must be present. For Hegel, this something is none other than desire, for 'Desire is always revealed as *my* desire, and to reveal desire, one must use the word "I."'[77]

Thus the absorption of the subject by its contemplation of an object-Other is a relational mode of being, one which is fruitless in terms of knowing the object-Other in-itself simply because— the subject will immediately be 'brought back to himself' soon after this *desire to know* the object-Other, as such, manifests itself. It is at this moment, Kojève writes, when 'suddenly,' the subject 'will see that, in addition to the thing [the object], there is his contemplation, there is *himself*, which is *not* that thing. And the thing appears to him as an *object*, as an *external* reality, which is not in him, which is not *he*, but a *non*-I [which the subject desires to know, as evidenced by his/her contemplation]. Hence, it is not purely cognitive and passive contemplation that is at the base of *Self*-Consciousness,' but rather the subject's *desire* to overcome its self-alienation,[78] to attain Self, and to thereby discover what kind of *thing* it is.[79] As Žižek puts it, 'the paradox is thus that there is no Self that precedes the Spirit's "self-alienation": the very process of alienation creates/generates the "Self."'[80]

## §12. The mirror in our fantasy

This is what we've established so far: Objectivity is none other than a perceptual dimension in which subjective Spirit creates for the subject the notion of "Self," precisely so that the subject is able to recognize itself, *perceive* itself, in its notion. What this means is that: *objectivity is what gives to us our subjectivity.*[81]

Another way we can put this, is to say that, for the subject, the external, real images of objects are substituted by virtual, "mirrored," images; images that are mediated by and through the subject's consciousness. Consciousness denotes not only the way in which the subject perceives (things in) the world, nor the ways in which the subject ponders over the fundamental questions he or she may have about one's reality as a means to simplify these questions and thereby accumulate knowledge and understanding, etc., but also—and this is of most importance— consciousness is the very set of personalized beliefs, beliefs that are rooted in and influenced by ideology, which structures reality *for* the subject.[82]

The traditional epistemic-phenomenological dialectic that indicates to us that our lived reality is structured by and through what we know—which, to put it crudely, has long been erroneously thought of as the "synthesis" of experience and the factual, "objective" information we gather about the world, which, in effect, enables the transfer of our experiences, observations, etc., into a socio-Symbolic field in which they are transformed into information to be communicated and so on—should be left behind. It is our *desires* and our *beliefs*, moreso than our knowledge as such which ultimately structures our reality for us. In other words, *it is the socio-Symbolic order that structures our experiences for us.* For example, we all know that the burning of fossil fuels jeopardizes life on this planet, including our own lives. Though we choose to behave in the world as if we believe this is not so, desiring things like automobiles and strip malls, ATVs and international-travel-by-plane—desires that influence the promotion of, say, the industrial-scale generation of electricity that powers shit like our microwaves and air-conditioners and other stupid things such as the lambent glow of television screen after television screen in nearly every household of every neighborhood of every little suburbia.

In so many nuanced ways, our desires and beliefs determine how we behave in the world; in this instance, how our use of fossil fuels and other resources shapes the structure of our entire political economy these days. Another example: We know that the ocean is not only depopulated of ninety-percent of its large fish, but that, additionally, the waters of the ocean are thoroughly contaminated with noxious chemicals and other toxic agents, plastics and radioactive wastes, *ad nauseam*. Russia alone has dumped into the Arctic seas '17,000 containers of radioactive waste, 19 ships containing radioactive waste, 14 nuclear reactors [I couldn't make this shit up], including five that still contain spent nuclear fuel; 735 other pieces of radioactively contaminated heavy machinery, and the K-27 nuclear submarine with its two reactors loaded with nuclear fuel.'[83] Despite the impact commercial fishing has on the world's oceans, and, despite the deadly consequences the befouling of these waters has on life in general—and, despite the inescapable risk associated with seafood toxicity, we often *choose* to behave in the world as if we believe all this is not so. We continue to experience, and act on, the *desire* to eat fish from the world's oceans; we continue to experience and act on the *desire* to harness nuclear energy; desires that are sanctioned by the *belief* that those being affected by all this are objects or not at all.

Our experience and knowledge is always-already contained within, and subordinated by, our fantasies—in which our desires and beliefs are staged. What's more is that fantasies, which are created and maintained by our larger socio-Symbolic narratives, teach us how to relate to the world—*they tell us what and how to desire*. As if we are in front of the silver screen itself, we suspend all disbelief, thereby disavowing those self-evident truths (traumas, alienation, deficits of satisfaction of desires) that are responsible for the production of our fantasies. And fantasy, despite its deceptive quality, has a direct effect on the real, physical world. Hitler's fantasmatic belief that Jews were poisoning the race, that they were a problem to be solved, resulted in the deaths of over 6 million European Jews. This fantasy placed a firm grasp on reality itself for Hitler and his followers. And this was, plain and simple, psychotic. Marshall Applewhite and his 38 followers believed in the fantasy that the comet Hale-Bopp was escorting a UFO that would save their souls, and that the only way to board the ship was by suicide. This fantasy, too, placed a firm grasp on reality itself for Applewhite and his followers. And that, too, was psychotic. No doubt delusions and fantasies can be dangerous. They can have a dangerous consequence in and on the real physical world when they claim ownership of reality itself, for when the critical distance between the Symbolic and the Real collapses, when fantasy is mistaken for reality, psychosis sets in.

Today's fantasy that the burning of fossil fuels can go on indefinitely takes precedent over the fact that it cannot. This fantasy has placed a firm grasp on reality itself. This is psychotic. The fantasy that oceans are resilient pools of water qua receptacles for deadly wastes and plastics takes precedent over the fact that they are not. This fantasy has placed a firm grasp on reality itself. And this too, is, plain and simple, insane. All in all, however, our fantasies sustain the very framework in which our objects of desire come into their existence. And whether these objects of desire appear in the form of cellular-telephones or cans of Coke, or whether one's object of desire is international travel or the consumption of sea food, or, cruising on a yacht; whether it's another person or the abstract end to one's means, objects of desire serve to conceal, in an illusory way, an inherent lack and self-alienation around which, and for which, one's fantasies are constructed. And if the way we relate to the world, if what we desire, and how we desire, is inexorably eroding away the moral and ethical obligations once held between individuals in communities large and small, and if it is undermining the ecological infrastructure that is responsible for maintaining our very lives, then it's time we confront the fraudulence interwoven in these narratives.

## §13. An ontology of objectivity

To summarize the material up to this point, what we have been discussing implies a rather radical idea in terms of object creation, or, just the same—an ontology of objectivity. Let's lay this idea out in front of us, and go through its moments step by step: (1) As indicated through the use of Hegel's logic of "self-relating negativity," there exists an initial pre-ontological void in which the subject's self-alienation is invariably based—the place of the subject's inscription as such—from which the subject desires to extricate itself in order to understand itself by re-appropriating its Self within this empty place of inscription. This void marks an innate, not to mention immutable, lack of absolute knowledge of one's Self, and thus a lack of absolute Self-identity, and, equally so, a lack of absolute understanding of one's Self-*with*-and-*in*-the-world. For if all animated bodies are organized bodies, and all organized bodies are, essentially, a plurality (of pluralities), then how can we truly know what is the *one-and-only* Self? Thus there is no complete ontology here. (2) Such a void introduces a 'gap/cut into the given-immediate substantial [organic] unity' of the world: As illustrated through the logic of the signifier, the place of the subject's inscription is none other than this void, an irreducible gap situated at the heart of the subject itself, connecting both sides of the binary opposition between the subject's presence and absence. The only way to attempt to fill this gap, to suture this gap—in order for the subject qua "self-standing" entity to "return" to what in reality *seems* to be an organic unity to which it inextricably belongs—(3) the subject uses, and relies on, its desires and concomitant fantasies to overcome its subjective alienation, which, *in toto*, conduce to the creation of the very place to which the subject's Spirit arrives (read, returns) through its attempts to overcome the subject's self-alienation as such, thereby creating the very context in which the subject's presence is to be realized.

However, because the subject's presence always-already appears against the background of its own loss—that, at any given moment there is no ontologically consistent origin in the first place;[84] that, all there is and ever will be in the place of a "Beginning" is the eternal absence of a first cause—the subject's Spirit (4) "creates the very dimension to which it returns" by erecting the "fantasy screen" previously addressed.[85] *And the creation of this fantastic dimension is what serves to conceal, precisely by taking the place of, an original void at the core of the subject.* And *that* is what's behind the process of objectification, the production of objectivity as such.

In other words, rather than fully accepting the disjointed structure of reality—the postulate that the existence of the thinking subject introduces a sort of "glitch" in the network of reality itself[86]—we impose upon reality the *idea* (the Platonic form) that there is either some sort of Edenic, naturally balanced order to the world that we must strive to fit back into, or, that there is some hidden piece of information we are on the brink of discovering which will disclose a complete and consistent order to the nature of ourselves, of the universe, and thus of reality itself. The nature of the idea itself, however, serves as a sort of "plug," so to speak, employed to seal off, to conceal, the subject's inceptive void, that vortex which ruins any and all consistency behind any explanatory notions.

And it is through both the establishing of thought-products as such, and the belief therein, that we stage our desires (e.g., the desire to attain a sense of being-in-the-world, a sense of belonging—to know what sort of "object" we are to everyone and everything else around us; and through that, a sense of Self), and thus *find ourselves in the world*. Thereby creating consistency out of that which never was consistent in the first place.

To put it somewhat differently, as a means to overcome our subjective alienation, we seek to fill in, as it were, the blank spaces in the world, including our very own, for we are none other than the "night of the world." And we fill these spaces with products of thought. We seek to create a dimension in reality in which we can find for ourselves the notion of Self, through which, in which, and by which we are able to navigate within what is "retroactively presupposed" as being a consistent order of things. This is precisely how we structure meaning within our lived experience, through the process of objectification as such.

What this essentially means is that, for us, our perceived reality is ultimately structured in and by our ideation, in and by our dreams and fantasies, in and by our beliefs in the very concepts that shape and inform our perceptions. Is this not why Lacan posited that 'truth has the structure of a fiction?' And does this not, then, bespeak of the inalienable importance of the fraudulent nature of the Imaginary and thus the structural influence it has over our lived reality?

# Part II: Absence: The Symbolic Order

## §14. Objective certainty

What Serge Leclaire wanted us to bear in mind when he wrote that one's experience of reality 'presupposes the simultaneous use of two correlative functions, the Imaginary [...] and the Symbolic,' is the fact that, though there is no Imaginary without the intervention of the Symbolic order—that the Imaginary itself is hinged on the Symbolic—there is also no symbol which can do without the support of the Imaginary, simply because we must *believe* in the efficacy of the symbol for it to have any sufficient faculty of codification in our practical lives. And despite being propped up by Symbolic agency, belief is essentially a function of the Imaginary. Take democracy for example. It's Symbolic through and through. It functions as it does by virtue of its subjects' *belief* that it works, regardless of the symbol's "falsity." For if we were to suddenly subject our certainty that democracy is real to veritable doubt, the very act of calling democracy into question would undermine the frame of our democratic form of life.

To understand the complex relation shared between the Imaginary and Symbolic, it's crucial to note Žižek's retelling of the difference the late Wittgenstein introduced between "subjective certainty" and "objective certainty." Subjective certainty refers to a kind of certainty we're able to call into question without running the risk of undermining the form of life we partake in by the very act of calling this kind of certainty into question. Although it concerns things we may not be entirely sure about, the act of submitting subjective certainty to doubt poses no serious risk of abstracting the carpet out from beneath our feet, so to speak; for when subjective certainty is submitted to doubt, we are able to call upon a normative criteria of knowledge, facts, presuppositions, etc., to help us answer questions of this caliber. And this brings us face to face with "objective certainty."

What constitutes objective certainty, however, cannot be submitted to doubt without entailing a fiercely tectonic shift in the form of life we engage in day-to-day; that being the social reality we experience. The act of calling into question the beliefs that comprise objective certainty inevitably undercuts the very form of life it gives rise and consistency to. Imagine suddenly that language was subjected to serious doubt and, as a result, we lost all access to language. The result would be a chaotic Babel of noise, an ensuing radical uncertainty. In the words of Robert Plant, it would be a 'communication breakdown, baby...' And so as Žižek puts it, calling into question the things of objective certainty would result in what psychoanalysis calls "loss of reality."[87] Moreover, when philosophers posit the claim that objective certainty concerns not "truth" but "attitude" — what this means is that, what comprises objective certainty is *not* indebted to things that are unquestionably "true," to things that "universally hold." On the contrary, objective certainty is beholden to the subjective 'attitudes and beliefs [that] form the very background against which we may consistently doubt something, test it, and so on.'[88] As such, it is none other than a socio-Symbolic pact by which and in which our reality is able to acquire its sense of consistency and reliability. This social pact, which creates for us a world full of sense and meaning, can be likened to a "Universal Lie," or rather, to Plato's "Noble Lie": a lie that is nonetheless necessary for obvious reasons, which serves to secure its position of being true by dint of a consensus belief in its presuppositions. Taking this into consideration, it is none other than a good ol' sublime act of faith and trust in "objective certainty" that keeps our form of life coherent and continuous.

Beneath this well-crafted order, however, is the abyssal reality of pure, radical, contingency. The 'consistency of our language, of our field of meaning, on which we rely in our everyday life,' writes Žižek, 'is always a precarious, contingent *bricolage* that can, at any given moment, explode into a lawless series of irregularities.'[89] As Wittgenstein was well aware, it's as if all forms of life 'float in empty space'; there is 'no firm ground under their feet.'[90] The only thing that keeps our form of life afloat is a sort of fideistic social allegiance to the "objective certainties" underpinning the very meaning of our (socio-Symbolic conditioned) reality. And this allegiance, this tacit social pact, rests fragilely upon one thing: the belief that it exists. And belief—seeing something where perhaps it is not entirely, if not at all—is a function of none other than the Imaginary. Once belief attains the level of consensus belief, it becomes a constitutive function of the Symbolic.

## §15. The infrangible alliance between the Imaginary and the Symbolic, as facilitated by the "real-abstraction"

If belief is essentially a function of the Imaginary, how, then, do we explain its symbolic articulation? It's crucial to note that, to borrow a term from Marx, the "real-abstraction" occurring at the elementary level of "negating negativity" is that which is *unconsciously* doing all the conceptual-perceptual work for the subject: a sort of signifying chain persisting in "another space."[91] In other words, the subject is not solely the "knowing subject" (the "knowing subject" being that entity which—through *logos*, through words that have meaning within a reasoned discourse— recognizes its very Being). The subject is also involved in the unconscious process of "real-abstraction" as the Other of the "I": the 'revealing being that [the subject] *opposes* to the revealed being' that it calls Self.[92]

As Žižek puts it, this "real-abstraction" '*is not* thought, but it has the *form of* thought,' a 'form of thought [of which its] ontological status is not that of thought.'[93] Or as Lacan put it, this unconscious mechanism consists in 'thoughts that, while their laws are not exactly the same as those of our everyday thoughts, whether noble or vulgar, are certainly articulated.'[94] In other words, despite its "subjective" provenance, this "real-abstraction" is that which bears the impression of a kind of "external support," one that operates in another space situated between the subject and its Other (between Imaginary and Symbolic), its role being to (first) "retrieve" and (then) give symbolic resonance to that which populates the subject's Imaginary order. As such, the "real-abstraction" yields for the subject a direct access to that (Other) larger body of objective-universal knowledge, the ideological superstructure as such, 'whereby the [subject's] form of thought is already articulated in advance.'[95] This cache of objective-universal knowledge, of "objective certainty," is none other than the Symbolic order: a formal order in "metastable" state that, within which, the subjective notions of things are precipitated in their primordial form before being objectified in the dialectical process of identi-fication. Thereafter, identifications are related to one another, classified for the pragmatic task of categorization, schematizing, producing a systematized context of "common knowledge" from which meaning derives and in which it continues to evolve. This entire process stages for the subject a sort of "belief before belief," a paradigmatic network comprised of various experi-ential inputs that translate into facts about the reality of the world in which the subject dwells. In other words, one's belief in an ideology is staged in advance for him or her as such: by and through the process of "real-abstraction," which unites the subject with the world in the universal "oneness" of ideology. That is to say, the Symbolic is always-already at hand for the subject, making its intervention into the subject's reality, colliding and mixing with the Imaginary, determining the subject's reality and his or her designated place therein.

In this sense, ideology, "objective certainty," *is* consciousness, which mediates for the subject the dual relationship between its subjective experiences and facts pertaining to "external" reality. This process initiates the subject into what William Alston designated as a *"doxastic practice"* (or Wittgenstein's *"form-of-life," which is propped up by its respective Language Game,* or Lacan's *Symbolic order/big Other;* or Kierkegaard's *Public;* the "social construct" as such): a collection of integrated experiential inputs consisting of *prima facie* perceptions whose epistemic justification is reliable in virtue of, to put it simply, both their practical effects (i.e., how instrumentally sufficient these experiential inputs are in terms of achieving a *desired* outcome) and consensus *belief.*

Can we not, in a sense, expound on this by turning to the classic opposition Kierkegaard held toward Hegelianism? Those familiar with Kierkegaard will recall how, for him, Hegel's speculative philosophy came across as completely missing "what it means to be a human being." In other words, Kierkegaard found in Hegelianism what he thought be a heavily burdensome objectivism, which neglected to take into account subjectivity: 'objective thought translates everything into results, subjective thought puts everything into process and omits results—for as an existing individual [the subject] is constantly in process of coming to be.'[96] For Kierkegaard, Hegel 'does not understand history from the point of view of becoming, but with the illusion attached to pastness [Hegel] understands it from the point of view of a finality that excludes all becoming.'[97] For Hegel, consciousness is none other than the reflection of what has already happened: viz., history as objectivity. Is this not what Hegel was getting at when he said that 'the owl of Minerva spreads its wings only with the falling of the dusk'? That is to say, knowledge comes to understand its formative conditions only *after* these conditions begin to pass away, which finds its apogee of expression in the Symbolic (objective) order itself. In other words, objective reality *is* the Symbolic; it is ontologically constituted within a closed *"fullness"* as such. And what is "present" is none other than a positivized domain in which, objectively speaking, all that *"is" is*: the reflection of what has already happened; which is thus presupposed to be "objectively certain" thenceforth. And so for Kierkegaard, what he believes Hegel does not take into account here is the subjective domain, something that, *in itself*, is "open"; ontologically speaking, for Kierkegaard the subjective domain is not fully closed. But can we not posit the claim that, here, Kierkegaard had overlooked something of which Hegel had already addressed? For Hegel, this antagonism was always-already the inbuilt principle behind his dialectic: That is, we shouldn't overlook the fact that the open, subjective field of future possibility, something that is governed by radical contingency no less, is none other than the space from which we can, and should, wage our ideological battles, a space that is *internal* to the Symbolic order itself. In other words, what we should take away from Hegel's dialectic is the notion that we should *'reintroduce the openness of the future into the past*, to *grasp that-which-was in its process of becoming.'*[98] In other words, we should deploy objectivity against itself— *precisely* as a means by which we can perceive the radical contingency that generated objective certainty (history) in the first place! By these lights, the Symbolic order is a fragile realm, in which all of its presuppositions upon which it is based can be turned upside down, precisely by revolution.[99]

## §16. The significance of Symbolic authority

It is within the Symbolic dimension that the subject seeks out its identity. This is precisely what Lacan meant when he claimed that the subject is "decentered": the subject's decentrement is both the original and constitutive feature of the subject: the subject is, from the beginning, "outside oneself"; the Symbolic order 'is a kind of spiritual intestines of the human animal outside its Self, the spiritual Substance of my being [...] [is] outside myself, embodied in the decentred Symbolic order.'[100] It's from outside our subjective selves that we acquire our identity; thus our decenterement as such.

Let us be perfectly clear on this point, the subject, without the Symbolic order, is *substanceless*, empty. And this "objective" knowledge, ideology as such, which comprises the Symbolic, that which gives substance to the subject, 'supplements and/or disrupts the dual relationship of "external" factual reality and "internal" subjective experience.'[101] That is to say, *objectivity qua ideology is none other than the phenomenon of consciousness itself, as experienced and borne by the subject.*

This of course brings us face to face with the second significance of objectivity, one that is homologous with the dimension of the Symbolic, a dimension that emerges from, though is part and parcel of, the stage of Imaginary mirroring discussed earlier.

There's a joke that can help demonstrate the absurd logic behind the functioning of the Symbolic in which a woman goes to her analyst because she's having some serious problems with her sex life. The analyst spends an hour or so asking her questions, but he doesn't seem to be getting any closer to the root cause of her problem. Finally, with just a few minutes left in their session, the analyst says, "Do you ever watch your husband's face while you're making love?"

"Yes," she replies, "I opened my eyes and watched his face once."

"Well, how did he look to you?"

"He looked angry. Very, very angry."

At this point the analyst feels like he's finally getting somewhere, so he says, "That's very interesting. We must look into this further. You say you've seen your husband's face only once during sex, and that seems somewhat unusual. How did it happen that you saw his face that one time?"

The woman says, "He was looking through the window at

us!"

Here, we can assume that the wife's husband is still married to her; that much is obvious. And one may wonder why, despite her infidelity, he's stuck around in such a lousy marriage? A little speculation here should help explain how the Symbolic dimension properly functions: If the husband were to "believe only his eyes," to act solely upon what he saw—his wife screwing another man—then the efficiency of the Symbolic fiction—that of the rituals of love and marriage and so on, and the way this fiction structures for the husband his experience of his marital reality—would perhaps begin to withdraw from his reality. This functioning includes within it the structure of fetishistic disavowal—"I know very well that things are as they appear, that this person is a sleazy cheat, dishonest and promiscuous, but nonetheless I treat her respectfully and stay married to her since she bears the emblem of "Wife," so that when she speaks to me, it's not her that speaks, but it is Love itself which speaks through her."[102] In a sense, it's his wife's words, not his own eyes that the husband places a stronger belief in; he believes in "another dimension," the dimension of Symbolic authority, the dimension of marital love, which is more important to him than the reality of its spokesperson.[103]

It's crucial to note that Symbolic fictions attain their authority by dint of their subjects' belief in them. Hence, as mentioned earlier, both the Imaginary and Symbolic orders are not opposed to each other; they are not two separate dimensions that exist external to each other. Rather, 'within the Imaginary itself, there is always a point of double reflection at which the Imaginary itself is, so to speak, hooked on the Symbolic.'[104] To revisit an important point touched upon a little while ago—there is no symbol that can do without its Imaginary support, and vice versa: *There is no Imaginary without its Symbolic support*. What the latter proposition implies is that the Symbolic order is always-already "there" before the subject is properly installed into it (e.g., before the individual has been subjected to the law of castration, before he becomes a speaking-subject, before he is socialized, etc.). And yet there is a way to formulate another, possible, level of meaning behind the claim that the Symbolic precedes the Imaginary. For example, I recently finished reading Quentin Meillassoux's book *After Finitude*, and there is this one passage near the end in which, to paraphrase him, he poses the question: "Look, do you really think precursors come before their successors?" To which he replies to his own question: "They don't, they come *after* their successors." The point Meillassoux is making, I believe, is that—and my point should hopefully become clear in a few moments, and hopefully I won't sound like Howard Hughes here!—precursor qua "precursor" cannot be determined as such until there is an established successor that can determine its precursor as actually being a *bona fide* "precursor." In other words, it is the emergence of the successor that (retroactively) gives rise to its determinate precursor. Is this not homologous with the logic behind the retroactive movement of Hegel's figure of Spirit? Could one not claim that the Symbolic "precedes" the Imaginary in the same sense that the 'successor precedes its precursor qua "precursor"'? That is to say, it is only through the Symbolic that the Imaginary can be named *as such*. In other words, before fully becoming a subject-of-the-signifier, the individual is still engaging in a sort of "archaic-/proto-Imaginary" realm (arguably, the individual engages in the Imaginary before he or she is ever properly taught the codes of the Symbolic)—the individual is observing, sensing, perhaps even engaging with "internalized" images of external entities, and so on, though without any sort of proper symbolic under-standing and symbolic engagement of these things; and it is only through the Symbolic that this "archaic-Imaginary" is retroac-tively given all its meaning, after which it is *named* "imaginary." One should thus read this against Hegel's logic of subjective Spirit: "Spirit's return-to-itself creates the very dimension to which it returns": That is to say, the intervention of the Symbolic creates the imaginative space in which the Imaginary can be determined *as such*.

We therefore have two levels, or perhaps modes even, of what it means to claim that the Symbolic precedes the Imaginary: (1) The Symbolic is present well before the subject is, and (2), once the individual becomes subject to, and thus a subject of the Symbolic, the individual's rampant mental activity involved during the "archaic-Imaginary" stage preceding the individual's inscription into the Symbolic takes on a more consistent and defined form, thenceforth known as the Imaginary. Viz., the Symbolic gives rise to the Imaginary as such, in the same sense that a successor gives rise to its precursor, in the same sense that Spirit creates the very dimension to which it returns.

In any event, the entire dimension of the Symbolic is erected on a foundation of rituals, abstract formulae and differentiated signifiers that pivot on the signified and *per se* signification (the latter and former belonging to the dimension of the Imaginary). As such, the Symbolic dimension is none other than the invisible ideological network that acquires the form of *doxastic practice* by and through its subjects' belief in its Symbolic efficiency, an efficiency that is laid down by the Master-Signifier—which ultimately structures reality for us. It is a "world of words that creates a world of things"; a normative world made up of language, of categorical universals, of rituals (i.e., "objectified schemas of action"), of objectivity and nomic necessitation (universal laws such as cause and effect relationships, and so on), rather than subjective contingency and amorphous particularity.

# §17. Getting up close and personal with the big Other

I want to clear up whatever confusion might exist with regard to the notion of the big Other. When we get down to the essential details, there is an unmistakable difference between two faces of the big Other: the *Symbolic* big Other and the *Imaginary* big Other. The Symbolic big Other is that 'locus in which everything that can be articulated on the basis of the signifier comes to be inscribed': the locus in which speech is constituted.[105] As such, it is the invisible framework that must be presupposed if the subject is to engage in any communicative activity or social exchange. This framework is "invisible" because language itself is embedded in a network of historical/socio-cultural conventions, which provide an unspoken, unseen, context of meaning that we understand by dint of "common sense." I was delighted when I came across the following passage written by professor of computer science at Stanford University, Terry Winograd; he nails down exactly what I'm driving at here with the following pair of simple sentences: 'Tommy had just been given a new set of blocks. He was opening the box when he saw Jimmy coming in.'[106] As Winograd puts it, we can easily assume that what is in the box is Tommy's new blocks, and we know this precisely because of convention: gifts often come in boxes; and thus the immediate assumption that both sentences are connected, despite no apparent reason to think so. There's also a joke that helps explain this: A linguistics professor is lecturing to his class and says, "In English, a double negative forms a positive. But in some languages, such as Russian, a double negative is still a negative. However," the teacher points out, "in no language whatsoever can a double positive form a negative." To which a voice from the back of the room replies: "Yeah right!" Here I should point out the not so obvious though all the while evident characteristic of this joke: it is, of course, the sarcastic intonation that is negating the meaning, and not the double positive construction. In other words, there is an unseen semantic element at play here, which is solely responsible for providing the negative meaning behind the double positive construction, "yeah right." And so, in a nutshell, that is the Symbolic big Other—as such, it is a sort of invisible background of structured understanding that helps facilitate our speech within a meaningful context. For that reason, the Symbolic big Other is something that is shared by everyone, and moreover, it embodies the (false) guarantee of ideological consistency of the socio-Symbolic order of our lives; rules and etiquette—especially juridical Law itself—customs and beliefs, everything you should or should not do, what you aspire toward, and who or what you aspire to be, all of this and more, individually or in combination, constitutes the Symbolic big Other. The big Other "exists" solely to ensure the guarantee (in lieu of the utter lack of an external guarantee) of intersubjective relations.

To fully understand this, we need to also recognize that, as Žižek puts it, within any ideological space there are signifiers that just sort of float around—e.g., "freedom," "peace," "justice," "society," "politics," etc. The chain of these signifiers is given consistency by a Master-Signifier, the big Other as such, which retroactively determines their fixed meaning. For example, these terms may mean one thing under the Master-Signifier, "capitalism," and may be given an entirely other set of meaning under, say, "communism."[107] In a capitalist society, freedom may refer to one's right to economic initiative, whereas in a communist society, freedom may refer to 'surmounting bourgeois formal freedom.'[108] In any case, the Symbolic big Other is what ensures a fixed meaning to the terms that are tossed around within its given context. Without a big Other to anchor meaning within the ideological space, there is nothing to preempt against the slippage of meaning of the terms therein.

The Imaginary big Other, the subject's big Other, however, is a sort of private investment in this Symbolic big Other; a personal allegiance to the ruling ideology which sustains the narratives, beliefs, and lived fantasies of the very culture in which the subject is immersed. Each Imaginary big Other is distinct in its own unique way: My Imaginary big Other may be, say, a patriotic bricolage—a composite of things like, e.g., Uncle Sam, the American soldier trope, "God", and the good ol' American football hero Tim Tebow (not really, but you get the point). And your Imaginary big Other may embody, say, just Emily Post, or maybe Eleanor Roosevelt, or some vague ideological package of some other normative principles. In any case, the Imaginary big Other, the subject's big Other as such, designates a private virtu- alization of the ideological socio-Symbolic field in which he or she is inscribed. Whether it exists in one's private notion of God, or one's notion of government, or family, or "what's cool," or a combination of these things, or whatever, the Imaginary big Other refers directly to that distinctly (im)personalized social standard by which each of us respectively measures ourselves— 24/7/365 (yes, the big Other can make itself known even in our dreams).

Virtually everybody shares in the Symbolic big Other, for it's that very point from which the general "will-of-the-people" is reflected back to the people, *so that we can see ourselves as we appear in this reflection—as a consistent social "whole."*

In other words, the big Other is that which gives substance to the body politic. We are its subjects. And despite *not really existing*—that, at the imaginative level of the individual, it's really none other than one's own internalization of society's dos-and- don'ts—the big Other is nonetheless experienced as a sort of independent, impersonal phantasm which situates itself smack dab in the middle of any social interaction like some kind of incorporeal incarnation of a necessary third-wheel that both instructs and scrutinizes our every thought, utterance, and move. As such, the big Other ensures that the rules of a given society are being followed, that we are conducting ourselves properly in this society. Without the big Other the social fabric begins to fray, presenting the veritable threat of losing the constitutive substance of society itself, its governing laws, and its subjects. In other words, the loss of the big Other would reveal the utter lack of stability, the antagonisms, inherent to the constellation of intersubjective relations; because there is no universal schema, no *real* external edifice of any sort that *really* guarantees intersubjective relations, the big Other is that which takes the place of this void, thereby embodying this absence in its opposite: as something that serves to "guarantee" the relations constitutive of societies.

I suppose I should've been a little clearer earlier on: when we combine the Symbolic big Other and gaze, the result *is* the Imaginary big Other—that remote sense of being watched and evaluated by something that's not really there. It's sort of like a cross between a Jiminy Cricket figure of conscience and an iconic role-model of sorts, who, as such, seems to loom over your shoulder, telling you what and what not to do simply by "looking" at you, normatively shaping and informing your every thought and behavior. We all have a big Other. It is, to repeat an emphasis from earlier, that standard by which we measure ourselves: our own private piece of the larger, public social space we inhabit. To paraphrase Žižek, the gaze of the Symbolic big Other is my own view of myself, which I see through eyes that are not authentically my own. It is what defines an individual as a subject of capitalism, or communism, or anarchism, and so on.

## §18. Supremacy of the Symbolic, repression of the Real

Let's now return to the "quantum mechanics" underlying and facilitating the relationship held between the subject and the Symbolic order in which the subject is inscribed. Grasping this

relationship will imply something that is not so intuitively accessible, for its comprehension requires, as we've seen, a dialectical
reversal, an inversion of sorts, of the subject-object relationship:
that the subject's awareness of the other is reflexive *not* of a real,
positive self-standing Self, verified by one's own awareness, but
rather: as we've shown for so far, the subject's awareness of the
other is reflexive of the subject's own possible *non*-existence, of its
non-coincidence with itself, the subject's own absolute-
negativity—precisely in the sense that, to reemphasize a point
made earlier, the subject's notion of Self, arrived at via the notion
of the object-Other, is essentially an empty structure, designating
absolutely nothing at its most elemental level: Remember that the
subject's notion requires an engagement with something other for
it to acquire its substantial content, whereby it becomes a
substantial notion predicated of its particular content. As Hegel
would have put it: the subject's notion of Self is a union with the
content that it gives itself. This notion, like any other, must
determine itself, and this determination is not something external
but rather, to be precise—*it is the notion itself*, i.e., it is a *Self-determination as such,* the union of subject and object, of form and
content, which creates the subject as such.

And although the subject's own *thoughts* about the object-
Other would seem to demonstrate, to reveal, and thus confirm
the subject's self-actualization, at further glance this is actually
not the case entirely: The subject knows that it *is* simply because
his or her own thought-content of the object-Other is the result of
the removal of an original lack of a notion of the object-Other, a
second-order loss as such. But it's not simply the case that, "the
subject cannot *know* the object-Other directly, *immediately,* and
thus despite whatever knowledge of the object-Other that the
subject does conceive, such newfound knowledge always
appears against the original lack and/or removal of itself..."
Rather, to fully grasp what the latter claim is spelling out we need
to invert it: *The second-order loss that must occur in order for the*

*subject to grasp the object-Other in its notion instantiates the subject's own absolute-negativity—it refers to that original lack of Self against which the subject's subsequent notion of Self emerges,* that void at the heart of the subject which the subject desires to fill by directing itself outward in thought, toward the object-Other, which, in effect, "gives body" to this void by means of the very notion that takes the place of the void, thus "holding the place" of the subject in its notion of Self as such. That is to say, the object-Other is what substantiates the subject's actualization; the subject is an effect of its own objectivity as such: What is Other is what draws forth Spirit, which, in its act of return to the subject in the guise of Self, creates the subject *as the very effect of this giving-Self-substance-to-the-subject.*[109] This is what Lacan meant by: 'the subject, *in initio,* begins in the locus of the Other, in so far as it is there that the first signifier [Self] emerges': the object-Other draws out the subject, making what is implicit in the subject become explicit in its objectivity. To quote Alenka Zupančič, it is the subject's "becoming-the-Other," and what's 'at stake in this "becoming the Other thing" is not a kind of (mystical) *transformation* of subjectivity: the Other thing is the subject itself.'[110] Or as Hegel put it: 'On approaching the other [the subject] has lost its own self, since it finds itself as another being; secondly, it has thereby sublated that other, for this primitive consciousness does not regard the other as essentially real but sees its own self in the other.' Which in effect raises the following question: After the subject arrives at its notion of Self through this dialectical process, as the rational *"I,"* what is it, exactly, that this established "I" designates?"

This division between "I" and what this "I" designates bears a lack within the subject itself, a negative qua "generative" void, an "ontological excess" as such (an excess because the Self attempts to encompass *all* that it is not in its quest to "find" its Self, as a means to fill in the gap inherent to itself; and a void because the process of subjectivization presupposes this primordial lack, a gap in the order of the subject's *Being*; a lack, however, that is "generative," which serves as the very impetus behind the dialectical movement of subjectivization). This (original) void generates, for the subject, the positive elements of its identity by "pulling in" and receiving its content from the external world, from the field of the object-Other, as it is mediated by a Symbolic intervention. The whole point behind this activity is to (retroactively) conceal the place of such a void located within the gap between the subject's notion of Self and what this notion actually designates, which is located at the core of the subject.

We should now turn our attention back to the unconscious agency of real-abstraction, the "place" from which language emerges. And why is this? For the obvious reason: language runs through us. And also because, no less important, language can get pretty damn close to the roots of things—*it's a tool, with a lineage.*

Signifiers, like subjects too, operate within a complex network of historical and cultural contingencies. And moreover, language is indivisible from the Symbolic: it structures our reality for us moreso than the objects we perceive do, for the word itself supplants the thing itself, and becomes more real than the thing itself. As Lacan once remarked, the use of language 'implies the symbolic murder of the thing.' Thus the Symbolic, in this sense, has a certain supremacy over what is otherwise Real.

## §19. Speculative Identity: the heart of the subjective-objective analysis

What this essentially means is that the *name* of something tells us more about the subject of language and the chosen discourse from which the applied name derives (and thus about the social reality in which the subject lives, the Spirit of the epoch around which this social reality is both constructed and situated, its history, and so on), than it does about the actual entity being named. To expound on this, let's turn to another of Lacan's examples as explained by Žižek: If one were to say: '"The word is an elephant" one is essentially demonstrating that an elephant is "more present" in the word which evokes it than in its immediate physical being—it is present in its Notion.'[111] And to follow this up with Lacan's formulation: '... the notion is not the thing as it is, for the simple reason that the notion is always where the thing isn't, it is there so as to replace the thing [...] the notion is what makes the thing be there, while, all the while, it isn't.'[112] The notion is that which lays the groundwork for the assemblage of knowledge in which the thing in its symbol is inscribed. To name something is to cancel it out in its immediate notion, to subtract it as such, and to then elevate it to the status of symbol in the form of the word as designated by language, in order for it to enter into the stage of concept, etc. Spirit *is* the creative, relational activity behind the dialectical process of Naming.

When one claims that, for the subject, knowledge of a particular object always emerges against the background of its original lack of knowledge, a lack that's concealed by the notion that takes its place, what this means is that: *for the subject*—i.e., solely from the subject's perspective (whether this perspective is "superficial" *or* "objective")—an external, *real* entity can never be fully represented as *itself* in the subject's notion for the simple reason that the subject instantly transforms this original entity into an object of desire the very moment the subject *wants to know* (what it is the subject is dealing with, what he or she is relating to, and so on). This of course means that, paradoxically, the subject is dealing with his or her inner-self, one's own desire to know, as it appears in the guise of an external entity.

Sameness and opposition, identity and difference, are thus included as "one" within the subject's gaze. The subject is, in a sense, merely revealing the self-relating truth of the subjective-Symbolic condition of *him/herself*, of the subject's place in the Symbolic order, through the thought-products of that with which the subject associates the images of an external entity. In a sense, reality is in the eye(s) of the beholder here—though, as Žižek puts it, these eyes aren't necessarily one's own: Though it is the case that, the way one perceives the world shapes the way one behaves in the world, one's perception is made in large part by the very social narratives he or she is subjected to, the ideological field of which one is subject. For example, if the social narratives propounded by the ruling ideology of your culture persuade you to believe in a brutal utilitarianism, that the world is a container of objects to be used, a stock of insensate *things* to be exploited, then the world easily settles into this viewpoint of being a container of "dead" objects to be used and exploited. And thus your worldview and discoveries therein will often be in proportion to what you're taught to perceive. Therefore it's important that the ideological stories that shape the way we perceive the world remain open to other, new expressions of Being, rather than closed totalities that seek to encompass and contain all differences in a static oneness.

In any event, the question is not to discover something "objective" about the external world and its inhabitants but rather, it's to discover what the speaking subject is disclosing about his or her own subjective situation, about his or her own ideologico-Symbolic status, in such conceptual-perceptual productions. This is, after all, the best objectivity can ever do for any of us anyway.

What about the hard sciences? you may ask. Doesn't science boost its claims to truth by being objective? Let's try to answer this question honestly. The thing is, no matter how much one tries to prove otherwise, subjectivity inevitably leaves its stain on the "objective" mechanical materialism of the hard sciences. It's said that science begins when we can start talking about objects from outside our subjective first-person experiences. When we can talk about things in terms of measurements, approaching things from a vantage point philosopher Thomas Nagel called "the view from nowhere." For example, you may say that it's cold outside, while I may make the claim that it's actually quite warm. We measure the outdoor temperature and see that it's $58°$ F/$14°$C. We are now able to discuss the weather in terms that are 'less beholden to personal experience.'[113] The vulgar materialism of which a lot of today's "science" is one manifestation, nonetheless obscures the immutable subjectivity that this objectivity interpellates, creating a beastly confusion—that a mechanistic-vulgar-materialist science seeks to explain the world not in terms of qualia and appearances, but in terms of quantity only. But I think this complaint is a bit naïve, the result of weak thinking—for, isn't the real issue here the fact that, science, today, deals *only* with appearances, seeking to explain the phenomenal processes behind appearances only through quantification, thereby depriving appearance itself of its inner reality, ossifying it within the symbolic deadness of quantification?

Mechanistic materialism may have been the predominant doctrine for quite some time, but it's starting to fall from favor as science itself shows us that this breed of materialism has its limits. For example, in order to measure something, to quantify something, it must first appear, and appearance is inextricably united with perception, which presupposes awareness, which presupposes an imbedded subjective aspect, a real substance that is involved *in* the immediate appearance of the world itself. Here, one may be quick to offer as a rejoinder John Searle's analogy that neural activity and subjective conscious experience stand in the same relationship as molecules of H2O to water with its features of wetness, translucence, crispness and so on. This analogy ultimately fails, however. Yes, there is the level at which water can be seen as an assembly of particular molecules, and yes, of course there is the level at which water can be described as wet, translucent, etc. The mere existence of these descriptions, these secondary qualities, however, nonetheless presupposes a conscious awareness of something-to-be-defined. But that's not even the point, though it is a point. Here we should focus on the fact, that, likening the relationship between consciousness and neural activity to the relationship between sensible properties of water and its molecular structure ultimately backfires for the following reason, provided by professor of geriatric medicine at the University of Manchester, UK, Ray Tallis:

> While neural activity of a certain kind is a necessary condition for every manifestation of consciousness, from the lightest sensation to the most exquisitely constructed sense of self, it is neither a sufficient condition of it, nor, still less, is it identical with it. If it were identical, then we would be left with the insuperable problem of explaining how intracranial nerve impulses, which are material events, could "reach out" to extracranial objects in order to be "of" or "about" them. Straightforward physical causation explains how light from an object brings about events in the occipital cortex. No such explanation is available as to how those neural events are "about" the physical object. Biophysical science explains how the light gets in but not how the gaze looks out.[114]

In other words, mind is more of an "exchange" with the world. As Catherine Malabou (who's best known for "Hegelianizing" today's brain sciences) puts it in *Que faire de notre cerveau?* (Paris: Bayard, 2004), the brain is more like a structure that is influenced by the external world, it doesn't just "reflect" the outer world but rather, as Žižek writes in *The Parallax View*, it "sees" the world as a series of "possible projects" which in effect animates and modifies brain activity itself. In this sense, one's sense of Self is not merely a genetic determination, but rather: a malleable structure, open to endless possibilities of modification. Here, we should recall Brecht's famous comedy *A Man's Man*, in which the innocent Galy Gay, just another common person who casually frequents the market, ends up as a soldier: The point is that, like a machine that can be transformed and given a different function, the individual too, can go from being an "innocent" denizen to a fierce warrior "thriving on iron and blood."

No less important, however—although it's true that, as Marx put it, environment determines man, the contours of one's environment too, is partly determined by man's determination of himself (e.g., the transmogrification of the natural landscape into cities). The main point here is that, the modern vulgar-materialist, objectivist, mechanistic, descriptivist standpoint only works if one disregards the evaluative, *intentional*, element altogether. That is to say, to speak solely in terms of mechanical, quantitative description omits altogether even the consideration of the *intentional* force behind the act of description, or determination, or any other *intentional* behavior. Once we bring intention into the mix, its "parasitic" nature ruptures the self-contained unity of our mechanical-material, cause-and-effect objectivism.

Here, we need only to stop and ask ourselves—is it not the case that the very framework of science itself presupposes the existence of a radically subjective, rationalist freedom, a freedom that, in its decisive moment, gave rise to the very *intended* invention of the scientific method? To ask this same question differently, as Badiou might phrase it—how is it that, despite being just another animal in the kingdom, the human individual is able to exceed beyond and cast aside one's "animal nature" in order to put its life in the service of some (universal) idea itself such as science? Therein, too, resides the crucial question for today's cognitivists: How is a free act possible? How is it that, as

Žižek puts it, we are able to break free of the 'network of the causal connections of positive reality, and conceive an act that begins by and in itself?' Again, then, we must follow this up with the following questions: Is science itself not the direct result of a radically free act as such? Science is, after all, none other than the chosen freedom to systematize the concept, which points reflexively back to its basis in subjective cognition, which coincides with consciousness, which, as Tallis wonderfully shows us, is not one and the same with neural activity, for in order to even conceive of a science that can explain neural activity, thought must break free of the 'network of the causal connections of positive reality,' in order to 'conceive an act [in this case, the methods of science] that begins by and in itself.'

So what does this tell us about the nature of objectivity? That objectivity, as such, is essentially ideological: it is a "frame" within reality itself, one that enframes reality *for us*. In the same Žižekian sense that canned-laughter is not some Pavlovian trigger designed to prompt us to laugh, but rather, *it is that that laughs for us*, the objectivism of science is essentially that which "sees reality for us": it is that which schematizes, for us, the Real; viz., that which sees, for us, the result of subjective Spirit's *free* creation of the very objectal/objective field in which we are inscribed, which, it too, this "objective" field, is nonetheless inscribed in the whole of reality itself; that is to say, this "gaze" — that of the sciences which "sees" reality for us as such — is nonetheless a part of the very reality that is caught up within this gaze.

And so, of course, even science itself is riddled with antagonisms: there is, within science per se, an irreducible gap between the phenomenal experience of reality and its scientific representation, which has reached its pinnacle today in cognitivism. Is objectivity, then, at the present time, none other than the attempt to establish a sort of knowledge creation that can deliver to us a "Truth" that will remain the same in all possible scientific realms? And, as such, is today's notion of objectivity not the very universal that *is* the struggle between all its particular elements? Is objective quantification not merely an attempt to balance out something that is radically out of balance, precisely as a means to establish a common denominator for the whole of reality: All appearances are different but all appearances can be measured? And *what* of appearance, i.e., what *reality-beneath-appearance*, is being suppressed by its measurement?

The idea that there obtains in the world both problems and their respective solutions is none other than a symptom of academic philosophy and science, and is thus the philosopher's and the scientist's—the objective intellectual's—*sinthome* (the latter being a modality of the subject's enjoyment, jouissance—the way in which this particular subject *enjoys* his or her symptom; in this case, the enjoyment that is issued to the subject from trying to "solve" an unsolvable problem, an enjoyment, as such, that substantiates and sustains the subject's identity of: "problem solver"!). Philosophy should not be about solving problems, it should be about formulating new ways to look at the same old problems that science and philosophy have been striving to solve since the days of their inception—the structure of the universe, the nature of Being, Absolute Truth, Ethics, and so on. New ways to look at the same old problems, developing new questions for these, will, in effect, illuminate things about ourselves, about the nature of our ideologies, about what it means to be human and, most importantly, why, for us, these things are structured as problems in the first place.

Is this not precisely the import of "Socratic ignorance"—to assert that we know that we don't know? Or rather: To *not* know all along that which we always-already know: to forget that our knowledge is always-already incomplete, as marked by the empty place of its inscription; that we conceal what we don't know with what we come to know; and that truth, and its very movement, its development, conforms to this process of knowledge creation?

We can now see how the object-in-itself, that elusive thing imagined with strong conviction to be *the ultimate object*, something presumed to exist by virtue of the very idea of objectivity, is none other than an illusory and enigmatic *something* that is more in the object than the object itself. And what exactly does that mean? The short answer one more time is: *What is more in the objet than the object itself is none other than the trans-positioning of the subject's desire into an external object.* And the drawn-out answer can be inferred by the use of Hegelo-Žižekian speculative logic: Once an entity, in its passive, ambiguous presence becomes the object-Other of a subject's (observational) activity, and once this entity qua object-Other *is taken into account* by the subject's (observational) activity, the entity (qua object-Other) then changes altogether, it relinquishes its passivity. In other words, the subject desires to know the (entity qua) object-Other, what the object-Other is, what it does, how it exists, and why it exists, etc & c. The subject's thought extends itself beyond its bodily restrictiveness, beyond its own finitude, in thought, toward concept, where it will unify its idea of Self-in-the-world by and through Otherness as such, i.e., by and through the entity (qua object-Other) that is not the subject. In this sense, caught within the stream of the subject's inquiry, the entity-qua-object-Other is constantly changing, constantly on the move. It is now no longer an entity in-itself, for-itself; it is rather an object-Other of the subject's desire to know, an object-Other of the subject's thought. It is one thing and then another. Paradoxically, however, this initiates yet another shift! This time in the status of the subject, bringing about a full-on role reversal between subject and object-Other: the subject becomes passive as the object-Other becomes active. That is to say, the object-Other becomes the active agent in the subject's unification; it inscribes itself in the very void of the subject by means of the dialectical reversal of the subject's positioning of his lack in the object-Other—thereby giving rise to a consistent and positivized reality, a "oneness" in which the subject and object-Other overcome their antithesis in a Symbolic oneness as such. As Žižek has pointed out on numerous occasion, the subject, having initially *subjected* itself voluntarily to the fundamental mode of the object-Other's passivity, desires to flesh out through the activity of his inquiries the "objective" knowledge he believes pertains to the object-Other. At this very moment, it is the subject from which movement comes. Though, as a direct consequence of the object-Other's "*objection*" to a full disclosure of itself, *in itself*, the subject then becomes 'defined by a fundamental passivity, and it is the object from which movement comes'—And which object are we now talking about? We are talking about the object of the subject's desire (to know), which is none other than the very thing responsible for, the enigmatic *object-cause* behind, the transformation of the original entity at hand into an object of the subject's desire, giving rise to that anamorphic object-Other that is more in the object than the object itself.

What this essentially means is that the object as such is a sort of parallax of the subject itself. Thus the subject can never truly know an object-Other in-itself, but only the truth of the (Symbolic) oneness in which the subject and object-Other are both united. To expatiate on a previous example, if the desiring subject sees an object-Other as something to be *exploited* in order to satisfy his or her desire, chances are the subject's ideologico-Symbolic condition is that of being situated within an exploitative social order: and thus the subject's thoughts, perceptions and behavior will be shaped and informed by this ideology of exploitation. On the other hand, if the subject were to perceive the object-Other as something to enter into a non-exploitative relationship with in order to satisfy his or her desires, the subject would thus be cogitating and perceiving from within an entirely different ideologico-Symbolic order. To wit, if you perceive, say, a river as some *thing* to be exploited, as some *thing* to dam up in order to generate electricity, rather than seeing a river as a dynamic habitat harboring diverse life, then more than likely you will treat such a river one way. But let's say that, on the other hand, you *do* perceive a river as a dynamic bastion of habitat, a world unto itself that provides for the continuation of many different lives (e.g., the lives of mollusks, salmon, trout, mayflies, riparian vegetation, etc.), then arguably so, you will treat that river, use its resources, in a completely different way.

To drive this point home, here in Vermont the indigenous Nulhegan tribe of the Memphremagog Abenakis once subsisted off their immediate landbase and watershed; they perceived the land and its inhabitants as something with which to enter into relationship: i.e., it was in their best sustainable interest to maintain the health of the landbase and watershed, to keep it as healthy if not healthier every successive year as it was the year prior. Today, the entire Abenaki nation has become subsumed under the dominant culture, a culture that seems over-keen to balk at the idea of "entering into relationship" with the landbase and watershed and their nonhuman inhabitants. Instead, the dominant culture seeks out the satisfaction of its desires through acts of exploitation, hyper exploitation even, of its immediate material reality, taking more from the natural environment than it gives back. As a result, at the present time, the surface waters of Vermont's rivers and streams are not drinkable, despite the fact that roughly a couple hundred years ago many were. Today, Vermonter's receive 90% of their food *not* from Vermont's own landbases but trucked from afar. Today, 32% of Vermonters cannot afford either enough food or enough nutritious food.[115] The point to all this: How one perceives the world he or she inhabits can become a matter of life and death. None of us can live without drinkable fresh water, or without intact, fecund landbases to grow the very food that provides our bodies their needed health. Ignorance or denial of these self-evident truths does not exempt one from this ecological reality we are circumscribed by.

Objectivity, *in toto*, refers to the active means by which the negative space in which the subject's ego is based generates and then receives its positive content; as Hegel put it: 'the Ego is, so to speak, the crucible and the fire through which the indifferent multiplicity is consumed and reduced to unity.'[116] As such, objectivity is the very process by which the "original hole" at the core of the subject is woven into the fabric of the subject's Symbolic reality in the guise of its opposite: into that which conceals this original hole qua void at the heart of the subject.[117]

Either way one looks at it, objectivity refers to the efforts belabored by the subject's Spirit of whose activity is in the service of taking the place of an inner lack, of satisfying the subject's desires — precisely by and through the transformation of external entities into "desired non-I's," into objects of desire, as such.

## §20. The desired object is the subject

Another way we can formulate this, is that to resolve the antithesis between subject and object, its reconciliation, is, *as a thought-product*, first staged by the unconscious work of "real-abstraction" (Spirit) as it passes into the Imaginary order, whereby the gap between subject and object-Other is then sutured by the mediating force of Symbolic intervention. To refresh an old Lacanian simile, it is sutured like that of the patchwork that takes the place of a large rip in a cloth that has resulted from the way in which the original fabric itself was woven. This gap is a sort of *"original hole,"* the negative space at the heart of the "I" of desire, which is never capable of 'finding its own substance again since it was never anything other than *"hole-substance."* This hole can be covered over, so to speak, but never more than imperfectly, only by a "patch.""[118] This process of suturing, beginning with the unconscious process of real-abstraction, gains its initial stitches, as it were, in the Imaginary order. It is then secured as that Freudian "patch"—identification becomes ratified, so to speak—by dint of a Symbolic intervention, one that dissolves the imaginary relation, whereby this relation is elevated to an epistemological status that has "social durability and legitimacy," thus providing consistency to the subject's (material) reality in a Symbolic network.

What we're essentially dealing with here is a matter of stripping away the 'alien character of the objective world that confronts us,' and thus *'finding ourselves in the world.'*[119] Therefore, it is the purest form of oneself—the subject emptied of all its substantial content—that is essentially an infinite recess, a *Thing* unknowable and inaccessible by any other thing, inaccessible by oneself even. What truly belongs to this order, writes Lacan, is that which 'is neither being, nor non-being, but the unrealized.'[120]

My point should be getting clearer: It is this infinite recess, a gap in the order of one's being, from which objectivity emerges. Why? Because, as a "quilting point," provided by a Master-Signifier, objectivity serves to close this gap, it takes the place of this void as such, and thereby secures a "total" order that, in effect, gives rise to an objective reality *for the subject*.

This is what Žižek means when he claims that the Cartesian subject, the thinking ego, is not some positivized existing entity surrounded by illusory objects one must put into question. Rather, it's the other way around—*everything else exists except for the subject*.

[T]he subject is the immense—absolute—power of negativity, of introducing a gap or cut into the given and immediate substantial unity, the power of *differentiating*, of "abstracting," of tearing apart and treating as self-standing what in reality is part of an organic unity.[121]

To flesh this out some more, let's turn our attention to another of Lacan's responses to Descartes' formulation—"*cogito ergo sum, ubi cogito, ibi sum*":

> this formulation limits me to being there in my being only insofar as I think that I am in my thought [...] It is not a question of knowing whether I am speaking about myself in conformity with what I am, but rather that of knowing whether, when I speak of it, I am the same as that of which I speak...[122]

The cogito is therefore a pre-ontological void we name the "place of the subject," that "original hole" woven into the fabric of the subject's reality, a pure ego as a negative space which receives its positive content by negating its desire through transforming a real object into a "desired non-I," into an object of desire as such.[123]

Subjects, then, are *literally lacunae*, "gaps in the positive order of being." Or, as Hegel put it, subjects are the "night of the world": '*The human being is this night, this empty nothing, that contains everything in its simplicity—an unending wealth of many representations, images, of which none belongs to him—or which are not present.*'[124] The (unconscious) subject "sees" itself and the world as an unfinished reality full of holes needing to be filled— God is either all too human, or a Gnostic demiurge whose project came up short; he was at a loss. Thus God (if there is any such "being"), *is* this unfinished business to be done, he *is* this unfulfilled lack in the order of his own creation—and the subject's correlative object-Other is none other than one of these "holes" in the order of Being, too: a 'proto-real spectral object-stain' which, like the subject itself, *like God itself*, is waiting to be actualized, waiting to be inscribed into (the subject's) unfolding reality.

It is precisely in this sense that we can posit the claim that the subject represents an ontological void, which, as such—as the nothing qua exception to everything—constitutes the universal order of its Being. The subject's correlative objects, as inscribed in the field of the object-Other, represent the subject's radical loss in the appearance of its opposite—as *positivized*: as a self-standing Self, verified as such in an act of awareness of the object-Other, a recursive and self-*reflexive* means by which the subject is able to recognize its own Self, *as such*, in its determinate immediacy. It's not unlike the message conveyed in the chorus of the song by The Magnetic Fields, "The Death of Ferdinand de Saussure": *We don't know anything / You don't know anything / I don't know anything ... But we are nothing / You are nothing / I am nothing ...* without knowing anything.

## §21. Fetishizing content

In the same sense that a signifier only appears 'against the background of its possible absence'—an absence that takes on its 'positive existence' in the form of its opposite, so does knowledge of an object (of desire) only appear against the background of its possible absence, in the form of its opposite. In other words, that a signifier cannot ever "attain itself," so too, representation of an object (of desire) cannot ever attain itself.[125] Here, we could say that representation always ultimately fails in terms of an accurate depiction of its object precisely because—representation always culminates in the completion of a reflexive arch; not back into itself, but as a return to the subject doing the representing, *without fully arriving at the subject, that is, it misses the subject in its reflexivity*—for the subject is never fully aware, in the moment of representation, that the images of the objects it perceives take on a Hegelian "speculative identity" in which identity and difference are at *one* with each other, a *one* that takes the place of the radical void at the core of the subject (thus the void is internal to the one as such, thereby rupturing the one from ever fully coinciding with itself).

In other words, the network of signifiers in which the Self of the subject resides is a *oneness* that also includes its opposite, which is to say: The subject's Self is not only a signifier for itself but, to emphasize a point made earlier, it's a signifier for other signifiers too, which means that the subject, and the very object-Other being perceived, are inscribed together in this network of signifiers. The subject and object-Other are both inscribed in the signifying chain, in which the subject — *the place of enunciation* — is never fully able to recognize how he or she is inscribed in the very thing they perceive — *the place of the enunciated.*

As Hegel writes, truncating the scope of this speculative logic — i.e., the 'omission of the dialectical and the rational' from the full scope of speculative logic — leaves us with *'what is usually called logic, a descriptive collection* of determinations of thought put together in various ways, which in their finitude count for something infinite.'[126]

We can even take this further and claim that the frame of objectivity is merely the subject's gaze of "external" reality (as it is situated *in* this reality) — *without* the dialectical and the rational aspects of this speculative logic. What Hegel's speculative logic reveals, then, is that the subject puts the truth of its own Symbolic condition on display, precisely in the very manner in which he or she contemplates over the outward appearance of the objective reality being perceived, without fully recognizing him/herself in the images that comprise such a reality. How one "objectively" sees reality is nonetheless inscribed in reality itself, and vice versa! Is there not a parallel to be drawn here between the activity of seeking the "objective" truth of an object under scrutiny and seeking the object-cause of one's desire in a desired object? Both deeds are unalterably reflexive of the subject: the mainspring of objectivity, the source of the desire to know. Thus the "truth" of the perceived object is, in every case, a tautology (the repetition of the same), a self-reflexive feature of the perceiving subject's difference from itself, systematized in and through the Symbolic network the subject is inscribed in.

This explains why objective thought can never fully correspond with its object: the subject itself, he or she who is doing the thinking, is inscribed in the very object he or she is trying to grasp. It is not: Ideology gets in the way of "real" objectivity, but rather: Objectivity, as an ideology, *as consciousness itself*, gets in the way of the subject's realization that "real" objectivity *is* ideological. Thus the object-in-itself, that "hidden" essence about the object the subject is desiring to know, forever eludes the subject's grasp because the object has acquired the subject's desire; and once this has taken place, the object-Other is no longer a thing-in-itself, but a thing *for* the subject. That is to say, the subject's desire has vacated its subjective origin and has occupied, has found its way into, the very object under the subject's consideration; the object-in-itself has been transformed into a "non-I," into an object of the subject's desire as such—which is then inverted in its outward appearance, presented back to the subject in the "flamboyant reflection" of its reality—in the guise of its opposite: as an external positive object-Other, rather than as an inner subjective moment of self-reflexive negativity.

This is precisely how the object assumes the (illusory) appearance of its thought-product: by means of the subject's "trans-coding" of the object-in-itself into an externalized moment of the subject's desire, as an object of representation as such, whereby it assumes the autopoietic nature of its *self*-organization: a continuous process of "unfolding," which entails the dialectical development of an object's relation with its image and its abstraction—*borne in upon the subject's cogitation as such.*

When Marx claimed that matter is the base of all thought, perhaps he glossed over the notion that, though this may be true, thought itself gets caught up in a sort of self-reinforcing, positive feedback loop, whereby it takes on a dimension all its own, able to be an object unto itself, another constituent of reality, one that can influence the movement of the very material conditions it arises from.

In any case, the question, then, is not to discover what is in a particular object that is of a particular object, but rather to discover that objective thought per se can be likened to the result of what Freud called "condensation" and "displacement": the idea that, through the process of the transformation of thoughts about what is "out there" into consistent ideas and images, while also undergoing the 'shifting of accent' by which these said thoughts are 'cathected with quotas of affect of varying magnitude and are [then] correspondingly judged to be important and deserving of interest,' the thinking subject reveals the truth about its own Symbolic condition in the way in which he or she perceives the image of a particular object without recognizing him/herself in this perceived image.

Here we are dealing with what is contrary to the common notion that a thing's external form conceals its true content:

the dialectical approach conceives content itself as a kind of "fetish," as an object whose inert presence *conceals its own form* [...] Hegelian dialectics implies the experience of the ultimate nullity of "content" in the sense of some kernel of In-itself one is supposed to approach via the formal procedure: this kernel is, on the contrary, nothing but the inverted way consciousness (mis)perceives its own formal procedure [...] The reverse of the dialectical passage to the "truth" of an object is thus its *loss*: the object, its fixed identity, is dissolved in the network of "mediations" [...] [T]ruth does not consist in the correspondence of our thought (proposition, notion) with an object, but in the correspondence of the object itself to its notion [...] [T]he "unthought" of a thought is not some transcendent content eluding its grasp but its form itself. The encounter between an object and its Notion is for that reason necessarily a *failed* one: the object can never fully correspond to its Notion since *its very existence, its ontological consistency, hangs on this non-correspondence.* The "object" itself is in a sense *the incarnated non-truth;* its inert presence fills out a hole in the field of "truth," which is why the passage to the "truth" of an object entails its loss, the dissolution of its ontological consistency.[127]

Therein lies the authentic nature of the inaccessible object-Other: There does not actually exist some ideal content-to-be-known belonging to some piece of "external reality" in-itself; that is just mere objective fetishism. Rather, the true nature of the object-Other is a void—a void whereby the (dialectical-subjective) process of an object of perception, thought, and/or discourse assumes, for the subject, the form that it does by taking the very place of this void. This is what it means to say that: *'Being-for-itself equals the being of a thing for its symbol'*: The object-Other in its otherness is sublated (subtracted from its inaccessible in-itselfness and elevated) into the ideologico-Symbolic system whereby this object-Other is "more itself" (*for the subject*) in its symbolic form, thus attaining a unity with the subject in its notional oneness as such. Therefore the void (the "hole substance") in which, by which, and through which the subject and object-Other meet in their antithesis, dwells in the unity of their Symbolic "oneness," the ideological form of objectivity as such. This oneness takes the place of a void, or rather: the void, the zero qua nothingness—as that which gives rise to oneness—is the only true content of the one. This "one" is none other than an empty signifier, a signifier for other signifiers, a "name" that refers only to itself. This, then, is the *real* status of the object-Other: It is none other than that elusive, chimerical *Thing* that "gives (symbolic) body" to the liminal negative space that separates the subject from itself. Objectivity therefore serves to fill in the gap that cuts through both the subject and everything Symbolic.

## §22. Because it's desire, in the guise of the concept, that structures objectivity...

Objectivity, as the *idea* that there is a deeper knowledge belonging to any object under scrutiny waiting to be ascertained—a putative knowledge presumed to exist beyond the pitfalls of subjectivism and relativism—is a will-o'-the-wisp, a never-ending pursuit. Why? Because all projects aimed at ascertaining an unerring and invariable "objective" knowledge of an object of discourse and/or science, etc., are, from their respective beginnings, doomed to fail on account of a single factor: the *desire* to seek out such a type of knowledge in the first place.

To help spell this out, today's common doxa on objectivity is riddled with an inherently flawed conviction. The impulse behind the very intention to accurately represent an object in-itself—that which both stimulates and supports the belief that there dwells within some *thing* concealed knowledge that is presumed to transcend the tendentious drawbacks of subjectivism, an objective knowledge as such waiting to be discovered—will never fully coincide with such a presupposed end. The very *idea* of objectivity is staged within a specific, though specious, notion itself: the notion that the objects we perceive, *as they exist within the confines of our gaze*, are enigmatic things in-themselves containing "secrets" that are just waiting to be discovered.[128] As long as such objects are caught in our gaze, however, they cannot, for us at least, ever be things-in-themselves; rather, they can only be things *for us, for our consciousness*, simply because the subject's gaze is always-already inscribed in the perceived object itself as the point from which the object itself returns the subject's gaze. And thus the desire to accurately represent an object as an in-itself cannot be fully satisfied precisely because: representing an object entails (by virtue of it being an object of desire as such) the subject's disavowal of its own inscription into whatever object is being observed (which means that, in point of fact, objectivity will always remain tethered to subjectivity like a balloon tied to the wrist of a child). Thus the only thing that can attain the level of a transmissible "objective" truth is the representation *itself*, precisely in the sense that, once it's introduced, the gap between reality and its representation is reflected into itself: that is, once we get a glimpse of objective reality, situated at the level of the Real, through the frame of its representation, this reality *becomes its own objective appearance*.

What this means of course, is that, once again, what is more in the object than the object itself is none other than the trans-positioning of the subject's desire-to-know into an external object; *thus an object of desire is never the object as it appears in and of itself.* Kojève writes to this effect:

Desire dis-quiets [the subject] and moves him to action. Born of Desire, action tends to satisfy it, and can do so only by the "negation," the destruction, or at least the transformation, of the desired object: to satisfy hunger, for example, the food must be destroyed or, in any case, transformed. Thus, all action is "negating." Far from leaving the given as it is, action destroys it; if not in its being, at least in its given form. And all "negating-negativity" with respect to the given is necessarily active. But negating action is not purely destructive, for if action destroys an objective reality, for the sake of satisfying the Desire from which it is born, it creates in its place, in and by that very destruction, a subjective reality.[129]

Objectivity, then, designates a sort of anamorphosis of self-relating subjective truth in the following way: Today's take on objectivity exists as the idea that one can provide an accurate and full-dress representation of the *object in-itself,* the object at its zero-point. And does the term *"idea"* itself not refer to a basic element of subjective truth here (the subject's Symbolic position that helps foster and facilitate the idea itself), one that is, always-already, inextricably involved? Objectivity, then, is, of course, none other than the result of objectification itself, a "repetition of the same" that *is* subjective Spirit's activity: The subject recognizes its Self in its desire as such, mediated by a Symbolic intervention—*the Symbolic intervention of naming the object, creating knowledge of the object, etc.*

In effect, objectivity is an articulation of our subjective position in the Symbolic order we are inscribed in. When we're being objective we are merely *thinking through objects, with the aid of Symbolic mediation.* It is precisely in this sense that objective truth cannot exist fully external to subjectivity. The belief that it does is mere fantasy. Let's take an example from Mao. When writing about the universality of contradiction he made the following claim: that when studying a problem 'we must shun subjectivity'; that, 'to be subjective means not to look at problems objectively [...] not to look at problems all-sidedly [...] not to understand the characteristics of both aspects of a contradiction.' The resolve to this "superficial" deadlock of subjectivity, Mao claimed, is to be found in objectivity: the "removal" of the subjectivist position in an act of "looking from afar" to resolve a contradiction. Here, however, Mao was erroneously glossing over the irremediable subjective aspect of objectivity: *the way in which subjectivity is hinged on objectivity.* He is wrongfully conflating subjectivity with the denial of the necessity of probing deeply into something and assiduously studying the characteristics of its contradiction. His formulation of objectivity—the "removal" of the subjectivist position in an act of "looking from afar" to resolve a contradiction—is precisely the definition of fantasy: the "removal" of the subject from the very "reality" being observed. What Mao should've considered, then, is that objectivity is perhaps a subjective gesture *par excellence!* The universal of objectivity is none other than the subjective struggle leading from one formulation to another.

The point here is that it's important not to erase the thinking subject from the big picture, for the subject is always-already inscribed in the very world he or she observes, in the very worldview he or she gives rise to, objectively or not. Thus the Marxist notion that truth resides in some sort of subject-less objectivity is fantasy *through and through.* And fantasy, in the guise of objectivity, is none other than that which stages, for the subject, its desire to know.

## §23. Gaze and voice

When certain philosophers claim that we are not simply born into reality, but that we have to be "properly installed" into our reality, what this means is that we do not enter the world in all of its raw reality, we're not born into some multiform flow of life devoid of any meaning. On the contrary, meaning awaits us. Ideology has already assigned meaning to our lives, well before we take full form in the womb even. Names are already chosen for us, gifts from friends and family await us; depending on one's family, gender roles may or may not be assigned to us, respective family creeds will give rise to particular character traits, and the list goes on. In other words, when we're born into the world, we're born into the Symbolic order, a (social) reality in which there already exists, for us, a designated order of reality to be lived and experienced. The socialization process that "installs" us properly into this order begins well before we are even aware of it. Moreover, at the initiatory stage, at the most elementary moment of our induction into the social order, a part of ourselves must be sacrificed; that is, we *lose* a part of ourselves, a part of our primordial being for which the Symbolic order has no "meaningful" place. Once we become fully aware of the place we've come to, we're already metabolized into this place, we've been taught its conventions, its principles, its rules, its laws, and so on; we've been taught to conceive of the world a certain way, and thus perceive the world a certain way, and thus behave in the world a certain way.

In a sense, what is "lost" of us, in order to come into the Symbolic order, is a piece of our autonomy, *voice*. And in return we are given perception: *gaze*. One should thus equate the voice with that alien "thing" within our material bodies: that which is indicative of the subjective Spirit that animates the otherwise inert matter that constitutes our bodies. As Žižek puts it, 'Our ego, our psychic agency, is an alien force, distorting, controlling our body.' The dimension of the voice is an infinite abyss of pure autonomy, of radical freedom as such; a place in which all moral and/or social restraints are nonexistent, or, held in a state of abeyance; a place where everything and anything is not only possible, but permissible too. There are no restrictions here, no prohibitions. The deepest level of our desires, those primordial desires of which we are at no time conscious, come into play in all their obscenity and vulgarity, in all their "innocence" and "evil." In other words, were the subject to experience such a place, the place of pure, unadulterated voice, he or she would be confronted with all their desires in the absence of any proper self-regulation or constraint thereof. It is pure freedom as such. Thus in order to be properly installed into the socio-Symbolic order, a piece of this autonomy must be given up, "sacrificed." In this sense, the dialectic of ideology can be formulated as follows: The power of the autonomous subject (voice) is sublated (sacrificed and elevated) into an objective framework—ideology— whereby the "energy" of subjective Spirit is injected into an objective dimension as such. This sacrificed voice is then given back to the subject in the capacity of the gaze. Here, however, the subject's power of pure autonomy has gone through a dialectical reversal of sorts: The power of the subject's voice is relinquished and then returned to the subject as gaze: that is, much of the subject's power has been lifted up and handed over to the objective framework of ideology in exchange for perspective—*for it is the gaze that directs the subject where to look*; the subject has become "domesticated" as such.[130] As Lacan put it, the gaze *is* the "lost object," and the subject is the gaze. In other words, what is objective, is, radically speaking, none other than the very make of subjective Spirit. And through this chiasmic exchange of properties, so to speak, there is an exchange of voice for gaze, autonomy for perception. One should therefore apply a properly Hegelian reading to this: *Ideology is the objectification of Spirit; it creates the objective dimension in which Spirit can recognize its presence in the Real as such.*

# Part III: Impossibility: The Real

## §24. The three modalities of the Real

Without the phenomena of differentiation and "codification"—which are specific to the Imaginary and the Symbolic, respectively (albeit operating together, in tandem)—the distinction of singularities—what Franciscan philosopher and theologian John Duns Scotus called *haecceity*, that individuating essence that makes an object or subject become *this* particular object or *this* particular subject—would be plunged back into that which is structureless, formless; into the indeterminacy of a nameless and non-realizable life force: an amorphous mass of innumerable particulars that eludes any truly rational grasp; effects isolated from any context as such. This is why it's often claimed that, if the Symbolic fictions that structure our realities for us were to be removed, our realities would disintegrate, and thus we'd be swept away by the constant torrent of a raw reality that bears no structure and meaning whatsoever.

Therein we have hit upon an aspect of the third signification of objectivity, what we can liken to the Lacanian notion of the (objective) Real. A simple and naïve conceptualization of Lacan's Real would be to describe it solely as a non-realizable dimension that eludes full inscription into the Symbolic, as a dimension that incorporates everything that ex-sists outside of language, outside of ideology, outside form of thought, and so on. In Derridean terms, *"what is outside that which is outside what is inside"*; that which bears no mark; that which has no name, and thus no meaning.

But the Real is a bit more complex than this. We should think of the Real as having "three modalities":[131] The "real Real": that which denotes the impenetrable, enigmatic core of reality itself, including the impossible, non-realizable "No-Thing"—e.g., the primordial object, like the black obelisk depicted at the beginning of Kubrick's *2001: A Space Odyssey*, or The Horror! of Kurtz's voice in Joseph Conrad's *Heart of Darkness*. As such, the "real Real" is the infinitely vast and enigmatical field of particular effects isolated from any consistent context whatsoever, it is, as Lacan put it, the "unschematized Real." Then there is the "imaginary Real": an enigmatic "something," an object experienced at the level of the sublime, e.g., the time-honored oracular crystal ball, or the spiritual/religious object-figure that can effectuate miracles, and so on. And last, though surely not least, we have the "symbolic Real": the "consistent" Real, e.g., what Žižek explains as scientific formulae and theories that are not translated into, or related to, our everyday experiences,[132] like, e.g., the mathematical codes in Darren Aronofsky's film *Pi*, or Badiou's set theory qua metaontology. The "symbolic Real" deals primarily with "how to schematize" the "unschematized Real."

In effect, the Lacanian Real designates all three dimensions at once: (i) the "abyssal vortex" that disrupts every consistent structure; (ii) 'the mathematized consistent structure of reality; [and] (iii) the fragile pure appearance.'[133]

And can we not, to spell out a little more these three modalities of the Real, draw another set of examples around the Lacanian notion that, from within our structured place of the Symbolic, one is not just presented with a simple choice between choosing the illusion behind Symbolic authority and what is "real," but that that there is, at a more radical level, a third option: the Real in the illusion itself? Here, we find that there are three different ways in which the Real is in the illusion itself:

1. Imaginary-Real in the illusion itself: The way in which Žižek puts it at the beginning of his book on Deleuze, *Organs Without Bodies*: In 1964, when David Lean was shooting *Doctor Zhivago* in a suburb of Madrid he wanted to emulate a crowd of protesting Spanish statists singing the "Internationale." The

hired extras sang the song with such fervor that the police ended up intervening—they believed they were dealing with a *real* mass demonstration! Later on, people nearby, who had heard the din of the crowd, began to partake in what they, too, thought was a *real* demonstration, mistaking the shot scene for the real thing![134]

2. Symbolic-Real in the illusion itself: in which Marx revealed how the republican Party of Order, during the French Revolution of 1848, 'functioned as the coalition of the two branches of royalism (Orleanists and Legitimists)': During parliamentary debates, the republican Party of Order often scoffed at the Republic itself; what they really wanted was to restore the old monarchy. But what they weren't able to recognize was precisely how they, themselves, were hoodwinked by the very Symbolic weight of their own authority: that is to say, they were unwittingly reinforcing the creation of the very order they loathed, the order of bourgeois republicanism. In other words, despite believing that they were royalists passing as republicans, their royalist passion appeared as republican passion—for it was none other than the very mask of republicanism through which their royalist passion was expressed outwardly![135]

3. Real-Real in the illusion itself: the enigmatic way in which the Real appears in our reality as such: Recall Tommy Lee Wallace's TV mini-series adaptation of Stephen King's *It*. In the first half of this film, during the opening scene of "Stan's story" (in which we discover that Stan, played by Richard Masur, can't bear the return of the trauma of the monstrous It and slits his wrists in his bathtub), there is an episode of the TV sitcom *Perfect Strangers* playing on Stan's home television set in the background. Here we are presented with the illusion of Bronson Pinchot ("cousin Balki") appearing in a Stephen King movie, though not really—and yet, we have Pinchot reappear as a *real* character (Craig

Toomey) years later in the TV mini-series of Stephen King's *The Langoliers!* What was at first a contingent event—Pinchot appearing randomly, unintentionally, uncasted as a background image in the 1990 TV mini-series *It* was then redoubled as a necessary character, Craig Toomey, in another of King's made-for-TV adaptations, *The Langoliers*. Can we not claim, then, that the Real was always-already in the illusion as such? (!)

## §25. The grimace of the Real

According to the way in which Lacan formulated it, the Real is the inherent limit to our structured reality: that "unfathomable fold" that prevents our reality from achieving identity with itself. This irreducible gap that separates the Symbolic from the Real is paradoxically situated within the Symbolic. It is this void of the Real, which cuts across the Symbolic, that is none other than a rupture internal to the Symbolic, which forestalls the Symbolic from "becoming itself." This makes the Symbolic order of our universe merely another (virtual) reality with respect to the Real. To put it in Žižekian-Deleuzean terms: the Symbolic is the Real of the Virtual: *it is how the raw reality of non-meaning all around us is structured into meaningful categories of thought and application, which in effect have real consequences in and on the physical world.* Without the mediations of the Symbolic, an outpouring of the Real would inundate us; for pure reality, in its absolute multiform flux, as a pure multiplicity that lacks any intrinsic sense and order, and which therefore cannot lend itself to any definite meaning or understanding without being redoubled in and structured by the Symbolic, is too much to bear all at once. *In toto*, the Real is the swirling vortex of pure reality that appears in the form of radical inconsistency;[136] and the Symbolic is the virtual, that which structures this bare reality for us in the form of consistency, in the form of a "closed" order.

Take for example the conflict between one's moral right to unauthorized initiative and one's moral duty to submit to authority. These moral imperatives do not coincide with each other; they can only be asymptotes at best. Thus the irreducible gap between the two presents a cut in our social reality—a "grimace of the Real" as such. The Symbolic is, so to speak, the mask that conceals this "suffering face," it seeks to suture this "grimacing" fissure that is marked by an existential tension separating how we *want* to be—an array of desires that courses throughout our "inner" space—from how we *should* be in the outer social space. As Žižek puts it, this "grimace" of reality is what masks are made of: 'a mask is [...] neither imaginary nor symbolic [...] it is strictly *real*.' Which is to say, the real horror is the mask itself, not the tormented face beneath it.

Recall Christopher Nolan's *The Dark Knight*; in this filmic space all the elements we've discussed so far, and then some, reverberate: Batman's mask serves to conceal the pathetic anguish of Bruce Wayne, and that, as such, the Batman legacy presents itself as a stunning analogue to how the Symbolic authority behind ideology serves to conceal the trauma of the Real gaping beneath.

Nolan's *The Dark Knight* is a narrative in which the law, when left to itself, cannot arrive at justice without the demand for a heroic exception to the law: Batman. As an exception to the law, Batman presides over Gotham City as a hero; though, and here's the rub, if placed within the context of a legal order Batman's behavior would nonetheless be criminal, and there'd be no way, writes Todd McGowan, 'to differentiate this behavior from evil.' Batman's state-of-exception behavior is not unlike, say, when SCOTUS overstepped their constitutional boundaries, went partisan and "settled" the Bush v. Gore recount. Nor is Batman's state-of-exception behavior unlike George W. Bush's prosecution of the Iraq War, or the NSA's ongoing warrantless wiretapping, and so on. Should any of these events have occurred within the context of an inflexible legal order, each of these extra-legal activities would have been overtly criminal, unable to be differentiated from "evil," so to speak. What's of most importance to consider here is that, this exceptionality has an inherent tendency to proliferate exponentially. McGowan writes to this effect:

> In the United States during the War on Terror, exceptionality takes the form of an ever-increasing extension of surveillance and security. Once we grant the necessity of the position of the exception, the law can no longer define those who will occupy this position nor restrain their activity. Once we violate rights of non-citizens, we will soon be violating the rights of citizens as well, and finally we will end up with a society in which rights as such cease to exist. The exception necessarily exists beyond the limits of the law, and if the law could contain its magnitude, it would cease to be exceptional...[137]

Okay. Either that, or the law would cease to be *The Law*. It all depends on what has more of a powerful influence over the other—the law or its exception?

Or... well... how about both?

Ultimately, and paradoxically, the law can't exist without its exception because crime, the exception to law, indexes and gives rise to the very thing it's an exception to: law! Thus law can only be applied to the very thing that generates its universal necessity: an act of crime. This perverted perspective of the law shows us that law is none other than universalized crime. It is precisely in this sense that the Symbolic is always hinged on an element of the Real. For is it not the case that the "closed order" of law itself is also tainted with a "grimace of the Real"? Law is constitutively split—the coincidence of order and its exception is situated within the whole of law itself, rendering this juridical "whole" always-already fractured from within as such.

In any event we can see now, that beneath the heroic mask

Batman wears is the underbelly of a legal order that, whether left to its own rules, or overtly endorsing the Beyond-the-Law tactics of Batman, inevitably corrupts itself under its own venality and/or inordinate tactics and force. The crucial point to be made here is this: Our submission to the law is always compromised from the beginning. Law itself, beneath its mask of order, rests gently and fragilely upon a radical base lacking any principled order whatsoever. Like the psyche's *Id* this substrate space is a chaotic vortex of pure instinctual forces in which all elements of human meaning collide and cancel one another out. To wit, Freud claimed that the basis of our assent to the law lies in the envy of the satisfaction of others, which radically disfigures all social arrangements. Before Freud, Kant himself had written in *Religion within the Boundaries of mere Reason* that,

> The human being (even the best) is evil only because he reverses the moral order of his incentives in incorporating them into his maxims. He indeed incorporates the moral law into those maxims, together with the law of self-love; since, however, he realizes that the two cannot stand on an equal footing, but one must be subordinated to the other as its supreme condition, he makes the incentives of self-love and their inclinations the condition of compliance with the moral law — whereas it is this latter that, as *the supreme condition* of the satisfaction of the former, should have been incorporated into the universal maxim of the power of choice as the sole incentive.[138]

Therein Kant claims that we cannot escape the originary evil that follows us like a tail to its cat, which ineluctably impels us to subordinate the law to our own self-love; and therefore we are always acquiescing to the law not for *its* own sake but for pathological reasons, i.e. — "What can I personally gain, or lose for that matter, from abiding the law?" (Which is why within the dominant culture, legal institutions actually serve to protect only the rights of society's privileged, the ascending classes, the rich, and the powerful. Benefits that spill over onto the less powerful and the less rich are a "bonus." Recall Rousseau's quip: "laws are always useful to those with possessions and harmful to those who have nothing...") That is why, for Kant, the brunt of obedience to the moral law is radically evil.

As a friend of mine recently put it, Batman is all about enforcing an idealized status quo, which both the movies and comics suggest as being not as great as imagined to be. Which ties in to another theme, one that is heavily explored in the comics but only skirted around in the Nolan movies, which is the existential malaise of Bruce Wayne. He sees a clear problem and attacks it, and on the surface that is what Batman is all about. But there is a lack within Bruce Wayne, and thus a pathology he clings to, one that just craves, on a personal level, Batman as an escape, or as his *raison d'être*, same difference. He cannot let it go, and when he does, he's rudderless and miserable. The Nolan movies of course focus more on Batman as the heroic soldier, but the message is still there about whether or not he even knows what he's fighting for. Batman's supposedly selfless mission co-exists with the selfish impulses of a troubled billionaire. Beneath Batman's mask exists the hidden identity of an anguished Bruce Wayne, a character that, like many of us, embodies the very banal evil Kant admonished against. And so on the one hand, because there is much at stake for his dual identity, Batman has an impulse to enforce the status quo: As a "one-percenter" that protects the "99-percent," Batman's position as such can only be supported by Bruce Wayne's "one-percent" status: Without the elite status of Wayne Enterprises, Batman could not be Batman— all his hi-tech appurtenances and weaponry/gadgetry would be unattainable. (This point is made clear at the beginning of *The Dark Knight* when the real Batman encounters a bunch of ineffectual Batman wannabes—whose utter futility hinges precisely on the fact that they *can't afford to be the real Batman.*) Viewed from this angle, hidden beneath Batman's mask of heroic probity is his hedonistic billionaire Bruce Wayne self, which Batman relies on to coddle his addiction to fighting crime, which Bruce Wayne relies on to escape the banality of his own evil.

The legacy that is *Batman* has come a long way since the Adam West days of slapstick grooviness and joyous campiness. Today's Batman myth has a tendency to reinforce the perverted desire—one that is both extravagant and ecstatic, though often shallow and vapid—for the hedonistic permissiveness that defines our current epoch: Batman is the profligate exception to the "one-percent" that promises to help rather than exploit The Common People; but if we pervert this perspective, that is, if we turn this perspective around on itself, Batman's "charitable service" is merely the preservation of the "one-percent"—for the sole purpose of securing the ruling class as the iconic standard that The Common People, the petite bourgeoisie, the status quo itself, not only measures itself by, but aspires to be.

To put it bluntly, Batman embodies not the ideas and desires of the ruling class, but the ideas and desires of the lower classes. The point is that, the ideas comprising the ruling ideology are not necessarily the ideas of the ruling class, but rather an assemblage of motifs and desires of the oppressed as they are conditioned by the oppressive structure of the ruling class. The ideas and desires of the lower classes get rearticulated in such a way that they became compatible with the existing relations of domination. Which merely serves to sustain the ruling class. Thus Batman fights the crime that Bruce Wayne's lifeworld generates. A vicious cycle, yes. And as a result, Batman therefore necessarily upholds and protects the very social arrangements Bruce Wayne revels in, which ultimately engender nothing but class disparity and privation and the rampant crime that not only pervades the pyramidal 1/99 social dichotomy—but it's also the very crime that Batman grapples with night after night with fetishistic fervor!

Batman's "heroism" is an ideological fake, a purely selfish narcissism serving as a remedy for his own subjective desolation. Batman is not only literally fighting himself, but, most importantly, he also represents the excess of a law and order that is radically corrupt: he is merely the necessary supplement that serves to ensure and guarantee the promises of safety given only to today's bourgeoisie; thus Batman is the object of the status quo par excellence. And because Batman himself does not work toward exposing the radical evil lurking beneath the legal order that his actions help amplify—that his actions only supplement where this legal order falls short in making sure that the middle class and the rich stay safe and secure—Batman is thereby not at all selfless and altruistic. He is, at best, a different side of the same pathetic coin of the people he fights. And Batman persists and appeals as a mythical character precisely because of these elements of duality: these subjective elements inhere in each and every one of us—*for none of us are strangers to the universal conflict between one's moral right to unauthorized initiative and one's moral duty to submit to authority.*

Which brings us to the Joker, who is perhaps the only true exception to the good/evil duality endemic to the Batman saga and the overall status quo. The Joker acts for the sake of acting, disregarding entirely all consequentialism. Despite his personification of chaos, and despite his predilection for sadistic violence, the Joker may be viewed as the ethical agent par excellence, precisely in the capacity of the *persona non* who reveals to society, for society, its own corruption and disorder that is concealed beneath the illusion of law and order. If the Joker shows no concern whatsoever for his victims, is he not, in a sense, only mirroring the real conditions of civil society itself? Recall the utter lack of concern some people have for the casualties of Boeing's, or Lockheed Martin's military drones.

In any case, the Joker specializes in precipitating events in which people are faced with no other option than to either (a) act ethically for the sake of the ethical act itself, or (b) cling tightly and feebly to the conventional morality of calculation, and to act for the opportunistic sake of self-preservation. Here, recall the late scene in *The Dark Knight* in which the Joker gives two boats that are fleeing Gotham City their respective detonators, challenging the passengers of each boat to blow the other one up first. One boat is full of normal citizens, while the other boat is full of criminals. If both boats are still afloat after a certain lapse of time, stipulates the Joker, both of them will be blown to pieces. In other words, one group must die to save the other. This test, writes McGowan, 'actually paves the way for citizens of Gotham to transcend the morality of calculation in the way that the Joker himself does.' In the end, both boats pass the test unscathed (unscathed because Batman nabs the Joker before the Joker can blow both boats up as punishment for not blowing each other up), and thus their respective passengers survive, having decided not to blow one another up. However, as McGowan astutely observes, this scene evinces the

antithetical relation between the institutions of democracy and ethical action. The authorities on the civilian boat decide [...] to vote on whether or not to destroy the other boat [...] [And] the [...] act of voting on a question such as this under-scores its inappropriateness. But when [...] a large majority [...] votes to blow up the criminal boat, we see [...] that democratic procedures have no ethical status at all. In fact, the secret ballot allows each subject to retreat from the trauma of the ethical decision rather than confronting it directly. The film shows one passenger writing out his vote and handing it in with great determination, while a shot of another reveals his emotional struggle with the difficulties of the moral issue. Both of these attitudes toward the vote serve only to illustrate the absurdity of voting on the decision to blow up a boatful of other people. The vote is an inadequate mechanism for approaching a decision of this magnitude. The ethical act occurs not through the hastily put together franchise on the civilian boat but through the revolutionary seizure of power on the prisoners' boat. The way that the prisoners are depicted accentuates their menace: they stare ominously at the authorities; they whisper to each other while staring; they maintain a determined grimacing expression. These visual clues, added to the fact that the film establishes them as dangerous criminals, suggest that they are planning to seize the detonator and blow up the civilian ship in order to save their own lives. But the film turns the tables on the spectator's expectation.[139]

Are we not, then, presented with a clear example of an ethical act that transcends the pathological limitations of conventional law, *brought about by no other than the Joker himself?* — An agent who shows us that, beneath the illusion of order, there is an inconsistent disorderliness, a Real that does not cease to exist. And as an aside, can we not find a better example that reveals how the real evil, you know, the kind that, say, Jesus warns about in his parables, is that which is any kind of fanatical dogmatism?

To make an ethical point here, real evil is an unyielding obedience to the unquestioned assumptions that comprise the imperious character of any status quo and its ruling ideology, especially when it's exercised in the name of some supreme Good, when backed by a Claim to Virtue. This is a lesson that goes as far back as Socrates' dialogue with Euthyphro, and which continues to find its pulse in recent affairs such as Edward Snowden's whistle-blowing case, or Chelsea Manning's heroism. Here, one should recount the quote from Oscar Wilde's *The Picture of Dorian Gray*, spoken by arguably one of my favorite characters, Sir Henry: "Morality consists in accepting the standard of one's age. I consider that for any man of culture to accept the standard of his age is a form of the grossest immorality."

And so, as Hegel observed, the real source of evil is the putative "innocent gaze" that sees evil everywhere in the world. Did we not witness this very evil unfold in Germany from 1933 to 1945, or under Stalin's command of Russia, or with McCarthyism in the US? And does it not now refer *at times* to the very gaze which today sees "terrorists" everywhere in the world? One has to beg the question: If this is what evil *really* is, would this make an ethical agent of good appear as "evil?" One can only suspect that, if a truly righteous and virtuous character were to emerge today, he or she would perhaps be mistaken for a Joker-like character, only to be strung up on a cross in no time soon, their anguished grimace-of-Real pushing out those famous last words: "Forgive them, for they know not what they do."

## §26. The Real as non-sense

Here we should introduce the Lacanian distinction between the Real and reality. The Real is designated for that which has no room in our socio-Symbolic reality. It is literally a thing of non-sense. That is to say, the Real is that piece of raw reality that gets "lost," a piece of that unfathomable abyss of subjective freedom which we must sacrifice in order to immerse ourselves into the Symbolically constructed social field we experience as reality. As a result, this little piece of the Real returns to us 'in the guise of spectral apparitions,' as "symptoms" which haunt our everyday experience, threatening to undermine the internal consistency of a reality organized around the (fantasmatic) interconnectedness of its ascribed symbols.[140]

Once (a piece of) the Real is experienced, however, it simultaneously transforms into something symbolized: what was at first a matter of chance and contingency becomes inscribed in reality as something "Named." Take the example of "miracles";

miracles are that which conform to the universal order they index, but transgress the internal consistency of said order; as a transgression, they are conditioned by what they transgress. As such, miracles confound the regulations that are necessary for maintaining the very universal order they conform to. This fortuitous paradox can perhaps serve to instantiate the determinate moment when non-meaning, an element of the Real as such, intervenes in reality, becoming inscribed in the Symbolic, thereby receiving its meaning.

It should be carefully noted and kept in mind that objectivity, at its purest, directly relates to this dimension of non-sense, of non-meaning, and/or the perplexity that arises along the boundaries of contact between the Real and the rest of the triad. In other words, objectivity, at its purest, is the Real in all its *multiple* dimensions at once. As such, it is impossible.

## §27. A conscious encounter with the Real

Sometimes we experience a *soupçon* of the Real. As a dimension that is always-already with(in) us, as that which cuts through the subject and everything Symbolic, the Real oftentimes percolates into our lives now and again. Though such encounters with the Real are often traumatic, inconsistent, too overwhelming or too stimulating, or, sometimes too abstruse for a pedestrian understanding when it's formulated, as in the case of mathematical formulae used to explain quantum mechanics.

A great analogy for this can be found in what Žižek styles the 'ontological paradox of quantum physics': The "physical reality" we see as emerging from the fluctuation of the reduction of a wave packet—or rather, put a bit more concisely, the "image point" (particle) of a system—is represented by what Schrödinger described as a "wave group" with infinitesimal dimensions going in every direction. The "visible" particle moves with the group velocity of the wave packet, and although it seems like a distinct particle, this "particle" is really just the superposition of numerous different waves, a position that corresponds to all the particular possible states of the particle being observed (which embodies a contradiction par excellence—for it's been proven that an object manifests both wavelike and particle-like properties, hence the term "wave-particle duality"). The problem, of course, as pointed out by Henrik Lorentz, is that the idea of representing particles in terms of the superposition of waves appears invalid simply because the wave function spreads out as time increases. In other words, according to quantum mechanics, the mathematical formalism according to which the universe evolves determines only the *probability* that a particular particle's future will occur; that is to say, it cannot predict with perfect precision which future will *definitely* occur, only that which *may* occur. (*In other words, this immutable aspect of probability is merely the reflection of our incomplete knowledge.*) Moreover, in order to *see*, say, an electron, something must be done to it, such as bounce photons off of it, i.e., shine light on it. But because of the infinitesimal size of the electron, no matter how gently you carry out your determination, the photon will inevitably affect the electron's subsequent motion and likely its position. As string theorist Brian Greene puts it, 'any attempt to verify this seemingly basic quality of reality [i.e., the electron] ruins the experiment.' In other words, the more precisely the momentum of a particle is determined, the less precisely its position can be known, and vice versa. What we are dealing with here is none other than Heisenberg's "uncertainty principle," which states that both the momentum and the position of a particle cannot be precisely determined at the same time.

How then, does one resolve this contradiction? How about this: The particle is none other than what Bertrand Russell once coined it as—an *Event*, the 'intervention of consciousness,' a rupture in the particle's unfolding journey: the very moment of its observation (for more on this, see Žižek, *Parallax View*, pp.

172-3). One should not (simply because one cannot) erase the thinking subject from the fabric of reality being observed: the subject is as much a part of the fundamental force impacting the very fabric of reality; to "remove" the subject from the reality being viewed is to elevate reality into a dimension of fantasy. Thus the Real of quantum multiplicity (waves, oscillations, etc.) preceding the emergence of "hard reality," is ontologically ambiguous—previous to its perception this reality is fluid, protean, its evolution aleatory and rhizomatic, radically uncertain. Following the intervention of consciousness, however, this "hard reality" assumes its perceived, albeit *affected*, identity—though it is none other than a "tensed identity": i.e., it assumes a particular identity at a particular time by its particular observer(s); or, to return to a passage from Hegel: *'it is a descriptive collection* of determinations of thought put together in various ways, which in their finitude count for something infinite.'* And as Heidegger would have perhaps put it, its form is none other than a concealed history, which is always situated upon the edge of a precipice of an undetermined future.

Let's back up a step, because things get even more strangely exciting here. It's been shown that each electron actually journeys over *every possible path it can take, which is infinite in number, to get from its point of departure to its "destination"—simultaneously!* Theoretical physicist Richard Feynman's formulation for quantum mechanics (Feynman's "sum-over-paths" approach) shows that one can assign a number to each path belonging to a particular electron

in such a way that their combined average yields exactly the same result for the probability calculated using the wave-function approach [...] The probability that the electron [...] arrives at any chosen point [...] is built up from the combined effect of every possible way of getting there [...] The result of calculations using Feynman's approach agree with those of

the wave function method, which agree with experiments [...]
[H]is rule for assigning numbers to each path ensures that *all
[infinite] paths but one cancel each other out* when their contribu-
tions are combined.[141]

Let's play with that. Here, we need to revisit the concept of the
multiple: the claim that there exists no animate body that is not
organized, and there is no organized body that is not, in essence,
a plurality (*plura entia*); viz., all material bodies have extension
and are therefore divisible to infinity: that is to say, there is no
*One* (*unum ens*), but only a plurality (*plura entia*); and for that
matter, there is only a plurality of pluralities, and so on. This
infinity of plurality might as well equal pure nothingness, for if
there is, as shown here, no *real* discernible oneness, then any
determination to show for oneness quickly dissolves into an
amorphous indetermination. It's like trying to swipe at
something and catching only a handful of air; the moment one
tries to explain for a determinate *one*—a body of matter—logic
shows that this "one" immediately dissolves into an infinite
regress of pure multiplicity—pluralities that are constitutive of
and constituted by plurality—ultimately unable to be enveloped
in any sort of *real* determinate oneness. Thus an object's self-
standing appearance is mere illusion. It's not unlike our electron.
The electron, in its natural state, unperturbed by observation and
experiment, *is equal to the infinite number of paths it traverses*. But
once one makes a conscious observation of the electron in an
experiment, then all paths cancel one another out, save for one—
the path that indicates the electron's general location. And this is
precisely why consciousness must be a variable at play here. Our
state of conscious awareness gives us the impression, quite
convincingly so, that our reality is *not* experienced as a
multiform flux of radical multiplicity *ad infinitum*: we experience
reality in the form of "oneness," as a self-aware, self-standing
body that perceives reality; and moreover, from this sense of

"oneness" as such we perceive the physical reality around us, at least at the macro level, *not* as a chaotic flow of radical pluralities, but as discrete bodies interacting with other discrete bodies—*But what if this is the very nature of consciousness itself?* As Žižek puts is, the "mystery" behind the nature of consciousness does not reside in some sort of complex puzzle situated at the level of neuronal activity, but rather: The enigmatic feature of consciousness is that it is an agency whose sole function is to *simplify* complexity. Perhaps, then, the "one" exceptional path that the electron takes is reflective of the intervention of consciousness itself—that which intervenes and simplifies the complexity of the electron's infinite number of paths. That is to say, what if it is the act itself of observing the electron, an act of consciousness as such, that reduces the infinite number of these paths down to a single path? Could we not posit the claim, then, that consciousness arises from the multiple as the very exception to the multiple, in order to *simplify the multiple?* That, as such, consciousness is the *One* that intervenes and simplifies, enframes, the infinite complexity endemic to the multiple? If so, then *that* is how objectivity works!

Here, we should turn our attention for the moment to a passage from the book *Philosophy in the Present*, on page 44, in which Badiou writes about the Evental act, which seems to help support what's been discussed above:

Although the being-multiple of the situation [in this case, the being-multiple of the particle] remains unaltered, the logic of its appearance—the system [field of quantum physics] that evaluates and connects all the multiplicities belonging to the situation [the particle]—can undergo a profound transformation [...] It is the act [of observation] to which a subject-thought [consciousness] becomes bound in such a way as to render that act capable of initiating a procedure which effects a radical modification of the logic of the situation, and hence of what appears insofar as it appears.

Perhaps, then, Russell had nailed it when likening particles to Events—that they are the nodal points at which synchronicity and diachronicity intersect, so to speak; and perception, objectivity as such, is the integration of this sensual observation into a network of 'memories and anticipations,' into a Symbolic network that structures this pure reality into a meaningful and consistent "whole"—consciousness *as such*.

## §28. *Vis imaginativa*: the Real of Spirit

*The [...] separation of [...] interiority and outwardness, when history in its entire range becomes an object of consideration and of [...] representation as a coherent whole [...] [t]his progress stems from the power of objectivity itself, which gathers itself together out of its rarefaction in inwardness and seeks to condense [...] inner spirit in the object...*[142]

The reason why objectivity has become, for many, such a bone of contention can be best explained by its multivalent disposition; that, as a whole, objectivity accommodates multiple modes in which it can be expressed. Not only do all three significances, as laid out above (Imaginary-Symbolic-Real), reverberate within objectivity per se, moreover, what is purely objective, that which is situated at the level of the real-Real, is that which accounts for an impenetrable core that diffuses into a "multiplicity of appearances," into the other significances of objectivity that are none other than the series of attempts to fill in the gap inherent to the hard bone of objectivity itself. Thus Real-objectivity bespeaks the inaccuracy inherent to the very act of representing any object in-itself. What is *purely* objective is either pre-knowledge, or, is that which ceases to be inscribed into any kind of explicit, consistent knowledge whatsoever.[143] Why, exactly, is this the case? The answer is not: because one cannot know the thing-in-itself, as it ex-sists in its own center of being-in-itself; rather, the answer is: there is no stable center as such, no discrete thing *in-itself*. There is only a complete nullification of foundation. In other words, every seemingly substantial thing, every seemingly discrete, material entity, at its most radical level, breaks down into something that is both constituted by and constitutive of a multiple, a multiple that emerges from its own "place of inscription," a void as such. Thus something in-itself is irremediably unknowable, ungraspable—its precise representation is always-already elusive; all that we can truly know is that which exists in its concept: that which assumes the place of what eludes a complete and accurate representation. Therefore our knowledge of something other is restricted to the form of its notion, idea, concept, etc.—and thus marks the movement and inherently unlimited scope of thought, in which all of reality is "determined" for the subject. What this implies is that the Thing-in-itself is essentially ideal in nature: a thing's appearance appeals directly to the cognitive subject's intuitive contact with it, and, ultimately, as Kant put it, to the interpretation that "rationally apprehends" what the subject's intuition yields. And yes, the mere appearance of *something* presupposes that there exists some thing (that appears), and yes, we can never truly know this wholly other thing in *itself*. But that's not the point right now. What we should take away from this is that the unknowable in-itselfness of something wholly other, that which is in the object that is more than the object itself, is reflexive of the Thing-in-itself *that is in the subject more than the subject itself*. In other words, the enigmatic Thing-in-itself does not refer immediately to the inner integrity of some external object; quite the contrary—by dint of entering the province of human awareness, the in-itselfness of an external object *immediately* reflects the unfathomable void, the in-itselfness that is at the core of the subject. And by means of an inversion into its opposite—i.e., *through the inscription of this void into the external object, whereby the object-Other takes the place of this void*—this empty part of the subject is placed onto the side of objects, into the object-Other, whereby the apprehension of the object-Other in its notion takes place, and from which the subject's objective viewpoint emerges.

This process of inversion results in objectivity, a "frame" that enframes reality itself for the subject, a frame that, when viewed through, reality becomes its own appearance. This engenders, for the subject, a sense of subjective oneness, a sense of Self with and in the world, producing the subject in-itself and for-itself as such. To exemplify this, let us look to Hegel's figure of Spirit— Spirit being a creation of itself, to be likened to the subject's creative prowess familiarly known as imagination: a substance in-itself insofar as it sustains itself as such through the activity of the subjects involved in it. But first let's back up a few steps.

Put simply, there is a difference between the thing that is known, and the mind that knows it. This gap between subject and object, however, is internal to mind itself, situated at the core of the subject. Thus what is purely objective, the impossible *Thing-in-itself,* precedes the subject: ostensibly it refers to the gap between subject and object, but at deeper level it is a void as such indwelling the pure subject, a gaping place at the heart of the subject whence Spirit emanates and "accumulates" the very substance that becomes subject. Can we not say that Spirit, then, is what Freud called *Lust-ich,* a "proto-Self" which, as such, is, *literally* a "Self-organizing" agent that explodes forth from the deadlock of the subject's inherent non-coincidence with itself?

Consider, on the one hand, that "Self-consciousness"—one's palpable sense of "subjective oneness"—can appear as an object of consciousness *itself* in the form of the rational "I," as in the Other of the "I" that thinks: the empirical, discernible Self, which substantiates, gives body to, the immaterial, imperceptible "I" that thinks. This notion of Self, this oneness as such, however, is imaginary/illusory, it's not a substantial form in-itself—for not only is it hinged on the object-Other whence the notion of Self derives (the subject recognizes itself in its otherness), but also, as a *notion*, this notion of Self serves to supplement an original lack of substantial Self. Hence the sense of "oneness" we feel, our awareness of Self—our subjectivity as such—is essentially a nothing that counts for something, as it becomes something. That is to say, the subject without its Self cannot be conscious of itself. And one's Self is a series of *developments*, as such it is none other than a bricolage, an array of identifications that *are not*, ontologically, one and the same as the subject itself; for the subject is an *effect* of the plurality of identifications that comprise the Self, which is developed in and through pure difference, the difference of the subject from itself, the minimal difference between the subject and his place of inscription, as it's transposed into the field of the object-Other. As such, it is the accumulation of a series of attempts to fill in this gap inherent to the subject.

On the other hand, consider the Other of the Self, the agency behind consciousness itself, or rather, that which is in consciousness more than consciousness itself—the Fichtean *"Ich."* This is the subject's apperceptive "I", the alien *Thing* that thinks, that which consciousness is for: the empty framework of thought itself. A shadowy feature of the subject's Self which, through the activity of thought itself, moves beyond the subject's corporeal limits, arriving at the side of objects and, upon its return—that is, after thought grasps, so to speak, its object— reveals to the subject, for the subject, the subject's Self: the latter being the "I" of empirical, contemplative experience: an objectal correlate of the elusive "I" that thinks. Thus the Self is a *re-presentation* of the unfathomable subject-in-itself, which has arrived to the subject, for the subject, from the side of substantial objects, the objective field as such. In other words, the subject recognizes its Self in otherness, in *objects* that give themselves to the subject's notion in their objectivity; and thus the subject's Self, to which Spirit returns, is created in the very activity of this return, thereby giving, *retroactively*, substance to the subject. Hence the subject is an effect of objectivity as such.

As Žižek maintains and, as Hegel claimed, the Fichtean *Ich* is not some absolute "I" identical with the mere act of self-positing.[144] Rather, *it is what produces the subject*—for no other reason than the assertion that the subject, a production as such, serves to give body, "subject matter," to a radical lack (i.e., a lack of Self) that is, from the subject's inceptive moment, built into the subject. That is to say, for the conscious subject to "come forth," to appear, the empty framework of conscious thought itself must be filled in with the substantial content of all that its thought is directed toward. The subject's lack, as such, is what's responsible for the movement behind the development of the subject's "substantial" Beingness simply because, there is no substantial being, no original order of Being that the subject can return to, but can only develop into. In other words, "the subject is not its own origin" but is rather the *process* of Self-manifestation: *the subject is its history*. As such, the subject is the "active relationship to itself" found in the doubling of itself (its lack) in the (lack of the) object-Other: the subject emerges in the process, by the process, and through the process of objectification, a process engendered by the activity of subjective Spirit's return to the very Self it creates in the act of this return. Thus Spirit is *the* act of comprehending the history of its activity, and the subject *is* this protean history.

Another way to look at this is that, the subjective experience of givenness *is* a form of objectivity: as such it's the creation of a dimension, a frame in which and through subjectivity becomes itself via the recognition of itself in otherness. Objectivity is a perceptual mode in which, through which and by which the subject attempts to fully actualize itself by means of its juxtaposition with the objective field of otherness. And thus Spirit is none other than that which creates for the subject, objectivity, precisely as a means to transform this objectivity into the very vehicle by which the limits of its previous achievements of recognition can be overcome, whereby the subject will acquire his (unfolding) Self-identity. Hegel writes to this effect, claiming that '[P]rogress, therefore, is not an indeterminate advance *ad infinitum*, for it has a definite aim, namely that of returning upon itself.'[145] And because the subject *in-itself* has no substantial actuality, each attempt to *fully* actualize its Self inevitably fails — *and the subject emerges by means of and through this failure.*

Thus marks the repetition of Spirit: the subject *"is"* its constant striving to fulfill itself, to attain itself in-itself, by means of manifesting its subjectivity via objectivity. The subject *is* the effect of all its significations, an effect of objectivity *as such*.

What this means is that the incessant repetition of Spirit, of this *activity*, is the attempt at reconciling the gap that appears between thought and its object, which, as stated above, is nonetheless internal to thought itself — the latter being none other than an "object" of cognition, transposed into the objects of desire "out there" in the external, objective world. As Fabio Vighi aptly puts it, 'I can think something [...] only if the constitutive non-coincidence of my thought with itself is externalized [and transposed into an object in such a way that it] sets my desire to know (my thought) in motion.'[146] Such a movement is Spirit, which designates the very movement of the subject's "absent" center (lack) from the place of the subject into the object-Other, whereby the act of concealing-by-means-of-giving-substance to this absent center of the subject — the process of objectification as such — takes place. Thus objectivity, the perceptual mode in which, through which and by which the subject acquires his sense of subjectivity, his sense of oneness, is that which serves to conceal the void at the subject's very core. Hence "subjective" reality is none other than the inverted form of this absent center, substantiated and legitimized by "objective" reality. To reiterate an emphasis from earlier: the Spirit of the subject is that incorporeal, elusive *Thing* in and of the subject, which moves beyond the corporeal extension of the subject to the side of objects before returning back to the subject, whereby it creates—in the very act of its return—the space to which it returns: the subject's sense of oneness qua Self. Spirit produces the subject through objectification as such.

Can we not liken the subject's Spirit to the "real-abstraction" discussed earlier, as the subject's unconscious-at-work? As that which reaches beyond the (subjective) position where it appears as a means, absorbing itself into the larger ideological space of the Symbolic order before enclosing together in itself the subject's (Symbolic, objective) being in its lack of being, thereby providing the subject with a sense of place, a sense of oneness, a sense of Self?

Can we not assume, then, that objectivity as such serves to provide a stabilizing force, one which guarantees that everything in the world, including the subject, has its proper "objective" place, while also providing an image of "wholeness," the ideological assurance that the signifying system of the world is closed, that all antagonisms and divisions can be reconciled? And if so, have we not, then, hit upon the elementary ("paternal" and "maternal") features of ideology itself, therefore supporting our claim that objectivity is, essentially, ideological?

## §29. We are not so sure we know anything...

So where does one's faith in objective representation come from? The answer to this may be found by answering the following question: What does the lack of a signifier for a signifier *actually* indicate? Or better yet, what does it mean when we acknowledge that there is no system outside of language from which we can ever refer to language? It means that per se signification is not a completely closed system, it will always fail in terms of accurately representing the thing it's designated to represent. *And it is precisely by dint of this intrinsic glitch, so to speak, that 'the object inscribes itself in the blank opened by this failure.'* Objectivity thus arises as an ideological phantom, so to speak, as an anamorphic distortion of reality that serves to conceal the negative space at the core of the subject's reality and everything that is Symbolically contained therein. In this sense, objectivity is a moment of "constitutive reflexivity": it functions as a stand-in for what immediately eludes its *guaranteed* Symbolic inscription: as such, objectivity can be likened to a sort of "ideological police force," arresting that which is not *instantly* inscribed and concretized in symbolic form. For instance, there may be many ideological edifices that seek to explain the world—e.g., a variety of religious doctrines—but in today's "post-ideological" world there appears to be not a single ideology that can *guarantee*, for everyone, a believable story for the nature of the universe and so on. Although it's true that intelligent life is none other than the product of billions of years of evolution, the complete story behind this still remains somewhat "open," questions still remain unanswered—"Is there some sort of "creator" behind evolution itself, or is it merely the chance result of pure randomness?" "How does free will fit in the picture?" And so on... And that's where objectivity comes in. Its function is to secure in Symbolic inscription what any other ideology today cannot secure. Thus objectivity appears in the guise of its opposite: as a non-ideological ideology! It's an ideology like any other simply because of the enduring aspect of probability at play in the very constitutive elements of our reality—even objectivity can't *really* guarantee any complete knowledge; thus objectivity, too, arises by dint of its inherent lack of a complete knowledge, precisely as a means to conceal this lack—a hallmark of ideology if there ever was one.

Therefore, today's ideological system of symbols functions in the guise of its opposite: as Real, as *not ideological*—paradoxically speaking, today's ideology appears *as itself in the guise of its own constitutive essence: as objectivity.* Thus objectivity is a reflexive "empty-signifier," one that serves to mask the lack that is inherent to itself; thus objectivity takes the place of the very absence that precedes its presence as such.

By this light, an object-Other is, by its very nature, a sort of *locum tenens* for a primordial void, a "something" that seeks to conceal a radical *nothing*. Objective reality, functioning as a Master-Signifier, is none other than the Symbolic as it refers to itself. As such, objectivity is a veil for nothing in the guise of something, and that "something" is a "stain" on reality that corresponds more with the desiring subject and his or her Symbolic condition than with the object-in-itself. Thus the object-Other is none other than the inverted appearance of the perceiving subject's own immediacy. And objectivity, as we think of it today, is nothing more-nor-less than a "universal schema" in which, by which, and through which the subject makes the steadfast attempt to bypass one's own subjective perspective while striving to know the "truth" of the object-in-itself. Though in order for the subject to wholeheartedly believe that this mode of truth actually exists, he or she must behave *as if* they are not a part of the fundamental force impacting the very fabric of their reality: one's subjectivity, which is provided by the very objectivity the subject is an effect of!

The crucial element at work here is the function of fetishistic disavowal: the denial of the fact that objectivity is merely a moment of inner reflexive negativity inverted into an illusive moment of transcendent "objective" externality. As such, the object-Other, *in-itself*, will always remain elusive and enigmatic: As one strives to know the truth of some external thing, the respective thought-products one develops for it can never, will never, acquire a precise representation: i.e., one can never attain a complete knowledge of something other—for the concept in which all knowledge abounds takes its form against an original lack of knowledge that won't—can't—ever go away; and therefore thought can never fully correspond with its object precisely because this object is always more present in its notion, in its concept, which is borne from the subject forming the thought as such, and which arises from the indeterminable Real around which it's structured. That is to say, this radical lack of *purely objective* knowledge is what initiates the very movement of objective thought, pushing it forward; and once thought is caught up in this motion, this lack of purely objective knowledge is trans-positioned onto the horizon of knowledge, thereby drawing and pulling thought's movement forward. And thus the notion, the idea, the concept of an object—something that is infinitely protean—is impossible to comprehend in its entirety simply because the task of completion always begins from a radical misconstruction, from the Real as such.

## §30. The object of knowledge and its Real predicament

It is against this background that we should pose the following question: Why is it the case that, in the sciences, where objectivity is presented as a "no-brainer" in the painstaking quest for knowledge and truth, significant levels of disagreement between theories and their respective schools of thought persist in a realm of tenacious competitiveness and antagonism, moreso than in a realm in which they may find themselves in agreement with each other? The short answer is that there is no common methodology, and no common basic assumptions, shared between science and philosophy...

One should probe a little deeper, however, and consider that the reason for this—why there is no concise "theory of every-thing"—is precisely because the *real* object of intellectual objec-tivity is not some "external" entity under examination/consider-ation, but rather: the "object" of intellectual objectivity is none other than the very unconscious *desire* of the thinking subject, that part of the subject that is *in* the object under examination, the human point of the subject's *gaze*. In the words of Alenka Zupančič,

> what drives knowledge further and further, and could be called the object-cause of knowledge, is always something in the object of knowledge that keeps escaping our grasp [...] [T]he (search for) knowledge is structured like desire [...] Every new discovery is thus accompanied by the feeling that perhaps "this is not yet it," that it is always possible to go one step further, or discover yet another aspect of the object. What keeps eluding our knowledge, however, is simply our own gaze [...] The true question concerns not where we stand when we are reflecting on a certain object, but, rather, where we stand within this object itself.[147]

Scientists and philosophers, like everybody else, are not exempt from ideology. All "experts" and "specialists" alike have unconscious desires too, and these desires find their expression in the very way in which the scientist, the specialist, et al., has "deposited" his or her gaze *within the object being considered*, a gaze that is conditioned, enframed, by the very socio-ideological lifeworld he or she is inscribed in. In other words, the scientist's gaze is not the perspective of the scientific individual him/herself, but rather the gaze of science, but not necessarily of science *itself* even—more than that, it's the gaze of a particular *manifestation* of science: the idealized images of objective analysis are staged for the gaze of science as it is practiced under the ruling ideology of today's capitalist society. Moreover, the interfering aspect of the subject's gaze is obfuscated by none other than today's ruling capitalist ideology, which is the continuation of an old paradigm of classic thought: a consciousness that takes on the form of the dogmatic belief that objectivity, without fail, will lead to the discovery of knowledge about an external object under scrutiny, a knowledge unadulterated by any ideology.

Such knowledge is practically impossible however, simply because it's impossible to remove the subject altogether from the very reality being observed. And the subject is always-already a subject of ideology.

Here, one should keep in mind that, as Georg Lukács held, capitalist ideology creates the very social structure that promotes such "objective" views: the view that entities (and their environment) can be 'inspected without outside interference,' or rather, without the "subjective distortion" that is nonetheless at play in the act of inspection; 'it is in the nature of capitalism to process phenomena in this way.'[148] As Lukács put it—it's in capitalism's best self-serving interest, as a means to constitute and substantiate its own premises, to promote as unchangeable 'the laws of its society as the unalterable foundation of science.'[149] In other words, science, as it's expressed by and performed according to today's capitalist society and its laws, accepts the nature of objective reality as it is "given," while disavowing the fact that the very laws used to explain such a "given" reality are none other than products of an historical evolution—which will inevitably change since the relationship between these laws and their social context are involved in a much larger flow of continuous deformation and reformation. Lukács writes to this effect, claiming that today's materialists

do not go beyond the reproduction of the immediate, simple determinant of social life. They imagine that they are being [...] 'exact' when they simply take over these determinants without either analyzing them or further welding them into a concrete totality. They take the facts in abstract isolation, explaining them only in terms of abstract laws unrelated to the concrete totality.[150]

Taking facts in "abstract isolation" clouds the historical, protean nature of society, capitalist or not, in which the knowledge that is created around these facts is deeply embedded. The best that science and philosophy can provide for us are new discoveries. Though what these discoveries "mean" vary tremendously according to at least two criteria: (i) meaning inheres in the *effects* (and affects) scientific discoveries and philosophical postulations produce when these discoveries and postulates are put under further analysis, experimentation, and so on; and (ii) meaning also inheres not just in the many ways in which these effects are interpreted, but also, how such effects are interpreted in terms of their *use* for practical knowledge, a practical knowledge that is reflexive only of the scientific/philosophical community's Symbolic constitution and, the universal ideology that subtends the community. And knowledge is constantly undergoing change; it accords to how we relate to the physical world around us, which is a relation that is fixed within a protean history.

Here, one should bear in mind that "absolute knowledge," or T.O.E. (Theory of Everything)—that presupposed (desired) "goal" which effectuates the very *desire* driving objective, intellectual thought—cannot be sundered from its subjective position; a position that—if the reader were to recall the paradox of quantum physics explicated earlier—delineates contradiction—the coincidence of opposing features—as an 'internal condition of every identity.' Therefore, any "Theory of Everything" must include within it its contradiction as the innermost constituent that is essential to the order of everything: that, as such, contradiction designates the aspect of excessive contingency around which all necessity is structured.

In any event, the paradoxical logic of contradiction thus reveals that the object-*in-itself*, what can be termed as that little "piece of the Real," an impenetrable kernel belonging to all the sundry objects persisting under the skeptical gaze of the sciences, *does not really exist*—and yet it does exist, though only as that of what Maurice Merleau-Ponty described as being 'an unreflected life that is its initial, constant, and final situation.'[151]

In other words, on the one hand, the object-in-itself exists as a resistant, impenetrable kernel, unsusceptible to inscription into the Symbolic: it is a nothing that nonetheless counts for something, it's precisely that which 'does not cease not to inscribe itself (*ne cesse pas de ne pas s'écrire*);' and on the other hand, as that nothing-which-counts-for-something, it exists as the chimerical 'object cause of desire': as that enigmatic *Thing* in the object that is more than the object itself, which propels one to chase after it despite the impossibility of ever catching up with it. Which is another way of saying that the object is "more present" in its notion: the object exists moreso in the very *idea*, notion, concept, etc., that processes the object's image, than in its immediate physical essence. That is precisely how knowledge develops. And despite the fact that one's understanding of something in its concept is none other than an "illusion" of sorts that serves to conceal this "non-existent" piece of the Real, there is in fact a Real in the illusion itself: the way in which science itself produces, as a direct result of all of this, its effects in and on reality.

In this sense, what is considered today to be "objective" completely passes over, and thus neglects to take into account, the irreducible gap *inherent to representation itself*, an irreducible gap that spews forth a multitude of representations. It's not so much the case that there is a gap between knowledge and truth, insofar as the truth emerges *as* the series of attempts to fill the lack that is intrinsic to knowledge itself. Most people assume that truth and knowledge — that, e.g., signifiers and their respective signifieds — are seamlessly conjoined, that they are one and the same. But by this assumption, the very impossibility of ever knowing anything in-itself, the lack of knowledge inherent to knowledge itself, is disavowed, quite fetishistically. Thus the difference between knowledge and truth is not the difference between two opposed poles within the same field, rather: it is the non-coincidence of knowledge with itself. Truth therefore refers to this fact, and this fact only: that the "truth" *is the appearance of the representation itself,* precisely as the return of the "primordially repressed" element: What is primordially repressed is none other than the truth of this lack of complete knowledge; and the "return of the repressed" is the very signifier that stands for this lack (i.e., the representation) and its incessant *reduplication*. The truth appears *as such:* as the multitude of representations, and the proliferation of knowledge begot by this series of attempts to fill in the gap internal to knowledge itself, a minimal difference between knowledge and its empty place of inscription.

## §31. Ethics of a political philosophy

Louis Althusser, who was a bit of a theoretical innovator for his time concerning the analysis of ideology, made it very clear that class antagonism pervades not only the material realm of production and work, but that it also pervades the immaterial realm of intellectual thought within the sciences itself and, generally speaking, academe all together—i.e., how we appropriate facts about the external material world within our socio-political domain. If one were to think long and hard about it, the only real problem worthy of our intellectual attention in these times is that which is radically nested within much of the contemporary sciences and its supportive Anglo-American analytic philosophy: that materialist science and analytic philosophy both err in the same sense in that they strive to explain for a coherent, unified, and consistent order of things, which is nothing less than an *ideal* way of seeing the world. Or rather, it's an expression, an articulation, of an unconscious desire for order and control. The fact that pure Real-reality is constitutively split however, that there is no consistent and intelligible order (were we to strip away altogether the Symbolic order of our "meaningful" lives), is something these philosophers and scientists alike refuse to accept, somewhat if not entirely wholeheartedly. Therefore, philosophy should not be in the business of trying to explain an "order" to the world or the universe; rather, it should serve to expound on the world as it exists in its natural state of antagonistic disorder, how reality is inherently divided between its rational and organic material "wholeness," and its immaterial excess; and to help teach us new ways to live our lives appropriately in such a world—This is, after all, approximate to what Hegel wanted us to acknowledge when he posited that the 'Absolute involves a radical loss.' It's not just that the Absolute as such is impossible to fathom, but that, moreover, this impossibility is what drives our every attempt to fathom and be at peace with the inconsistent nature of reality, a nature that is both generously giving of the very lives we lead, and one that ensures the inevitable taking of these lives. From between both Being and Nothing we *become*, we become the free human beings we were always-already born to be, and this freedom can only amount to something through our acceptance of its guiding principles, ethical principles by which we should always be ready to sacrifice all we have for nothing, since, after all, it from this nothing that all this has come to be. This is what it means to love, and to defend that which you love. This is, simply because it *should* be, objectively so.

For that reason, philosophy should align itself with the political. It should serve to influence and determine how and why we should or should not, can or cannot, appropriate facts that science unearths about the external (and internal) material world within our socio-political domain, ultimately shaping both the means and the ends of the sciences. As such, philosophy should help us get out of today's existential malaise: It should wrangle itself free of academe, and return to its proper place, to honestly address the fact that, in these times, we no longer live in *this* world but instead live in television shows and videogames, the Internet and text messaging, automobiles and fantasy sports teams, and so on *ad nauseam*. Philosophy should therefore shine more light on what this malaise actually alludes to: That the dominant culture, in a gravely ironic sense, has robbed the world of a certain subjectivity of its own, only to reify the entire living world into a stock of objects to be exploited, to be enjoyed for the sole subjective pleasure of one domineering group. Furthermore, philosophy should address that this atrocity could not have happened if not for the exploitative capitalist ideology that serves to undergird today's intellectual objectivity. If philosophy cannot follow through with this, then it is dead.

## §32. The Real antagonism that is subject

Now that we are beginning to suss things out, at least in terms of a solid understanding of the features and the formative processes of ideology, we should take a moment here and make a brief lateral intervention into the material at hand, go a step further to illustrate just how, exactly, the first-person singular (nominative case personal) pronoun, "I," —as in, "I think..." or "I am..."—is both an ideological gesture *par excellence*, and, the radical base from which one can subvert their ideological allegiance altogether. We'll also see in this analysis not only how ideology interpellates the subject, but how the singularity of the subject as a unique, particular individual is, also, at the same time, universal by dint of its exceptional status in regard to the universal.

Now, it may be the case that all hegemonic structures are ideological, but not all ideologies have ruling, hegemonic power over an entire society or network of societies. That is to say, even when a particular ideology doesn't subtend an entire culture or society, or at the very least the majority of an entire culture or society, it still has a dominating force over those who do accede to its interpellative force. In other words, there exist particular ideologies, and each particular ideology is universal in the sense that it shapes and informs its individual subjects' worldview, their "*objective reality*" as such. Take, as an example, those tinfoil-hat-wearing conspiracy theorists: their particular view of "how things are" may not hold universally true for everyone, but this particular outlook on the world sure holds universally true for them.

In any event, there is no reason why ideologies, despite their often-hegemonic qualities, cannot be both universal and particular and, not to mention just as well—if I may add a third term here to make it a sort of ever-shifting ternary structure—*protean*;[152] protean by dint of the very individuality that is involved with each particular ideology, whether it's fully hegemonic or not.

First, the fact that the individual subject is, at its core, none other than an "ontological excess" qua void means that the subject is decentered: we are always connected to the social field because we are inherently split, not fully connected with our Selves—for the simple reason that the subject's Self is determined by the very ideological field he or she identifies with. In other words, the subject must embrace its own otherness in order to become, and to be recognized as, its Self: a subject of ideology. Therefore the subject is split, decentered as such, for we cannot separate the analysis of the subject from that of the social. On the other hand, the individual subject is, at the same time, an exception to the ideological universal—the particular individual is an element that is "outside" of the (self-enclosed) universal, and the difference between the universal's self-enclosure and its "outside" element—the individual subject as such—is nonetheless inscribed within the universal ideology, precisely as a means to account for ideology's "universality." But the individual subject is also an *antagonistic* subject, one that appears in the guise of a 'paradoxical element that functions as the universal's symptom'—i.e., as an exception to the universal which both indexes the universal it is an exception to, and, *mutatis mutandis*, gives rise to its own universal. For example, let's say that I overhear some other people saying that I have poor taste in music, and I think, "No I don't, I have excellent taste in music!" Here, I designate an "I" that others do not perceive, an "I" that *does* have good taste in music *by my own lights*. Thus this "I" is related to the others' taste in music antagonistically: my taste in music is an exception to the others' and thereby indexes the music they listen to as such—*as the very exception to the music they listen to*. And at the same time, my taste in music indexes the very music I listen to. What one should take from this is that, the antagonistic subject stands opposite to the subject of interpellation in its resistance to conforming to a given ideological, socio-Symbolic identity.

Regardless of that example, we can look at this in a completely different way: The subject contains within itself, its own lack of Self, and this lack is enveloped by ideology as a means to fulfill this lack in the subject. But this lack is precisely what *gives rise to, and thus structures,* the universality of the ideology: My worldview becomes "totalized" according to how the ideology I espouse shapes it. But all that really happens in the ideological exchange is that the lack becomes absorbed by the universal, it becomes internal to the universal, barring it from ever actually becoming a closed totality. The ideology thus has an internal blindspot where it fails to be at one with itself. This implies that the individual subject is always-already capable of subverting the ideological universal's concreteness at any given moment, simply by abjuring his allegiance to, withdrawing his belief from, the ideology at hand.

By withdrawing one's belief, the subject in effect reduces, deflates, the universal ideological notion back to its empty universality. And through this disengagement with the universal the subject is open to a subsequent engagement with an entirely different ideological universal. This of course means that ideologies—indeed as universals which pervade 'into our slightest gestures and most intimate utterances'—evolve contingently, their development aleatory, advancing (or not) via the subjects they interpellate; the outcome is 'a *political* struggle for ideological hegemony.' Each ideological development is articulated through particular sets of individuals and, *by how these sets of individuals produce and struggle, while exposed to contingent twists of fate.*

## §33. "Is" is all there is... or is it?

The conclusion to be made from all this, is that, the way by which one's lived identity is performed and articulated cannot occur without being undergirded by the belief in a set of given ideals, which structures the subject's reality through the interpellation of the subject as such. Here we have the paradox of material singularity becoming itself through immaterial universality: Without the mediating immaterial force of "distinction" (a universal function of idealism), singularity, particularity, escapes any rational grasp of intelligible comprehension.

The incessant oscillation occurring between materiality and ideality, an infrangible correlation between two things that are radically incompatible, owes itself to an internal antagonism between the two. As such, this antagonism is the basic constituent of reality: it is none other than that hard impenetrable kernel resisting (consistent) symbolization. As Žižek writes, 'Materialism means that the reality I see is never "whole" [...] because it contains a stain—a blind spot, which indicates my inclusion in it.'

*And what if this "stain" is precisely that inherent antagonism we are discussing, an innermost antagonism that is never capable of being resolved but rather: a deep-seated antagonism that—as the very intrinsic gap between two things that are radically incompatible with each other, idealism and materialism, an irreducible gap as such— nonetheless connects the edges of these two constitutive though non-coinciding elements,[153] which thereby stimulates a perpetual concate-*

*nation of "parallax shifts" that engender the positive results, the series of representations, of our empirical reality?*

Together, the union of the "I" and its Other is none other than the very veil that enshrouds this "stain," a blind spot as such, which is none other than the void at the heart of the subject: a paradoxical "generative void" that is both the source of Spirit and the receptacle into which conscious representations of one's *external* material reality is collected. Thus the ego's "I" is none other than the entire battery of identities that amount to the interpellated subject itself: a bricolage of elements from one's external Symbolic reality. This "I" is at the same time both one, me, a single individual, as well as One: a superposing ideological articulation qua performative, encompassing each and every particular ideological element subtended by it, which, in turn, bends reflexively in on itself (without fully closing in on itself), engendering its indicative mark, which is represented by the unary signifier "*I.*"

Is this not what Hegel meant when he wrote that, 'The universal determination should be recognizably contained in our particular way of acting'?[154] One's performativity, the way in which one 'objectifies a schema of action'—that is to say, the way in which one lives outwardly their lifeworld—directly corresponds with the universal ideology one is subtended by. In other words, we 'make the particular conform to the universal' in an attempt to actualize the truth of our lived experience. As Hegel wrote:

> we want to know what is inward as distinct from what is merely outward. So we reduplicate the phenomenon; we break it in two, the inward and the outward, force and its utterance, cause and effect. Here again, the inner side, or force, is universal, that which persists; it is not this or that [...] but what remains the same in all.[155]

And so if "I" corresponds with the universality of a ruling ideology (which plays a constitutive/structural role in one's reality) — *which is also constitutive of the particular individual "I"* — then "I," "me," is not so much indexical of my particular subjective finitude (in the sense of my moment in Being as a particular finite being), but rather: This "I" refers moreso to the imaginative activity of the (in-)finite Spirit and its creations, i.e., what is universal, what is *ideologically* true about me as a subject.

What this means is that the subject is not entirely equal to its ideological determination(s), only the *substance* of the subject is, that which the Spirit collects/creates for the sake of its subject's identity. Therefore, it is not "I" but *"Is"* which coincides with the pure Being of a particular subject and its ineffable lifeworld. The unknown primordial "proto-goo," of which the "generative void" itself is composed — a virtually if not completely immaterial essence that is vitally indispensable to the material stuff of the universe — is the only true (non) "content" of the subject. As R.D. Laing famously wrote, "Is" is the nothing from which everything arises. It's not that "is" is all there *is*, but rather: "is" is to be referred to as the "nothing that counts for something." And this "nothing" is not to be mistaken for the Nietzschean descent into a nihilistic "loss of meaning," it's not a complete surrendering of the desire for significance and meaning of one's life; on the contrary, what we are dealing with here is Kierkegaard's "infinite resignation": The complete void of Meaning, the inherent absence of meaning altogether, is none other than the fecund zone of meaning's origin. Do we not find here a striking similarity between this formulation of *"Is,"* that nascent zero point whence *"I"* derives, and Jacques Rancière's ontological formulation for ideology: 'The place of ideology is the void?'

So, once again, we are right back to where it all begins. It is the void, the coincidence of form and emptiness, which cuts through both the subject and the Symbolic: it is the "rip" that cuts through all of reality, an empty retainer that holds every thing in its place of inscription as such.

Not only does this aspect of the Real cut through the Symbolic,[156] but, to borrow a term from Dostoevsky, the Real "lacerates" even the subject itself, thereby connecting particular individuality to (particular) universality *along the edges of this "laceration" as such.* This allows for ideology to be both that of universality and particularity, for the sole reason that "I" does not refer to the pure subject itself (the "pure subject" being the subject at its zero-point, in its empty form of self-relating negativity); on the contrary, "I" refers to the substance, the identity-content, of the subject: *"I" refers to the interpellated subject inasmuch as it refers to the very "external" universality of ideology that is doing the interpellating.*

One therefore positivizes oneself through the Althusserian process of interpellation: i.e., *subjectivization*: The subject takes on his/her identity precisely by allowing ideology to interpellate him/herself; one's identity is staged in, by, and through ideology as such. Like fantasy, the role of ideology hinges on the fact that there is no primordial universal formula guaranteeing a harmonious sense of Self-identity; on account of the lack of this universal formula, ideology takes the place of this Real lack as such, precisely as a means in which, by which and through which the subject can fashion its own Self-identity.

# Part IV: Objectivity as Today's Ruling Ideology

## §34. Waiting for Godot and the infinite deferral

We all know that wholesale ecological catastrophe is immanent in these times, though we act as if we do not believe this is so. This was put on world display at the UN Climate Change Conference in Copenhagen, Denmark between 7 December and 18 December of 2009. What was drastically needed—a binding emissions limit that would keep the twenty first-century temperature increase below 1.5°C, was inadequately met with what senior fellow at the Center for Global Development, David Wheeler, called 'a sheaf of non-binding "commitments" which, even if they actually materialized, would produce an increase of 3.9°.' Wheeler sardonically likened the event to Beckett's *Waiting for Godot*: As delegates from around the world gathered in anticipation for the arrival of some notional solution to global climate change, it was, as if, in the spirit of Beckett's play, these delegates acted the parts of Vladimir and Estragon, waiting for days on end, in vain, for some auspicious solution that lied beyond their grasp to solve the very problem inherent to their own causes.

Is Beckett's recursive play not emblematic of the circular nature of drive; Vladimir and Estragon spin endlessly around the *objet a*, in pursuit of their object of desire, the cause of which is essentially nowhere to be found? Such a display of unwitting human futility demonstrates the failure of attaining any sort of salvation when the latter is expected from an external entity. Precisely in this sense, Copenhagen was ineffective. Besotted with the annular movement of drive, the world's leaders— rendered visionless by their own neoliberal desires sustained by the universal Real of capital—were unable to emancipate the world from the destructive forces of capitalism's global markets.

That Copenhagen can be likened to Beckett's *Waiting for Godot* is a salient indicator, if there ever was one, of capitalism's inability to "reflect into itself."

The precarious deadlock that was exposed in Copenhagen, however, is rooted in a complex system comprised of the ternary relationship between desire, jouissance and drive; one that is homologous to the deadlock which is at the core of the viewer's fantasy represented in, say, Hitchcock's famous 1927 silent, *The Lodger: A Story of the London Fog*, which follows the narrative about a death-dealing madman, otherwise known as the "Avenger," who has a penchant for killing blondes. Recall the scene early on, in which, displaying herself at a fashion salon, Daisy Bunting (played by actress June Howard Tripp) appears cynically 'indifferent to the possibility that she is in the Avenger's presence.'

> Showing no fear, she steps toward the camera. Only then does a cut to a longer shot disclose the real setting: this is a fashion salon, and Daisy is a model making her entrance. What we took to be Daisy in the London night, going about her private affairs, is Daisy in costume, about to display her outfit—and herself—to the wealthy men and women gathered for the show. The next shot shows us this audience—the men who take pleasure in viewing models like Daisy and the women who hope to buy the ability to arouse men's desire. We do not know who Daisy really is … Perhaps she models because she dreams of being the kind of sophisticated woman of the world, disdainful of those who would judge her, that we first took her to be.[157]

All of the psychoanalytic elements we've discussed reverberate in this particular scene; specifically drawn out by the fact that Daisy—the object of desire of her audience—is able to become an object as such only by means of her own desire to be a certain kind of 'woman of the world.' Her desire is the desire of the Other, her gaze as such is returned back to her from her audience. That is to say, the unattainable "mystery" (the object cause behind wanting to be a certain kind of 'woman of the world,'), the object-Thing, which concerns her, takes her gaze into account. Such a spectacle is staged for the object of desire as fantasy, which, as such, enframes this "nothing" of her gaze.

The relationship between Daisy and her audience simultaneously occurs in its reverse as well: Daisy's relationship to her audience is, in each of its moments, reciprocal. This is none other than the libidinal economy of drive, in which the "reflective" signifier, designated by Lacan also as "phallic" signifier (representing the object of desire of the Other) 'totalizes' the batteries of 'all others,' sustaining the void that is 'opened up by the failure of its representation.' Put differently, Daisy does not *ex-sist* outside the world of her audience, but *exists* within, quilting the heterogeneous field of particulars into a unified totality; as such, she is caught up within the very intersubjective network that constitutes the relationship between her and her audience in its totality, a network of intersubjective relations that spins endlessly round and round the Thing-as-Mystery, the *objet a*.[158] Such a network of relations is virtually impossible to disentangle solely because the *objet a* is impossible to attain. It does not exist. In other words, 'the "object" of fantasy is not the fantasy-scene itself [...] but the impossible gaze watching it.'[159] The more one moves closer to the *objet a* the more the *objet a* eludes the subject's grasp. It is, once again, this illusory object that is 'more in the subject than the subject itself.'

Are we not warranted in positing that this is precisely what lies at the very core of the relationship between the world's delegates who attended the climate change conference in Copenhagen, and the rest of the world as spectators? Were not most of us acting as if we were the very audience that watched Daisy put herself on display, when watching the world's political elite put themselves on display—these officials essentially epitomizing the same thrust as that of Hitchcock's Daisy? As the world's top policy makers attempted to search in vain for a solution to a problem engendered by an internal deadlock, much of the world watched attentively, hoping to no avail that they themselves would indirectly encounter the solution, as if it would somehow magically appear in the midst of diplomatic negotiations being discussed between a bunch of political elites acting in the service of capital. Such a multitude, "audience and performer," becomes totalized by the exceptional position of the elite as they embody the "impossible/irrational" in the guise of the Master-Signifier as such.

In other words, looking to Hitchcock's Daisy one more time, Daisy was seeking to fulfill her dreams in the very audience external to her, displacing the object cause of her desire onto her audience, while the audience, in turn, displaced the object cause of their desire onto Daisy. So, once again, does this not bear a striking resemblance to the political spectacle/deadlock exhibited at the climate change conference held in Copenhagen?

This is exactly how today's mode of neoliberal global capitalism functions: its *systemic* nature is that of drive, circulating endlessly around an absent cause of *desire*, rendering those who are subtended by its universalism enchanted by the illusion that the object cause of desire can be located in some external thing, thus keeping the self-engendering motion of capitalism whirling about, unable to "reflect into itself."

As Žižek writes: 'Drive inheres to capitalism at a more fundamental, systemic level: drive is that which propels the whole capitalist machinery, it is the impersonal compulsion to engage in the endless circular movement of expanded self-reproduction.'[160] It's important to note, too, that the aim of the drive is to serve desire, though it is impossible for the drive to serve desire in all respects; that is to say, it cannot bring the subject to a complete satisfaction of its desire, owing to the actuality that the object cause of desire does not *really* exist: 'no matter how close I get to the object of desire, its cause remains at a distance, totally elusive.'[161]

Thus drive circles endlessly around this absent center in search of the satisfaction-*qua*-object external to this inner lack, in an unrelenting attempt to fill this inner lack. And because the subject always fails to satisfy its lack, the elicited painful enjoyment, better known as *jouissance*, keeps the drive charged, forever in search of a possible something from an impossible "nothing."

By means of this very movement, that of drive, and the nascent energy provided by jouissance, which is always recre-ating the projects of drive, we are able to attain the level of productivity distilled from the very productivity obstructed by the *objet a*. This sounds confusing, but to unravel this paradox we need only look to the possibility of impossibility: 'what appears at first glance a purely Negative [...] functions as a positive condition of possibility of the entity it impedes.' Here we must do exactly as Hegel has suggested: "tarry the negative": execute the negation of a negation. To do so, it's important to distinguish the pure, closed field of impossibility from the fragile, open field of impossibility: Within the confines of the Symbolic order of simple pleasures, of the network of knowledge ("objective certainty"), and so on, what is already possible simply *exists*: viz., there exists only possibilities-as-what-is-already-possible, and it is here where we are up against *real* impossibility: nothing New can come solely from the extant conditions and arrangements thereof. On the other hand, however, "beyond" the Symbolic order is the field of (un)known impossibilities: the external-ization of the inner void: things that are yet to be possible, things that are yet to embody the void as such; things that may exist but are yet to enter inscription into the Symbolic order. It is the movement of drive, which thrusts its subjects toward the fragile realm of negative impossibility, impelling its subject to shatter this impossible realm into a positive condition of open possibilities, by means of which one can attain the level of productivity otherwise obstructed, though paradoxically propelled, by the *objet a*.

Albeit drive appears to delineate the very movement of capitalism, the impetus behind this movement originates in *desire*: drive is rooted in desire (which is why the movement of desire is propelled by the obstacle the *objet a* presents). And because there is no object cause of desire the movement of drive is thus that of an infinite deferral, a will-o'-the-wisp pursuit: the striving towards a goal which is impossible to attain. In this sense, one can be driven down the "wrong" path, to put it a certain way: As long as the subject's aim(s) remains tethered to the drive that spins incessantly around the *objet a*, and, more importantly, insofar as the subject seeks the *objet a* as something that exists *outside* oneself, rather than within, the subject will always already be *'waiting for Godot,'* as it were. That is to say, by the same token that Vladimir and Estragon sat endlessly waiting for Godot, the subject that endlessly waits in vain for an external entity qua salvation (for a response from the big Other) rather than searching within, will also be like Daisy from *The Lodger*: forever indifferent to the possibility that one is under the gaze of the big Other, unable to see "beyond-behind" the deceptive screen of the big Other.

And what, exactly, would result if one were to see "beyond-behind" the deceptive screen of the big Other? One would merely see nothing: the vast, internal abyss of *nothing* lurking within one's own empty formality. That is to say, one would see within, into their own subjectivity; one would identify with the specular truth of the big Other: that it does not actually exist, that there is nothing beyond-behind the big Other, other than the reflection of one's own inner subjective abyss from which the *objet a* manifests itself, presupposing its objective existence in the gaze of the (big) Other. This is where real freedom begins.

We of course witness the same thing occurring in Kafka's "Parable of the Law" from his novel *The Trial*, in which Joseph K. fails to notice that his externality to the big Other (the Law) is always already the 'disparity of the Substance with itself...' To reemphasize Žižek's keen observation, we are dealing here with the Hegelian speculative identity of Substance and Subject: 'the external gaze of the Subject upon the inscrutable Substance is from the very beginning included in the Substance itself as an index of its disparity with itself.'[162, 163]

In this precise sense, both the world's leaders and those who, as spectators, sat by the sidelines waiting to see what sort of solution to climate change would be drafted, were, in effect, like that of Daisy and her audience: 'indifferent to the possibility that she is in the Avenger's presence,' so to speak. In other words, the fundamental reason behind the ineffective policy borne out from the climate change conference held in Copenhagen is situated in the very fact that we are all, at some level, indifferent to the actuality that we are caught up in the gaze of the big Other: unable to escape the omnipresence of capitalism's self-engendering process.

## §35. Is it drive or desire, or, both?

What is responsible for the brute force of capital's self-engendering process has become a matter of dispute recently. The official opinion is that capitalism derives its explosive potentiality and reinforcement from desire; though recently some have posited in other respects, that the culprit here is instead drive (see, e.g., Jodi Dean's work). It does seem rather burdensome to disregard the notion that the systemic nature of capitalism, its very movement, is that of drive. Though, it also seems apparent that the constitutive energy behind capitalism's potentiality and constant reinforcement is inflexibly grounded in its subjects' desires. But what if the answer is that it's both, that of the tension inherent to the dialectical paradox of drive *and* desire? Capitalism of course attains its brute omnipresence in virtue of, like everything else, a robust inner antagonism—that of desire wanting to conflate itself with drive. Owing to the fact that the self-engendering movement of capital is indifferent to human and environmental conditions, however, we are able to find a sort of formal semblance to that of Kant's categorical imperative (though of course not a *sameness*).

Kant's categorical imperative, like drive itself, entails a complete indifference to one's pathological set, in the similar sense that the movement of capital's self-engendering process is indifferent to human and environmental conditions. The structure and function of Kant's categorical imperative is none other than that of drive. So, in some respect, we *can* liken the movement of capitalism to that of the drive. Is this not why the best suitable capitalist is the driven agent? the agent whose universal maxim is to generate profit at any cost, while remaining completely indifferent to those costs? (I nominate Don Draper from AMC's *Mad Men* as exemplar par excellence.)

The other reason I have for suggesting this idea is that, to me, it seems quite clear that we have a case of desire trying to fully integrate itself with drive, though always failing. For example: Argentine revolutionary, Che Guevarra, was indeed an agent of drive if there ever was one: He sought to radically change certain social arrangements *after* radically changing the coordinates of his choices (from young doctor to armed insurgent; from having "formal" freedom to possessing "actual" freedom). He attempted to make possible the impossible. He was *driven* as such. The fact that this figure of anti-capitalism par excellence is now celebrated on posters and tee shirts to be bought and sold from within the coordinates of capitalism itself is more than just sadly ironic. In my opinion, such a contradictory case of anti-capitalist revolutionary turned commodity alludes to desire wanting to fully integrate and identify itself with drive—its perverse injunction is therefore: *'Desire me, I'm (speciously presenting myself as) drive, and you can have me—for only $14.99, plus tax!*

The failure of desire to fully integrate itself with drive, however, results in the spurious presentation of the object-of-desire-qua-object-of-drive, thus resulting in a toxic mimic of drive. And what do we get with such a product? An ersatz political activism mimicking the failed projects of past revolutionaries: 'the very act of participating in consumerist activity is simultaneously presented as a participation in the struggle against the evils ultimately caused by capitalist consumption.' Is this not a perfect example of the attempt to *sell the desire of the perfect drive*? which of course ultimately fails, thus maintaining the self-engendering movement of capital, keeping it mobilized, forever in search of this perfect, Utopianesque object qua commodity that is representative of one's desire for the perfect drive?

If capitalism actually could succeed in selling the perfect drive (which would be none other than some sort of a representation of Kant's categorical imperative), such a transaction would invariably lead to capital's self-effacement! Thus, in the strict Hegelian sense of concrete universality, this absent object of desire qua drive—which doesn't really exist (because such an absence is designated by desire's utter non-coincidence with drive)—provides the very impetus behind capital's resilient movement and ongoing development. In this sense we have a sort of *literal* death-drive that is intrinsic to capitalism only (and of course, we all know that the drive does not actually represent the subject's movement towards real death, but perhaps this is the problem of capital: that it manipulates the very definitive function of the drive as such): capitalism's generative power is sustained by chasing after the very thing that would annihilate it altogether. (In this sense, perhaps the most subversive act one could undergo, an act that could potentially bring capitalism to complete nullity, would be to forego any cynical distance from the world of capital altogether and to fully commit to it, to fully identify with its innermost contradictions, its abject crises, and so on...)

The solutions to capitalism's crises will always-already be out of our reach insofar as we search for them outside of, while from within, the coordinates of capitalism. Žižek put it best when he wrote: 'as long as state political elites serve capital, they are unable and/or unwilling to control and regulate capital even when the very survival of the human race is at stake.'[164] This same behavior was exhibited here in the US in 2008: When much of the country's population stood to lose their jobs, their homes, their life savings, the political elite opted to save the banks. It's important to note here, that, as Vighi aptly writes, what at first glance seems to be a threat to the 'system's consistency' is 'turned into its raison d'être, ultimately the very matrix of our social life.'[165] That is to say, we mustn't delude ourselves into a false sense of reality; we now live in a world in which, despite the plethora of 'global realities,' it is 'Capital which is the Real of our lives.'[166]

Thus, in order to find a solution to the crises engendered by the capitalist machinery, we must first disassemble the capitalist machinery—which is a solution, an "off-switch," so to speak, that can only be found *within* the capitalist system itself. To do so means to remain vigilant to the actuality that crises such as climate change, famine, the pollution of the world's fresh waters, among countless other devastating crises, are inherent to capitalism itself; pure life gets mangled by capitalism because, *pure life is an inner moment of capitalism itself.* We must first look inward, deep into capitalism's inherent antagonism, its own inconsistency, rather than outward, in order to fully identify the ostensible "organic unity" of capitalism as nothing other than 'the mode of appearance of its opposite, of inherent instability.' As Dipesh Chakrabarty pointedly questions: 'Why could not the narrative of capitalism—and hence its critique—be sufficient as a framework for interrogating the history of climate change and understanding its consequences?' There are two answers to this question. One, Chakrabarty is merely being rhetorically accurate here with a step towards a solution, and we need not actually provide an answer. And two, if we were to actually read this question without its rhetorical spin, and answer it as such, such a framework would not be sufficient, *if and only if*, we were to remain indifferent to the fact that we are literally *in* capitalism's presence, thereby overlooking the historical conditions inherent to capitalism that have engendered today's crises, searching for those transcendent solutions, and bypassing the much needed and difficult preliminary work required to dismantle the capitalist machinery.

## §36. Intellectual objectivity as an ideology of exploitation

Some while back I was discussing with Derrick Jensen, the grave consequences of intellectual objectivity and the pursuit for "objective truths," how the two often deprive other beings, human and non-human, of their own subjecthood, their own volitional will.

'Our way of life,' Jensen told me, 'presupposes that it's in our best interest to coerce others into doing what we want them to do.'

'What do you mean by that, Derrick?' I asked, though having a pretty good sense of what he meant—that there's something to be said about this culture's fetishistic fondness for conflating science and control, about this culture's penchant for conflating the power to command with truth. I wanted to hear it from someone else though.

It took a few moments for him to respond; it wasn't that he was having a problem coming up with a good succinct answer, just that he wanted to choose his words carefully; he wanted to express his answer in the best possible language. Derrick continued. 'First, if the scientific materialist instrumentalist perspective is right and every other culture is wrong, the universe is a gigantic clockwork—a machine: a very predictable and therefore controllable machine. Power in this case, then, is like meaning in that there is no inherent power in the world (or out of it), just as no power inheres in a toaster or automobile until you put it to use, and the only power that exists is that which you project onto and over others (or that others project onto and over you). Power exists *only* in how you use raw materials—the more raw materials you use more effectively than anyone else, the more power to you. And science is a potent tool for that. This means, of course, that *might* then makes *right*, or rather, *right*, too, is like meaning and doesn't inhere anyway—if nonhumans are not in any real sense beings and are here for us to use (and not here for their own sakes, with lives as meaningful to them as yours is to you or mine is to me) then using, or destroying, them raises no significant moral questions, any more than whether you or I do or do not use or destroy any other tool, which means *right* is what you decide it is, or more accurately, it's irrelevant, *right* is whatever you want it to be, which means it's really nothing at all. But this malleable notion of *right* means that you can fairly easily talk yourself into feeling good about exploiting the shit out of everyone and everything else. If all of this sounds sociopathological, that's because it is. A lot of Western philosophy and scientific philosophy is sociopathological—it finds logic through the power of command. It makes us all insane.'

He paused for a moment, took a breath... My head was racing with thoughts... in a good way. Derrick resumed. 'Okay, let's turn to another example. Richard Dawkins writes, "Science boosts its claim to truth by its spectacular ability to make matter and energy jump through hoops on command, and to predict what will happen and when." Do you see the fundamental flaw in logic here?' he asked. I arched an eyebrow, indicating him to go on. 'I'm guessing that if we lived in a culture that wasn't sociopathological we'd all see through this in a heartbeat. Let's ask a simple question: How does science boost its claim to truth? Here is Dawkins's (and the culture's) answer: by making matter and energy jump through hoops on command, and by predicting what will happen and when. Do you see the problem yet?'

'Not entirely,' I said, unsure where he was going with this. 'You're gonna have to help me out some.'

'Okay, let's try it a different way: Let's say Dawkins has a gun. Let's say he points this gun at your head. Let's say he commands you to jump through hoops. Let's say you do it. He does, after all, have a gun pointed at your head. Now, with this gun pointed at your head, he tells you to jump through those hoops again. And then he predicts that this is precisely what you will do. You do it. Whaddya know—he's a fucking genius. He commanded you to jump through hoops, and he predicted right when you'd do it. You see, Dawkins was, with this sentence, incredibly intellectually dishonest—and sneaky as all hell. He has conflated the power to command with truth. He has conflated domination with truth. But neither the power to command nor domination is the same as truth. The power to command is the power to command, domination is domination, and truth is truth. Richard Dawkins could put a gun to my head. He could even kill me. But that wouldn't mean that he is telling the truth. This culture is dominating the planet. This culture's domination of the planet is killing it. That does not mean this culture is telling the truth, or is even capable of understanding it. And yet, at the same time, the power to dominate *is* a sort of truth; but there are other truths as well, truths that can be masked, obscured, or destroyed by this truth. I'll give you one last example.

'Let's say I force you to jump through hoops. Let's say I enslave you. Are there not other truths that have been foreclosed because I forced you to jump through hoops, because I enslaved you? Any path forecloses others. Some paths foreclose more than do other paths. The same is true with truths: some paths to certain forms of knowledge, and some paths to certain forms of truth, irrevocably foreclose other paths to knowledge, and other paths to other truths.'

The underlying message is this: We think we know a lot of stuff, though in truth we don't know much at all. And in terms of the "truth" that we are dealing with here, this has everything to do with a *truly* "objective" truth, a self-relating truth—the truth about our own subjective positions as they are in relation to the ideological superstructures by which our subjectivity is created and sustained. It is a truth that the subject engages with, day in day out, one that's measured not by facticity but by the way one's Symbolic position of enunciation, one's deployment of facticity, affects the world around oneself, and how that, in turn, affects the subject's position of enunciation. It's a truth that is "unleashed"—*it is 'only true inasmuch as it is truly followed.'*

In other words, I agree with Jensen up to a point. But I don't think the fundamental problem here is with science per se, insofar as this problem has to do with the dominant culture and its ruling ideology. As Jensen points out, meaning may not be inherent to the world itself, but rather in how we *relate* to the world itself. And that's the crux. And so in that sense, science, too, is like meaning: its effects (and *affects*) are contingent on how we *use* it, how we relate to it, sort of like language itself, which is determined by how we interpret it—and interpretation is more or less shaped and informed by our ruling ideologies, which is none other than a point of convergence of its subjects' collective desires.[167] And the dominant culture has a desire to control and exploit the world in such a way that it forces the rest of the world to conform to this desire (literally) by stripping away the subjecthood of others, by transmogrifying living beings into (dead) objects to use and to enjoy, forgetting that the life of another, human or non-human, is, as far as anyone knows, as meaningful to them as yours is to you and mine is to me.

## §37. The ideological notion of objectivity

The exchange between Derrick and myself illuminates the very nature of ideology, as well as the relationship between the latter and domination. Are we not able to see intellectual objectivity for what it truly is: as that which holds together its universal ideological notion? As such, it's an "element of fantasy" — something fraudulent, in which, through which, and by which our Symbolic reality, upon and around which one's reality principle is structured and maintained, gains an "illusive" consistency. To expound on this, Žižek writes that

> a particular content which is promulgated as 'typical' of the universal notion, is the element of fantasy, of the phantasmatic background/support of the universal ideological notion. To put it in Kantian terms, it plays the role of 'transcendental schematism', translating the empty universal concept into a notion which directly relates and applies to our 'actual experience'. As such, this phantasmatic specification is by no means an insignificant illustration or exemplification: it is at this level that ideological battles are won or lost[168]

In other words, owing to the fact that, in these times, objectivity is "typical" in the sciences, that it's "typical" throughout academe, and that it's considered "typical" in journalism and other media, and "typical" elsewhere, is evidence enough that objectivity is ideological. To borrow another quote from Zupančič: 'Every ideology works hard to make certain things "obvious," and the more we find things obvious, self-evident and unquestionable, the more successfully the ideology has done its job.'[169] Would it not be the case then, that were we to invert the current order, and perceive as "typical," as "obvious," *not* the primacy of objectivity but rather its *purely-subjective origin*, the ideological perspective, generally speaking, would then change radically? Let's continue along with Žižek:

> the Universal acquires concrete existence when some particular content starts to function as its stand-in... The fact that this link between the Universal and the particular content which functions as its stand-in is *contingent* means precisely that it is the outcome of a *political* struggle for ideological hegemony [which is why philosophy ought to be political]. However, the dialectic of this struggle is more complex than in its standard Marxist version — of particular interests assuming the form of universality: 'universal human rights are effectively the rights of white male property owners...' To work, the ruling ideology has to incorporate a series of features in which the exploited majority will be able to recognize its authentic longings. In other words, each hegemonic universality has to incorporate *at least two* particular contents, the authentic popular content as well as its distortion by the relations of domination and exploitation.[170]

Okay. Of course, the ideology of intellectual objectivity 'manipulates an authentic popular longing' for knowledge and good old honest truth against ardent prejudice, bias and/or abusive dissimulation. And of course the ideology of intellectual objectivity manipulates the expression of this desire 'in order to legitimize the continuation of the relations of social domination and exploitation.'[171] But the complexity of this lies precisely in the fact that, *the ideas comprising the ruling ideology as such are not necessarily the ideas of the ruling class, but rather a series of desires of the oppressed as they are conditioned by the oppressive structure of the ruling class*, 'rearticulating [these desires] in such a way that they became compatible with the existing relations of domination.'[172]

So, an ideological universal can only attain its concrete existence through the performative articulations of its particular subjects. And for a ruling ideology to work properly it must 'incorporate a series of features' that the exploited majority can identify with, while at the same time not disrupting entirely the status quo's structure of power relations.

In fine, what spells out a particular science and/or field of discourse is having an object, and we should, as Lacan put it, be 'prudent, because this object changes, and in a very strange way, as a science develops.' And no less importantly, at a deeper level, we cannot say that any object of any science, or of any discourse, etc., can be examined as an object in-itself, for, to say so is to initiate, disavow, and perpetuate a radical violence of domination over the entity being examined, a radial violence that also serves to conceal and repress the particular subjectivity that is involved with, and at the very core of, any conscious activity behind the examination,[173] which in effect further buttresses the ideological supremacy of intellectual objectivity. And so it is here that philosophy should make its intervention; it should police and arbitrate the ways in which we appropriate the discoveries of science for all social and political ends.

But that's not all. We can also see, now, how the conception of objectivity, the idea that one can "catch up" to a larger truth that lies beyond the subjective domain is, itself, merely an *ideal*, an ideal that has "caught on," like a meme, infiltrating the minds of its subjects, conditioning their desires. And like Achilles and the tortoise, this race to catch up with the truth puts the end of the race into an infinite deferral.

Objectivity is, as such, ideological; which in effect reflects the ruling ideology that subtends its loyal subjects.

'This culture,' Derrick told me, 'is based on the assumption that all of the world is without volition, is mechanistic, and is therefore predictable. The existence of the willfully unpredictable destroys a foundational assumption of this culture. The existence of the willfully unpredictable also invalidates this culture's ontology, epistemology, and philosophies, and reveals them for what they are: lies upon which to base this omnicidal system of exploitation, theft, and murder; it's much easier to exploit, steal from, or murder someone you pretend has no meaningful existence (especially if you have an entire culture's ontology, epistemology, and philosophy to back you up), indeed it becomes your right, even your duty (for example, war, genocide, death squads, mercenaries, etc). The existence of the willfully unpredictable reveals this culture's governmental and economic systems for what they are as well: means to not only rationalize but enforce systems of exploitation, theft, and murder—effectively stop Monsanto's exploitation, theft, and murder, however, and see how you are treated by governments across the world.'

It is against this background that we must conceive the argument that everything subtended by ideology—objective reality as we understand it, as we *believe* it to be—is based on a sort of universal Lie; as Lacan once claimed, *there is no truth that does not lie*. And this, claims Žižek, 'touches a nerve in our ideologico-political constellation: the undesirability of truth.' And the more we chase after these truths, the more we begin to reveal not only the lies upon which we structure our world but, no less important, that which these lies conceal.

## §38. Inconsistency as the innermost constituent of our reality: The passage from the universal to the particular

How often do we probe the depths of our collective memory to discover, avow, and talk openly about the relationship between the dominant culture's daily customs and the daily atrocities that play out upon the world? Do we ever wonder if the truth about climate change constitutes even the slightest substance of our anxieties? or if the deaths of thousands upon thousands of species, species driven to the brink of extinction, haunt our unconscious? Do we even care that those who produce most of the world's cereal grains often starve while the grains they produce sit inside granaries as "surplus"? If one were to read the daily news, one could not escape the patent inconsistency plaguing today's world that is broadcast with daily pattern. Such dangerous inconsistency is customary in today's world of capital. And the more we know this, the more we disavow it: "I know all along that my Playstation 4 requires the mineral coltan in its production, and that the mining of this metallic mineral is unquestionably implicated in the vast environmental and social devastation occurring along the border of the DRC (Democratic Republic of Congo) and Rwanda,[174] though nonetheless I act *as if* this is not so..." To use another example, I can easily imagine someone, who, from the comfort of their own office, is reading, say, the news of a violent air strike gone awry on some faultless village in Afghanistan. This village is mistaken to harbor "terrorists." This village has been "accidentally" bombed by a couple of F-15 fighter jets manufactured by Boeing, or maybe by a couple of drones operated from some remote location. In any event, let's say Boeing happens to be the biggest marketing client of this office-dwelling individual, who's reading about the loss of innocent life, experiencing this story *as if* he or she is completely "unaware" of their own involvement in this atrocity. Such a form of disavowal is commonplace these days. Of course, too, without a doubt we can substitute for this office dweller any other person who engages in the capitalist system; substitute his or her job with any other job that is fully integrated into the capitalist system. The result is virtually the same: complicity in the atrocities that occur the world over saturates the masses—including those who partake in the most quotidian banalities of capital. This is familiar routine these days, in virtue of the very ubiquity of today's predominant, neoliberal, capitalist, free-market economics. In order for anyone to simply coexist with the presence of capital, let alone partake in the world of capital, one must act *as if* capitalism does not thrive on the promotion of avarice and competition, one must act *as if* capitalism does not thrive on wealth disparity, widespread subjugation, and thus hatred and envy toward others whose assets, resources, etc, are coveted. To simply coexist with the presence of capital, one must act *as if* capitalism does not thrive on such wholesale atrocity, one must act *as if* capitalism does not thrive on the very crises it engenders, yes, one must act *as if* this is not the necessary condition in which capital is able to persist. And to maintain this *"as-if"* attitude, this *belief*, one must remain obedient to today's ideological injunction: *one must remain "objective."*

Deep down, however, we all know that, by dint of one's slightest participation in the system of capital, one is thereby complicit, to a certain guilty-by-association degree, in the iniquities that neoliberal policies engender. The entire system is subsidized by our tax dollars, sanctioned by our votes, strengthened with every purchase and sale we make, and so on and so forth. It's become ever more recognizable that, here in the US and elsewhere in the West, "democracy" and "freedom" are, as Vighi puts it, merely fetishistic references that "abound in the mouths of our politicians," which serve to prevent any alternative political discourse. We should, as Vighi calls for, confront what we love to disavow: 'the fact that even when democratic legitimacy seems healthy, our votes merely sanction the existence of an order whose framework has already been decided and imposed on us.' The liberal democracy we have come to familiarize ourselves with only allows us to choose those things that do not interfere with the interests of capital. And so we act *as if* the democratic challenge to capitalism will pull us out of this malaise, though we all know that challenging capitalism through democracy prevents us from ever removing capitalism from its seat of power.

## §39. The Last Man

I encounter all too often people pulling the "objective" card— "The world is what it is, try not to get too personally involved, be objective about the whole thing..." To which I remind them that they are nonetheless included in the big picture they "objectively" see.

Can we not see, how, in a certain sense, this deep-rooted inconsistency reflects the profound aversion the middle class has toward relating their ideological dilemma to their ambiguous social situation?—which, above all, engenders the pretentions of an ironic and cynical distance from any ideology altogether? Since, if today's bourgeoisie were to connect the two (their ideological dilemma and their social "(non-)plight"), they would fully realize their own position as subjects of a real universal ideology, as subjects of the ruling capitalist ideology. It is this moment, however, of "ironic distance"—this scoffing at the very practical stupidity in which we are, essentially, at any given moment, ready to actually believe and take part in today's ideology—in which ideology exercises its most assertive hold over us. It is at this very (post)ideological moment of liberating comic cynicism and irony when we become ensnared as "pure subjects of ideology."

What better way to exemplify this than with the proverbial cynic of our (postmodern) times who, in the face of seemingly insurmountable corporate malfeasance and political deadlock, and public displays of demoralized avarice and shameless competition, all beneath the Damoclean sword of wholesale ecological and social catastrophe, throws his hands up in a display of stoic resignation and says, *'It's human nature!'* Here Mister Last Man has unknowingly resigned to the ruling ideology: he has expunged the entire cultural ideologico-ethico-political background of these crises, thus diluting the entire set of ethico-political crises engendered by the culture of capitalism beneath the neutral sea of "human nature." This "human-ization," an *objectivized* "human nature" as such, serves to obfuscate the key question: *How is one's own life implicated in these very crises?* Such humanitarian and ecological disasters are not part of some oblique history of humankind that 'brutally disrupts our intimate lives—they are a field,' writes Žižek, 'in which we are always already engaged even if it is in a mode of ignorance.'[175]

Therefore, the objectification implied in today's notion of "human nature" is to be referred to the fact that the position of the enunciator is one of privileged exclusion in relation to the real victims of capital. Not only that, but such an assertion of an objectivized "human nature" is merely a covert way to eschew one's moral and political responsibility for one's own choices—it makes a human choice "appear to be outside of human control." This is why, as Althusser put it, the 'problem of humanism' is the cross it carries: '"Man," with a capital "M," is an ideological myth of the bourgeoisie that allows exploitation by masking it,' in objectivity as such.[176]

Such a cynical, coolly distanced, and somewhat misanthropic stance is of course the ideological gesture par excellence of our time. One should be quick to point out to Mister Last Man that his idea of an objective "human nature" (here, we should be quick to point out that today's objectivist concept of "human nature" is one that seems to gloss over any other real human behavior that is not characterized as greedy, selfish, competitive and sometimes destructive; it is a formulation of "human nature" that seems to take on very specific characteristics distilled from an erroneously refined Darwinian, civilized thought, which folks like Herbert Spencer, Malthus, et al. employed so they could formulate a "survival of the fittest" ideology for Laissez Faire capitalism, along with a litany of other things like eugenics, imperialism, and so on...) is, as Chris Harman puts it, 'a product of our history not its cause.' Our modern world, with all its troubles and hardship, all its instances of wholesale privation, environmental degradation and other capitalist disorders has been in such wretched shape for roughly 0.5 percent of our species' existence on this planet. For the other 95.5 percent, there were no rulers, no bosses, no class divisions; behavior was characterized by generosity rather than selfishness; there was no male supremacy over women, no private property.[177]

Though even Harman, despite being correct in a certain sense, claiming that today's "human nature" is the product of our history, is, for some reason, not able to discern that history is nonetheless also a product of human nature. To resolve this contradiction one should simply turn to R.D. Laing and D.G. Cooper's formulation, 'man is the product of his product,' which elucidates the real concrete arrangements that structure the dialectical relationship between history and human nature: 'the structures of a society created by human labor [and human thought] define for each one of us an objective point of departure': that is to say, the material conditions of our lives, the products of our history, circumscribe the field of emerging possibilities; viz., such an open field of possibilities is invariably fixed to the aim by means of which 'man moves in depassing his objective situation.'[178] To better explain this, it's not unlike the 1991 film *Delirious* starring John Candy, a screwball comedy about a soap opera writer, played by Candy himself, who gets hit on the head and knocked unconscious by the trunk of a car and wakes up only to find himself the pivotal character of his own TV drama. For Candy's character to effectuate any substantial change, for him to move beyond his "objective" situation, he must first accept his condition: that of a subject immersed in his own production; only then is he able to write his own future, to write his way out the current nightmare. But most importantly, along the way, he quickly learns that he is all the while vulnerable to the contingent twists of fate, which ceaselessly pour into the gaps of his story.

What this means is that, like the plot to the movie *Delirious*, the notion of historical necessity is mere illusion: history is the product of human agency, particular human responses that are enabled and effectuated by contingent events, which then re-mark human nature as being the product of history, all the while keeping intact the disavowal that such historical necessity initially arose from pure contingency as such, just like in *Delirious* when John Candy's character had a contingent encounter with the trunk of a car, that then sent him into the historical universe of his own making!

What is most perplexing, however, is that the ideological universe can supervene upon our reality virtually without any notice. By the time we are aware of ideology, it's already too late, it's secured its universal position. And even then, it does a good job obfuscating itself under the guise of a "harmony." To exemplify this, Kierkegaard had already understood perfectly well the threat of capitalist ideology at a time when it was still a way of organizing the entire production of just a single country, before it metastasized to the point of organizing the whole production of the world, with his abstract principle of "leveling": Capitalism 'has no personal relationship to any one individual,' he wrote, 'though only an abstract relationship which is the same for everyone.' Does not the basic tenets of Whig Liberalism, which have evolved for the most part into today's (neo)liberal capitalist ideology, reverberate within Kierkegaard's concept of "leveling": the historicist idea that, over time, 'humane intelli-gence' will progress and thus take control of all institutions,

Night of the World

thereby propagating the luxuries and conveniences of a dominant minority, in bland and diluted form, to the majority of the population? That is to say, leveling's outward appearance of harmony reaches no further status than that of being mere window dressing. Behind the mask of today's harmonious global village, united by "free" markets, exist hordes of deracinated peoples co-opted or coerced to subordinate at best, forget at worst, their particular traditions, their particular indigenous histories, for the sake of a universal order—to learn and to practice the governing laws behind today's socio-economic global capitalist order. As such, this ideology continues to threaten to dissolve the world's diversity—*in the name of diversity no less!*— reducing all the countless forms of particular lifeworlds into a static One. Even if capitalism unleashes the 'productivity of the multitude,' writes Žižek, this productivity remains 'constrained within the confines of a new "re-territorialization," that of the capitalist framework of profit which encloses the entire process.' Therefore, capitalist ideology is an ideology of uniformity for the sake of efficiency of its own growth. In effect, it either represses any real diversity, or, it assimilates this diversity into its own system, transforming what otherwise would present itself as an obstacle as the very condition of its growth. The ideology of the Last Man, through which history has come to its "end"—posited egregiously and erroneously as a lesser-of-all-evils persuasion through which liberal democracy and liberal capitalist economics have attained the level of a global civilized utopia—ignores the fact that if one were to line up all the historical formulations of this utopian landscape, the prevailing vision of the future is one of flat homogeneity and mechanical order, short-circuited by violent ruptures of revolt and resistance.[179]

Recognizing inconsistency, unraveling it to its final logical end, what it entails is not some gross contradiction. Well... actually, scratch that—*it does entail contradiction.* But that's the point. In every account, grappling with contradiction inevitably leads to the realization that, like our above mentioned example of the office-dweller, representation of something, anything—and it doesn't matter one way or the other how well-detailed the representation is—representation can never *fully* coincide with the actual *truth* of the thing *itself* being represented. Because the truth is never about that *other* thing itself, the truth is always— even when it's objective, or rather, *especially* when it's objective— a subjective truth: the truth of the subject's Symbolic condition, the truth behind the representation *itself.*

To exemplify this, we should turn to a passage from the ninth chapter of Book I from Dickens' *Hard Times*, in which the character Sissy, who is both the novel's device for fantasy and imaginative creativity, *and*, its voice of reason, makes a slip of the tongue while telling her peer Louisa about her performance at school; she confuses the word "statistics" for "stutterings"… But here, we can see that perhaps there is nothing to be confused over. Let's take a look:

*"Then Mr. M'Choakumchild said he would try me once more. And he said, Here are the stutterings—"*

*"Statistics," said Louisa.*

*"Yes, Miss Louisa—they always remind me of stutterings, and that's another of my mistakes."*

Sissy is far from making a simple mistake. To stutter is to interrupt speech with its own distorted repetitions. Is it not also the case that statistics is a sort of stuttering? Statistics distort (subjective) reality by interrupting this reality with its own (objective, reified) repetitions. What Sissy is alluding to is not simply a representation of the follies of her youth. On the contrary, her slippage of tongue calls attention to the fact that the difference between the way the world seems "out there," and the way it's represented through objective analysis *is* the very

condition of her lifeworld, that of the hardcore objectivist-utili-
tarian order of the very society in which she lives. Here, Sissy's
"blunder" points to the fact that the ideological order of the
Symbolic always-already operates at a level much different than
that of one's direct, imaginative experiential encounter with
reality: the difference between the way the world seems "out
there," and the way it's represented through objective analysis *is*
the innermost constituent of our reality. To look at things objectively is to not immediately recognize this innermost antagonism,
to not recognize that one's reality is always-already constitutively
split as such. Like any ideology, objectivity is an empty promise
that seeks to guarantee a *consistent* view of "how things are." The
moment we come up against contradiction, however, we often
feel that we haven't been objective enough!

Even with regard to one's most intimate knowledge of an
Other, such an intimate knowledge thereof is always an
asymptote to its truth, which is to say that knowledge and truth
never amount to the same, they never seem to "meet up" with
each other, they only change with respect to each other. Here,
recount Terry Eagleton's account of Žižek's astute formulation of
otherness: the limit that prevents our full access to the Other is
not just epistemological, it's *ontological*, too. As Eagleton puts it:

> what makes the Other difficult of access is the fact that [the
> Other] is never complete in the first place, never wholly deter-
> mined by a context but always to some extent "open" and
> "floating."[180]

Thus objectivity, precisely as an ideology, seeks to give to the
object-Other a determinate context in which its "objective" truth
and understanding can be accessed. Where the object-Other is
dislocated from itself, 'not wholly bound by [a] context,' is
precisely where the subject encounters the object-Other 'most
deeply,' since this lack of completion is also true of the subject.

And as Žižek puts it: 'The dimension of the Universal [objectivity qua ideology] thus emerges when the two lacks [...] overlap [...] What we and the inaccessible Other share is the empty signifier [objectivity] that [accounts] for the [enigmatic] X which eludes both positions.'[181] In this sense, whenever one is being objective, beneath its ideological distortion one is essentially dealing with the liminal space between knowledge and its place of inscription: the Lacanian notion of the gap of "Symbolic castration" that separates a subject from his Symbolic identity: the irreducible gap that separates one from oneself, which propels one toward the virtual dimension of the big Other as a means to fill in this gap.[182] This is the house of the "non-truth," the generative space (of play) between the knowledge of something and its truth that emerges from the gap intrinsic to knowledge: an open space in which and from which we are free to choose how to respond to our Symbolic situation—the abyss of one's radical subjective freedom from which one may be able to say *No!* to Symbolic authority (*acte gratuit*). In other words, the free subject can recognize him/herself as such only by one's resistance to Symbolic identity, when ideological interpellation "liminally" fails. That is to say, the gap between knowledge and truth, between the subject and the big Other, is 'the point of the inner limit, or inherent impossibility, of a given discourse,' and one can 'activate this precise point as the potential locus of creation.'

Here, one shouldn't confuse this with the inane silliness behind the postmodern notion—*"What-is-truth?"* The truth is simply that of the subject's Symbolic condition, which is always-already ruptured by this internal fissure from which one is capable of effectuating new ways of relating to the world. If this gap is not activated as the 'potential locus of creation,' as that space from which something entirely new can be fought for, today's ruling ideology of capital and its concomitant commodity fetishism will be allowed to continue to bridge this gap—a gap that merely reflects the lack of inner consistency that is inherent to the relationship between the subject and his Symbolic identity. It is only by recognizing that such a gap exists, and by confronting the universal ideology in which, by which, and through which we otherwise aim to conceal this gap, that we can enable any *real* change in the way we relate to the world.

It will be upon the bedrock of these observations, of our own subjective truths, that ideological battles will be won or lost.

## §40. The cunning of reason

Therein we have an example of Hegel's "cunning of Reason": the phenomenon by which the '*outward-directed activity*' of particular subjects 'is the *singularity* that is identical with the particularity' of the subjects in which, 'together with the content, *external objectivity* is *included* as well.'[183] In other words, despite the conjunction of the particular subjects' means with their purposive actions, their activity nonetheless remains directed outwards because, as Hegel writes, the purpose of their actions is never, in reality, identical with its end, with its object-goal. Is this not akin to the moral imparted by the fable of *Belling the Cat*: that a plan, an idea, is split between its desirable outcome, its end, and how it's *actually* executed? How an idea is fundamentally split between its theory and its praxis, split by the radical difference between an idea and its feasibility?

The gap marked by this split is where we often situate our fantasies, *our ideologies*; where we elevate reality to that "dream" level upon which the economy of our desires unfolds in the field of the fantastic ideology it's fixed within. That is to say, the idea itself holds invariable sway over its subjects' actions, which is the series of attempts to achieve the object-goal dictated by the idea itself. Therefore the true content of the fantasy, of the idea itself, unfolds through its subjects' actions; it uses its subject(s) (or rather, its subjects fully submit to the idea/fantasy) as a means to satisfy and fulfill their desires. The idea/fantasy assumes an autopoietic nature, it self-produces itself in its determination to fulfill its universal notion, as a means to realize its existential consequences, thus directing, like marionettes, the forms of life that will follow from its instructions, and how its end will pan out in its practice.

This is what Lenin meant by: 'Without revolutionary theory, there is no revolutionary practice.' There is no behavior without a guiding ideology. Without theory the world is left solely to chance. When Althusser claimed that 'we are merely concerned with filling in a "gap" between theory and practice on a particular point,' what he meant was that, this gap inherent to the idea itself is the very thing that necessitates the ideological content, the phantastic elements with which it becomes filled. Thus 'the subjective purpose'—i.e., the desirable outcome—the fantasy itself—precisely *as that powerful authority that presides over and directly influences these processes*—remains *outside of* the processes while at the same, preserving itself through them.[184]

To use as an example: Rather than placing *all* the blame solely on the power of transnational corporations and/or the "One-Percent" for capitalist globalization and its social and environmental catastrophes, Saskia Sassen was perhaps correct when she wrote that we should look more closely at the 'range of activities and organizational arrangements necessary for the implementation and maintenance of a global network of factories, service operations, and markets.'[185] These large producers partaking in the global market, not to mention all the individual producers and laborers working for them, as they strive to satisfy their passions and appetites for profit, are unaware of the way in which capitalist reason uses the exchanges of their desires to realize the true end of capitalist production, in which 'spirit achieves [its] "objective" existence [...] by means of the cunning exploitation of individual interests.'[186] What this means is that corporations are not entirely responsible for the continuous development of capitalism. Capitalism further develops *itself* through its subjects *belief* that they are producing for their own passionate ends when, really, the activity of capitalist production *itself*, sustained by its own ruling ideology, further develops its universal notion by using its subjects as a means to do so. The capitalist "Spirit" strives to achieve its "objective" existence, and its subjects thereby proceed to fill their radical emptiness with this "objectivity": Ideology interpellates its subjects *as such*.

To put it quite simply, the *real* problem, perhaps, isn't so much The Corporation, or, The One Percent—sure, no doubt they are parts of the problem itself. But the real problem, I believe, is situated at a level much deeper level, it's much more radical and systemic than any particular entity or group. For is it not the case that the enemy, the other, is always-already in us, precisely because we're always-already included in the big picture itself? Which means that the real problem here is the fact that we have not yet figured out how to effectively dismantle capitalism. *That's the problem*. Perhaps, then, our first step should be to refocus how we objectively view things, so that we recognize the problem more clearly.

To get a better view of this, in his book, *Living in the End Times*, Žižek makes the claim that the universal is always more real than the particular. He illustrates this by way of a very clear example, which involves an Indian software engineer who, on a daily basis, gives his private praise and worship to the local divinity. The significance of this example is the revelation that 'the concrete (cultural) content is ultimately an ideological fake: *a mask obfuscating the reign of abstraction*.'[187] The Indian programmer, writes Žižek, thinks that, 'in the core of his being he remains faithful to his traditional lifeworld, but his "truth" is his inclusion in the global capitalist machine.'[188] In this sense, the particular lifeworld of the Indian programmer is subtended by the universal of global capitalism: It is not his particular lifeworld which has real overarching effects on the world at large, rather it is his role as a software engineer, no doubt working for a company implicated in transnational affairs someway or another, that has real overarching effects on the world at large. In this precise way, the universal is more real than the particular.

The same, too, can be said about today's fundamentalist evangelical Christians living in the US. Despite the particular religious lifeworld these folks subscribe to, what is more real than their particular religious worldview is the universal of global capitalism—that is, their invested faith, their prayers and every other bit of theological devotion that goes on in all of its quotidian details, is subsumed under today's world of capital. Take as an example the Christian advertising go-getter, Bruce Barton, the man who turned Jesus into a "management guru," turning "prophet into profit." Such an 'entrepreneur-Christ prospers on a [broad] scale,' being the protagonist of 'best sellers such as *God Is My CEO: Following God's Principles in a Bottom-Line World*, and *Jesus CEO: Using Ancient Wisdom for Visionary Leadership*, and, most influentially, Rick Warren's spiritual time-management manual, *The Purpose-Driven Life*—more than 25 million copies sold since the publication in 2002.'[189]

What is to be considered in each of these instances, that of the Indian software engineer and Bruce Barton, is that, their respective particular lifeworlds are merely "ideological fantasies" that are always-already caught up in a more real universal ideology; these "ideological fantasies" are always-already being traversed by the universality of capital. Thus, as Vighi keenly point out, despite the plethora of 'global realities,' it is, nonetheless, 'Capital which is the Real of our lives.'

Here, one should pay careful notice to what is being evoked in each of these examples—Hegel's "cunning of Reason." Ideology qua universality realizes its true end-in-itself by means of the "cunning of Reason": 'it allows individuals to follow their finite ends, whilst it accomplishes its infinite end through the mutual "wear and tear" and failure of the finite ends.'

In other words, the Real universal uses individuals in their particularity as a means to advance its own notion. We indeed see this occurring in each of the instances provided above, in which the individual, believing in and thus performing from his or her particular lifeworld, is oblivious and indifferent to the Real of the universal, the latter using the "finite ends" of the individual, who is rooted in a particular lifeworld, as a means to further articulate its own universal notion, its "infinite end." Universal global capitalism therefore asserts its paramount "authenticity" by way of the "cunning of Reason." Albeit for most it seems virtually invisible, as if happening behind the scenes, this cunning of universal global capitalism is without question more real than any subject's particular lifeworld. The universality of global capitalism can achieve its end only by means of such deception: by means of 'the cunning exploitation of [individual's particular] interests and passions.' To put it bluntly, nobody works for the development of capitalism; rather, individuals mistakenly perceive this true end as a means to satisfy their own needs.

Therefore, it cannot be the case that capitalism prevails solely because of those who rule, insofar as capitalism exists because it deceives people into believing that the system operates with their best interests in mind; that it will give its subjects what they long for; that it will call upon the aspirations of the oppressed, the hard-working, and grant them their justice, their peace, and so on, all the while rearticulating the economy of these desires in such a way that it is all compatible with existing relations of domination. Those who rule just end up benefiting from this, and like a positive feedback loop, everyone and everything involved helps push the system forward. Therefore, it's easy to imagine removing every elite capitalist from the scene, and capitalism will just produce more elite capitalists in the wake of this. Remove capitalism, however, and there are no more framing conditions through which people can rise to the status of an elite capitalist.

# §41. And so that agitating "Thing" about objective news reporting

This is—to return to an example we have left simmering on the back burner for quite some time now—why objective journalism causes such anxiety: What is objective is merely an attitude, a belief even, that insists on providing a precise representation of that which cannot be precisely represented: that hard innermost impenetrable kernel which resists a full inscription into the Symbolic dimension of language and ideology: the heart of the "inner world" itself: the unfathomable void which gives rise to the appearance of the object, which is none other than the subject's own blind spot.

Anxiety is therefore, as Freud and Lacan put it, when the object proper gets too close to the subject, when the gap separating one's ideological identification from the virtual field of the big Other begins to close.

It's no wonder, then, that objective journalism provokes such anxiety to those it does—it exemplifies a larger threat, one that inheres to the ruling ideology of today's dominant culture: the threat of delivering to the subject the impossible object which thereby dissolves any and all particular legitimate worldviews and perspectives save one: the very "objective" worldview doing the delivering of the impossible object as such. This oppressive worldview attempts to conflate its Symbolic reality with the Real, and to then incorporate the self-sublation of its own objectivity into its own universalized essence, threatening to conflate its subjects' particularized Symbolic realities with that of the ruling ideology, which thereby threatens to reduce the tapestry of the world's perspectival narratives into a flat and static homogeneous narrative of One, a narrative that shares an eerie semblance to Nietzsche's concept of the Last Man who is unable to feel any sense of shame, who ceases to be human; a narrative professed to be so completely neutral, so impartial to any historical process, that it banalitizes the atrocities perpetrated by those who exploit this falsely presumed "neutrality" for their own ends, who see subjects as the object-Things they are falsely presumed to be, and *use* them as such.

Does this not delineate today's capitalist (post) ideological outlook in which Symbolic efficiency is rapidly waning? This can be best exemplified with Francis Fukuyama's 1990 message to the world that, 'great social conflicts and great ideological struggles were a thing of the past'; a world in which, to borrow a terse line form British sociologist Anthony Giddens, who served as director of the London School of Economics from 1997-2003, 'there are no alternatives to capitalism.' It is this very ideology, passed as an "objective" truth that no doubt imperils the passions. This is precisely what sparked Kierkegaard's reproach to modernity, an historical era he felt was defined not so much by action and revolution but rather, moreso, by publicity and advertisement— 'What our age lacks is not reflection but passion,' he warned, for, according to him, 'the conclusions of passion are the only reliable ones...'

It is this very ruling ideology, one through which our Symbolic reality is becoming dangerously too close to identifying with itself, and thus mistaking itself for being all too Real, thereby enervating the passions of the day, that is behind the capitalist-charged politico-economic agendas of today's overseers of "objective" journalism.

It should therefore come as no surprise, then, that the uncompromising problem at the essence of news reporting is all knotted up in perspective and passion. Most of us have come to know, one way or another, the tormenting inconsistency that can crop up and lodge itself in between not only the way in which we experience a particular situation and the way in which we see and/or appraise its truth value, but also in how an "objective" description or a linguistic account of a particular situation can oftentimes strike us as completely off target, lacking its essential meaning. Here, one need only to think back to the example drawn earlier about the guy in the office reading in the paper an "objective" account about a miscalculated airstrike in Afghanistan. Despite its "accuracy" or "correctness," such a news report can come across sounding as if it completely misses the point, as if the purveyor of this "objective" account is somehow lying to you, omitting a crucial piece of information; manipulating the story in a certain way. And there's the rub: How can any account of anything be true if it is steeped in mere perspective? Well, rather than arriving at the futile postmodernist conclusion, that everything is a matter of perspective and therefore nothing is essentially true, there appears to be two other, more precise responses to this as well.

The first response can be formulated in terms of ideology. The authority imputed to truth derives exclusively from what is universal about a predominant worldview, its laws, its categories, etc., for its own content. Truth, in this sense, means 'the agreement of a content with itself.' And so, to bring to light yet once again what Alenka Zupančič writes, 'ideology works hard to make certain things "obvious," and the more we find these things obvious, self-evident and unquestionable, the more successfully the ideology has done its job.'

The second response, and it is this one that we should be fully aware of should we want to promote any real radical reform and change in these times, pertains to the Nietzschean/Lacanian notion of Truth in the capacity of perspective. As Hegel claims, if one were to put a universal side by side with the particular, 'the universal itself becomes particular too.' That is to say, a worldview is merely a *particular* worldview, comprised of what is universal of and within its own respective content. Or, as R.D. Laing and D.G. Cooper formulate it: 'Each particular perspective, each particular point of view, is the center of a world, but not the center of another world. Each point of view is an absolute, and at the same time absolutely relative.'[190] Truth, in this sense, is the truth that emerges from *between* perspectives, that is to say: The very multiplicity of perspectives *is* the truth, that each perspective is none other than a moment in an ongoing struggle, a series of attempts to reconcile an original antagonism.

The problem here, of course, is that the more one strives to be objective, the more one asserts the difference between the "subject of the enunciation" (the subject who utters a statement) and the "subject of the enunciated (statement)" (the Symbolic identity the subject assumes within and through his or her statement). It is dialectical in nature precisely in the sense that the inner antagonism, as such, can never be fully reconciled. We are always-already left with an impossible choice between two different truths pitted against each other. The incessant oscillation of opposites that ensues thus sets in motion the perpetual striving towards an endlessly elusive objective truth qua non-truth. This is none other than the paradox of the relationship between Understanding and Reason: 'The fundamental illusion of Understanding is precisely that there is a Beyond eluding its grasp [...] Reason is simply Understanding *minus* what it is supposed to be lacking, what is supposed to elude its grasp: what appears to it as its inaccessible Beyond.'[191]

Is this paradox of the relationship between Understanding and Reason not best exemplified by objective journalism, which is often rebuked for missing the "real thing?" The dialectical answer to such a beast of a dilemma, then, could very well be obtained from the notion that objective journalism is not purely objective precisely because it negates the very objective element that defines it (!): the contingent, subjective encounter with the Real; the unanticipated eventual moment when the impossible happens, when the traumatic, disturbing, or, sometimes miraculously inspirational and encouraging event occurs: an event that is *news worthy*. This very object qua kernel of an event that is abolished is simultaneously preserved, lifted up as the ideal, transcendent object-Thing that retroactively defines what at first escaped any definition. That which retroactively gives rise to a particular news story. As such, journalism is the result of a dialectical process, one that alights upon each stage of Hegel's threefold formulation of objectivity.

## § 42. The *objet petit a* of journalism

The *objet petit a* is none other than that very mysterious *Thing*, that which is in the object that is more than the object itself, the "unfathomable X." The appearance of this object-Thing is the inverted mode of appearance of the subject's immanence. As such, the *objet petit a* is the 'objective supplement which sustains objectivity in its contrast to the subjectless objective order. [It is] that disturbing stain which forever blurs our picture of reality, [it is] none other than the illusory *object* on account of which "objective reality" is forever inaccessible to the subject.'[192]

What should not get overlooked here is Hegel's logic of reflection, the reflective "positing of presuppositions." Hegel was well aware that the immediacy engendered by the process of ascribing identity is always-already "posited," retroactively, so that, as laid out above, the object's immediate emergence, its "trans-coding" (to return to an earlier term), coincides with its radical loss.

Reflection therefore *finds before it* an immediate which it transcends and from which it is the return. But this return is only the presupposing of what reflection finds before it. What is thus found only *comes to be* through being *left behind*; its immediacy is sublated immediacy.[193]

As such, the *objet petit a* quilts one's ideologico-objective field: that is to say, *it gives consistency to one's objective reality*, the cardinal feature of which is the belief in the actual existence of the *objet petit a*.

Therein resides the immutable core associated with the whole enigma that is objective news reporting: What eludes the story is not some "intimate secret" but the "gaze itself," that stain upon reality that just won't clean up: it is a *blind-spot*—that which structurally escapes all perspectives: not just the unknown, mysterious inner integrity of the Thing itself, but the way in which the subject, the journalist him/herself, is inscribed in the very thing he or she is observing. Thus, to get at the "truth" of any news story, one should simply focus not on the story, but on the gaze itself—*precisely at that very medium which is delivering the message.*

The real issue at hand here is not pertinent to objective journalism, but rather to the supreme universal (ideological) medium in which, not just journalism alone, but our entire lifeworld is immersed today: that invisible intervening universal substance in which, by which, and through which our impressions are generated and conveyed. And how does one know what this substance is, how does one become aware of it? Marshall McLuhan once wrote that, 'the "content" of any medium is always another medium,' though it's often the case that 'the "content" of any medium blinds us to the character of the medium.'[194] That is to say: it's not that we must become more aware of the ideology that suffuses our subjectivity, but rather: we need to be conscious of the ideology that *gives* us, that interpellates, our subjectivity: the very ideology with-and-in-which we are always-already engaged.

Here we are dealing with the same logic as that of Freud's dream analysis, which is the logic behind the structure of the following twofold question—Why does the latent content of something manifest itself in the presentational form that it does, and what, exactly, is such a transformative process telling us? With regard to the dialectic apropos objective news reporting, an answer to these questions will reveal that the content of anti-objective news reporting deals directly with large multi-national corporate media, which, despite being presented as the "enemy," such a presented content is no doubt "blinding" the anti-objective journalist to the fact that such disfavored objective content is without question part of an even larger medium, a medium that the entire fourth estate, *including the non-objective journalist,* is immersed in: capitalism.

Capitalism is therefore none other than the universal 'medium that shapes and controls the scale and form of human association and action' in today's modern world. And this makes sense, owing to the fact that the majority of the content of the stories produced by today's independent and alternative media often deal directly with global crises engendered by the capitalist system, oftentimes exposing the big lies that structure the capitalist universe, though at the same time neglecting to fully acknowledge their own blind spot: the fact that the purveyors of this non-objective content can often partake in the very lamentable world of capital in order to keep one's company, career, etc., afloat.

Such a subject displays an outright (and sometimes fetishistic) cynicism toward those official institutions and universal ideologies in which they are nonetheless entrenched — portraying overt contempt for, though in their daily practice they are unarguably caught up in, the world of capital.

In other words, what is expressed by and throughout today's counter-culture is, to quote philosopher and historian Lewis Mumford, 'fast approaching [if it has not reached already] the point where the medium not only replaces the message but likewise the subject to whom the message was once addressed.'[195]

In fact, the bulk of news stories and other generated content dealing with the problems of capitalism circulate primarily within the parameters of today's (petit) bourgeois class (listeners of NPR, readers of *The New York Times,* subscribers to magazines like *The Progressive, The Atlantic* et al. embody the perfect example of this). It is very seldom, if at all, that slum dwellers, ghetto dwellers, the homeless and so on (who are often the *subject* of the said generated content, and are often discussed about in "objective" terms) have direct access to "progressive" or "radical" or "leftist" content and other intellectual information as such. This type of information frequently circulates only among the very classes that help maintain the existence of the "big Culprit" that is capitalism.

To repeat a crucial point from earlier, there's virtually no point in speaking the truth to those who are in relative positions of wealth and power (this of course includes even today's middles class, for they no doubt hold more wealth, thus more financial power, than the underclass—*hands down*); most of us already *know* the truth. Those who claim to want real change should give up the task of "holding the mirror," so to speak, to the powerful; such gestures are incontestably reflexive of one's own condition: that one's "enemy" is in fact the precondition of one's own (privileged class) position.

And so in a certain sense, without such a privileged position, one loses their enemy, so to speak: the very external point of reference whereby one's 'subjective position acquires its consistency.' *This is precisely how ideology works*. It is tenacious indeed. Taking this into account, perhaps it is the case that deep down many of today's "dissident" writers do not actually want real change, or at the very least, do not actually *know* if they desire substantial change or not. Perhaps what they truly desire is the desire itself. And for that matter, such a desire must remain unsatisfied, for if it's satisfied, this desire dissolves completely. And there's the deadlock! In other words, if real substantial change were to occur, if there were to be a complete radical shift in the coordinates of today's social arrangements, the entire raison d'être propping up many journalists' subjective reality would become as meaningful as the last waltz that accompanied the sinking of the Titanic.[196] This is precisely what we need to be aware of.

So what is the overall message here? In a certain sense, *the medium is the message*: which is to say, that most people are fully unaware, or perhaps in denial even, of the very reality of a universal ideology that directs and transmits the most intimate nuances of their performed lives. In the case of those journalists who trenchantly oppose objectivity in the newsroom, are they not aware that the very apparatuses they rely on to disseminate their "dissenting" message are at the same time instrumentally beneficial to the very "big Culprit" that makes one's dissenting stance so consistent, thereby benefiting the capitalist system and its livable worldview, a worldview which takes objectivity as a given in order to self-engender itself? Therefore, if one truly wants to bring about substantial change, one should first recognize the universal ideology one is subtended by. If this ideology is responsible for the conditions one truly wishes to change—then one should simply recognize it as such, *know* it as such, and withdraw from it completely. One should confront the terror that is at the core of one's identity, that disavowed void within: the radical abyss of subjectivity that remains once the subject is emptied of its ideological content. One will thereby become fully capable of initiating anew a project of self-reinvention, which will help restructure the external coordinates of one's inner subjective life-world.

And how does one know if they have successfully begun to do this; how does one know if they've begun subverting the very universal ideology that has been moving through them all along? When one no longer finds oneself "preaching to the choir"; when one has finally taken up the political project of "speaking truth" to the powerless, to the disenfranchised, to the marginalized; when one has finally gone out into the world with the aim not to proselytize but to politicize the excesses of today's capitalist societies, mobilizing the revolution through the very ghosts of society: those others who are at the same ourselves; those who dwell within the shadows cast by the light we shine upon the avowed; those whose social existence is disavowed everyday.[197] And so to put it quite simply, if our anti-capitalist messages do not seem to be getting across, then it is time to change the medium. And if we don't get it right... well—we shall repeat the failure again!

# Notes

1   Jack D. Forbes, *Columbus and Other Cannibals*, New York: Seven Stories Press, 2008, p. 24.

2   Slavoj Žižek, "The Three Events of Philosophy," *International Journal of Žižek Studies*, Vol. 7, No. 1, p. 9. Are we not talking, here, about the passage from "human being" (the human that is animal) to "being human" (the animal that is human)?

3   *Ibid.*, p. 10

4   *Ibid.*

5   In Stephen King's *Pet Cemetery*, a malevolent spirit named Wendigo inhabits the ancient Indian burial ground that Jud Crandall shows Louis Creed. That the Wendigo sounds a lot like Wétiko is perhaps no coincidence (in fact, Wendigo is a northern Algonquian term that refers to 'a cannibalistic giant; a person who has been transformed into a monster by the consumption of human flesh'): what gets buried in this Indian burial ground returns as the living dead, though inhabited by a diabolical evil spirit. This violence of the "undead" is what inevitably proceeds from Creed's repetitive attempts at getting rid of the death in his life, of trying to abolish the painful imbalances that plague his lived reality.

6   Take for example, Derrick Jensen's remarkable two-volume work, *Endgame*. Therein the author exposes how the problems of civilization amount to none other than *the problem-of-civilization itself*. But perhaps the problem of civilization is something more than just civilization itself? What if, rather, the problem of civilization is precisely that it is just another (failed) attempt at trying to reconcile the deep-seated antagonisms around which civilizations are built? In this sense, it's not: Civilization is responsible for

our alienation from ourselves—but rather: Civilization is another attempt at trying to "harmonize," to fill in the primordial gap that marks our radical subjective alienation that precedes it, thus engendering tyrannical expressions of control. And what, exactly, do we mean by subjective alienation? Subjective alienation is to be referred to the non-coincidence of the subject with itself, that there is a radical imbalance, a disparity *within* the subject itself, a gap that separates the subject from its empty place of inscription. This empty place of inscription, a void as such, is that unfathomable abyss of one's subjective freedom, which culminates in a deadlock: There arises from this same space both one's freedom to do what one wants/desires, and the limit-point to desire itself—self-responsibility, self-regulation (here I should note, as an aside, that freedom at its most *fundamental* is not freedom to do as one likes, but rather, the freedom to do what one does not want to do, a pure act of one's free will as such: the ability of one to stop one's own act in the middle of its execution, to undermine one's own partiality toward pleasure). As T.M. Knox writes in the "Translator's Foreword" to Hegel's *Philosophy of Right*, 'so long as men regard freedom as freedom to pursue selfish whims, society is possible only if external checks are placed on this freedom; government [civilization, even] is then an external organization to meet men's necessities.' The first thing we should consider, then, is that one's radical desire is almost always to be "free," and what we should take careful notice of after realizing this is that, the "external" organization that exists in order to regulate this desire, *is none other than internal to the very network of subjects that gives rise to this "external" organization*. We can debate all we want about, e.g., whether or not civilization is a problem, but the most crucial thing we should keep in mind is that the "enemy/other" is always-already in us. The key question, then, is—what if the (in)human excessiveness of catastrophe and atrocity, the barbarism of civilization itself, is none other than a remainder of some preceding (in)human excession, something of which was attempted to be abolished by the project of civilization itself? In other words: The very framework that seeks to regulate and govern the desire to be free always-already contextualizes one's notion of freedom as such. This governing structure, however, is also the very thing that can present itself as an impasse to one's desired freedom, especially when those in power manipulate the structure of governance in such a way that it serves their own self-interests. Thus, as Hegel posited: true freedom consists in the subjects' very acceptance of the laws and principles, which are their own nonetheless. This is why, in my opinion, real freedom cannot exist without a sturdy ethical edifice, though only after one accepts the fact that there is no external guarantee of ethical substance, that ethical judgment can only be borne in upon one's own "ethical reflection" upon one's own actions. Thus in today's capitalist age of moral bankruptcy, in which ethical reflection is often perceived as nugatory, we are not free, but often victims of those in power who manipulate the structures of power so that these structures serve only the powerful and the privileged.

7    In medicine, this word refers to the fracturing of a bone that produces multiple splinters. It is from the Latin verb *"comminuere,"* from *com-* ("together") + *minuere* ("lessen"). It is that which pulverizes its sameness, in its own *togetherness*, into a multitude of appearances.

8    Immanuel Kant, *Critique of Judgment*, New York: Hafner Publishing Co., 1951, p. 234.

9    German biologist Jakob von Uexküll discovered that, when shown a black spot, this spot means an entirely different thing for a hungry frog than it does for a satiated frog; for

the satiated frog, the black spot spurs no reaction. Here, the frog's desire is directed only toward its self-preservation: "I'm hungry; therefore I must eat!" Without the appetite, the frog does not desire to have the black spot.

10   Alexandre Kojève, *Introduction to the Reading of Hegel: Lectures on the Phenomenology of Spirit*, Ithaca, NY: Cornell University Press, 1969, pp. 6-7.

11   Karl Marx, *Capital*, Volume 1, Harmondsworth: Penguin, 1976, p. 63.

12   Joan Copjec, "The Subject Defined by Suffrage," http://www.lacan.com/frameVII4.htm

13   Claude Lefort, *The Political Forms of Modern Society: Bureaucracy, Democracy, Totalitatianism*, Cambridge, MA: MIT Press, 1986.

14   Slavoj Žižek, *For They Know Not What They Do: Enjoyment as a Political Factor*, New York: Verso, 2008, p. 267.

15   Georg Lukács, *History and Class Consciousness*, Cambridge, MA: MIT Press, 1971, p. 5-6.

16   Paul Ricoeur, *The Conflict of Interpretations*, Evanston, IL: Northwestern University Press, 1974, pp. 110-11.

17   A necessary addendum deemed as such by Yours Truly: Filmmaker Jean Luc Godard once said, "First there was Greek civilization. Then there was the Renaissance. Now we're entering the Age of the Asshole." Beginning with the advent of New World exploration, and culminating in today's liberal free-market global economy, a system of one-sided political, economic, and military domination has fatally arrested and initiated the systematic removal of any other worldview that threatens to present itself as a viable alternative to capitalism. The universal ideology of capitalism therefore disallows any alternative system to take precedent. And at its most extreme, capitalism pushes up against even life itself, by forcing life to metabolize into its very own system (is not the hyper-commodification of

natural resources, crucial to keeping the system of capitalism going, none other than the transformation of the living into the dead?)

It should come as no surprise, then, that throughout the developed world the falsity inherent to the ruling ideology of capital is virtually unrecognizable: those who dwell comfortably in the First World are fully metabolized into this ideology; which means that, for the most part, these individuals are unable to contemplate, in any meaningful way, even one viable alternative. The effect of this is the retreat, the failure of any *real* political project. Thus the vulgar majority often buys into the belief that there is no other alternative to capitalism; that the way the world is in capitalism is just the way things are supposed to be, and that *that* is "objectively certain."

What we have here is a prime example of a whole being contained by one of its parts: the Hegelian paradox of a 'totality which always comprises a particular element embodying its universal structuring principle.' In this case, the culture of capitalism, a particular culture amidst a plurality of other particular cultures, embodies its universal as a universality that is "objectively certain." Is this not, however, precisely what Badiou aims at with his claim that "every universal is singular, or is a singularity? And moreover, is it not the case that the common notion that, "a cultural or religious particularity is bad if it does not include within itself respect for other particularities," is none other than the "necessary counterpart," as Badiou puts it, to policy and protocol that is violently genocidal in nature? Let's face it, that a cultural/religious particularity includes within itself respect for other cultural/religious particularities is

obviously to stipulate that the formal universal already be

included in the particularity. Ultimately, the universality of respect for particularities is only the universality of universality. This definition is fatally tautological [...] a violent one—that wants to eradicate genuinely particular particularities... (Alain Badiou, *Badiou & Žižek: Philosophy in the Present*, Malden, MA: 2009, p. 30.)

*And that's the underlying racist message of today's ideology of "multicultural tolerance"*: Today's liberal, global-capitalist "democratic" society accepts (read, tolerates) anybody and everybody despite their difference, whether that difference be ethnic, religious, sexual, so on and so forth—except for one caveat: anyone can belong to this global community as long as one subordinates their difference(s), that is, subordinates their own particular lifeworld and self-determination to today's political economy of capital. Tolerance is thus none other than the mark of a brutal assimilation by means of either coercion or cooptation into the aggressor culture. And for those who refuse to integrate, well... those are the folks who comprise the homeless, the slum dwellers, the ghettoized, the powerless and disenfranchised; those are the people who carry most of the daily weight of today's humanitarian and environmental crises. They are capitalism's exceptions, the excess of the global capitalist society; forgotten; and if not forgotten, if thought of at all, these individuals are thought of in the popular imagination *as if* they live outside of society. Though any intelligent person *knows* that that is a delusive thought. Those who have been left behind in the wake of capitalism's "advancements" are, in reality, right here with all of us, breathing the same air, their feet standing on the same ground. So why is it that so many do not fully recognize this, or simply choose to not fully recognize this? The answer, to employ a little Marx: Because bourgeois freedom, that is, the freedom afforded to the middle classes and those echelons of class directly above, is merely the form of appearance of the *un-freedom* of those who have been "left behind." Many are perhaps too preoccupied with their own "freedoms" to recognize this.

In any event, the universal of capitalism (as it is hegemonized by and through the particulars involved in the global network of free market economics) is constituted by the dominant culture's act of subtracting *itself* from the set of particular cultures, whereby the culture of capitalism asserts its dominance through this very act of making itself the particular exception that embodies the universal *as such*. Do we not, hereby, have another illustration of Hegel's totalizing logic in which the dialectic is the central prime mover?

Still and all, one should take notice of how the culture of capitalism functions as a "pure" signifier: its entire actuality and authority consists in its Name (that of capitalism). As such, it embodies the function of Master-Signifier. Like Hegel's monarch it is the "One of the Exception," the 'irrational protuberance [...] which transforms [the multitude of particular cultures] into a concrete totality [...] By means of [capitalism's] ex-sistence of a pure signifier, [it] constitutes the Whole of the [new] social fabric in its "organic articulations," the "irrational" surplus as a condition of the rational totality...' (Žižek, *For They Know Not*, pp. 82-3.)

Let's look at it this way, humankind, as a diverse set of cultures ranging across the globe, is a set of non-totalized, non-universalized particulars; its multitude acquires the dimension of *universality* (as a "global village" by means of globalization) as soon as one *excludes* from the set of particular cultures an element which thereby embodies humankind as such: the capitalist culture. Such a culture, existing as merely one particular culture among many other particular cultures embodies an exception that, in effect, gives rise to the universal culture of capitalism. And the *truth* of this universality is on the side of the universal itself—precisely as the universal's constitutive exception: a disturbance in an original order, or rather, a violent transgression that violates an original order as a means to constitute a new order: e.g., *the rational whole of capitalism is founded upon an irrational structuring principle that embodies the universal as such.*

To help spell this logic out some more, we can think of Law as universalized crime; that is to say, Law can only be applied to the content generated by crime. In order for the universality of Law to be constituted, a radical crime must be an act-of-exception that calls for Law. Thus Law is constituted by an original criminal act, an irrational act that calls for a rational order, Law, which serves to arrest, in all senses of the term, the irrational exception that embodies the universality of Law as such. In other words, Law is essentially the attempt to rationalize the transgression of a primordial principle. For example: US Constitutional Law gained its juridical supremacy only after the genocidal removal and subsequent assimilation of the country's indigenous peoples. Therefore, it's not merely the case that Law can only be applied to the content that crime (as such) generates—*Law itself is crime*: it is more than just a binary relationship shared between the two, they exist as two-within-one, in a sort of "split personality" that is based on the utter lack of a purely juridical center: Law is more criminal than crime itself: it creates the criminal content needed to actualize its own existence. One could even say that Law and crime exist at the same level, and that neither one of them is substituted by the other, that Law and crime are therefore one and the same; they cannot be separated from each other for they are thus montages of the same fractured unity. Thus the tautology, the Law is the Law: Law does not coincide with itself; the difference between Law and crime is none other than the difference between Law and its empty place of inscription.

Here, one should recall the HBO series *The Wire*, a police drama that takes place in and around Baltimore, Maryland, in which the complexity of simple corruption can be parsed out from its deep integration into the very institutions that purport to oppose such corruption. The more the detectives start to follow the money implicated in the local drug trade (rather than chasing around the drugs), the more they realize that the money is collusively tangled up with the city's most powerful statesmen who are running the very institutions that are supposed to indict and prosecute the very criminals they've become! This paradox of the Law explains why, for example, states in the US with the highest budget for law enforcement also have the highest levels of crime. In fact, as far back as the first Kerner Commission Report on Civil Disorders (1968), studies have shown that increased police presence often leads to an escalation in criminal activity. Thus, Law is universalized crime: 'crime elevated to the level of an unconditional principle.'

What all of this means, is that, the dominant culture's entire ontology rests on an irrational structuring principle. Its truth is none other than its innermost antagonism: the dominant culture exists in virtue of a Universal Lie, so to speak—its rational order is precipitated by the irrationality of its existence as something it essentially is not: viz., the dominant culture is a *particular* culture assuming the form of its opposite: a *universal* culture. And it is the wholesale belief in this lie, that capitalism is a universal truth, i.e., that it is determined as objectively certain to be the only way we can live in this world, that elevates it to the level of universality, thereby accelerating its ideological expansion, sublating what is not a part of it into its oneness.

And does this not allow us to define postmodernism in the following terms? As Žižek puts it in *Living in the End Times*, postmodernism marks the moment in modernity itself when all obstacles that once stood in the way to achieving modernity have finally been overcome and sublated into the oneness of modernity; when the old threats no longer pose a direct threat to "progress," when these former obstructions lose their "menacing" qualities and eventually become benign and harmless items to celebrate and fetishize in a state of "postmodern" pastiche; which for many is the specious mark of *progress*. Though it's important not to confuse progress with complacent pride and hubris:

> The "spontaneous ideology" of this new bourgeoisie appears, paradoxically, as the opposite of their vulgar "passion of the real" (pleasure, money, power): a (no less vulgar) pan-aestheticism—all ideologies are equal, equally ridiculous, they are useful only to provide spicy aesthetic excitement, so the more problematic they are, the more excitement they generate (See, Žižek, *Living in the End Times*, New York: Verso, 2011, p. 252.)

Which reminds me of this one time, when a couple friends of mine attended a packed forum, assembled by the Park Slope cooperative in Brooklyn, New York, to vote on whether or not to vote on whether or not there should be a boycott on Israeli goods. (At which point I told my friends that there should rather be a discussion concerning boycotting Saudi goods, like, e.g., oil!) To my understanding, there are two things going on here. One, there is a situation in which the crisis is more in the solution than in the crisis itself: the deadlock that arises from casting a vote to cast a vote on whether or not to boycott. Let's amplify this conundrum of the solution-embedded crisis: While going through the motions of a two-state solution, Israel is nonetheless creating a situation which will leave such a solution '*de facto* impossible': As of 1 March 2009 Israel drew up plans to push forward with the construction of more than 70,000 new housing units in the occupied West Bank; if carried out, it could increase the number of settlers in the Palestinian territories by approximately 300,000, which would foreclose any realistic chance of there being a Palestinian state (See both Tobias Duck, "Israel Drafts West Bank Expansion Plans," *Financial Times*, March 2, 2009, and Žižek, *Living in the End Times*, p. 143).

The other thing one should glean from this story about my friends, and equally important to take note of, is that these friends of mine didn't even vote to vote. They simply showed up to watch. Their "playful indifference" to the ideologies floating around the room (not to mention to the existential crisis engendered by the very clashing of these ideologies) was useful only to 'provide spicy aesthetic excitement' to their lives. What could be more exciting than watching today's "post-political" liberal democracy do its thing, right? It is this "playful indifference" (articulated in this instance through political voyeurism) that nonetheless 'conceals the reality of the ruthless exercise of power': What is staged as an aesthetic spectacle for this voyeuristic duo is still a reality for the Palestinian victims, who are suffering thousands of miles away. It is precisely this ostensible indifference to ideology that reveals one's complicity with the ruling ideology. And it is the very structure of desire (for my friends, the desire to, pretense or not, be "politically" recognized in lieu of the complete failure of attaining any *real* political practice and/or object-goal) — the antagonism between drive and desire as such — that is the inner mechanism whereby the system of capitalism self-engenders itself, which keeps its subjects enthralled in its movement, and therefore complicit in the destructive policies of capital.

18    Viz., what I do *from here* will inevitably determine how I retrospectively view my life *later on*, but this *later on* does not exist *from here*; thus what I do *from here* affects my *later-on* hindsight—*contingently*; thus I only know what there is *from here*.

19    See Žižek, "How to Read Lacan; Troubles with the Real: Lacan as a Viewer of *Alien*": http://www.lacan.com /zizalien.htm

20    Gilbert Burnham et al., "Mortality after the 2003 Invasion of Iraq: A Cross-Sectional Cluster Sample Survey," *Lancet* 368 (12 October 2006): 1421-28.

21    Rupert Murdoch's News Corporation (FOX, HarperCollins, *New York Post*, DirectTV, and more than thirty TV stations), General Electric (NBC, CNBC, MSNBC, Telemundo, Bravo, and more than a dozen TV stations), Time Warner (AOL, CNN, Warner Bros., *Time*, and its plethora of magazines) Disney (ABC, Disney Channel, ESPN, over twenty radio stations, Hyperion, etc.), Viacom (CBS, MTV, Nickelodeon, Paramount Pictures, more than 150 radio stations, etc.), etc.

22    Robert W. McChesney, *Rich Media, Poor Democracy: Communication Politics in Dubious Times*, New York: The New Press, 2000, p. xv.

23    Or in the Hegelian sense: the more one attempts to escape Hegelianism, the more one engages in a "return to Hegel." As Foucault once wrote, 'We have to determine the extent to which our anti-Hegelianism is possibly one of his tricks directed against us, at the end of which he stands, motionless, waiting for us.' That is to say, any attempt to thwart or escape Hegel's dialectic, paradoxically, only strengthens the very logic behind it!

Hegelianism posits that, in terms of approaching binary

oppositions, if you wish to make the right choice, to pick the "right" option in order to arrive at the "truth" of some such thing, you would manage best to begin with the "wrong choice." The way this works is as such: By choosing the negative option, that is, by choosing the worst option possible, this option (if it really is the wrong option) will ultimately fail and thereby undermine its entire capacity for being an alternative, thus allowing one to overcome its terms, clearing away this negative option, whereby the space for something "new" to take its place will emerge. This is what Hegel meant by "tarrying the negative," which is also an apt description of the function of the Freudian "death-drive," a function that is twofold: as a unique feature of the human subject, unique precisely in the sense that it delineates a dimension of the subject that refuses to fully immerse itself into its own "lifeworld" (the drive is a "constant force" unto itself, following its own trajectory with no regard whatsoever to the laws and necessities of our material lifeworld), the drive functions by (i) seeking to clear the very ordered space in which all that is already possible persists; that is to say, it endeavors to disrupt a homeostasis of sorts, while simultaneously attempting to (ii) place within this disrupted, freshly cleared space new possibilities, which the drive uncovers by "tarrying the negative", i.e., by repeatedly attempting to transgress the limits of (im)possibility.† This of course raises some concerns apropos our conventional notion of time, specifically its assumed linearity. As Freud said about the drive, it 'has no day or night, no spring or autumn, no rise and fall.' The very activity of the drive entails the constant repetition of attempting to violate established laws, necessities, conventions, principles, and so on, in order to arrive at something New. The repetition of drive therefore suggests that the movement of "time" takes on not a feature of linearity but of circularity through repetition. The repetition of sacrifice, of work; those attempts and repetitions necessary to create something New. What is New, as such, is thus a supplement for the subtraction of the Old; the Old breaks down, and its elements are sublated into the New as such. In this sense, the temporal feature of linearity is illusory, effectuated by the emergence of something New, something which *appears* to emerge from the "future" to take the place of the former (Old) position that was, itself, always-already a stand-in for a radical loss. (Was not the Old at one point New? Thus it, too, the Old, must have also come about, when it did, through the same generative, dialectical process that manifests a New development.) By this light, circularity and repetition seem to be the salient features of the temporal dimension. For more on this, see Todd McGowan, "The Violence of Creation in *The Prestige*," *International Journal of Žižek Studies*, *Žižek and Cinema*, Vol. 1.3.

(Too, one should not misread/misconceive "death-drive"; it is not a force that propels the subject toward its own end; rather, the drive is a force that is "un-dead": as such, it is a constant, non-mortal energy that persists beyond the subject's own finitude; it is that libidinal *Thing* (of the subject) that is always-already on the *other* side of the horizon that demarcates the contours of the subject's own finitude.)

† It's important to distinguish the closed field of (im)possibility from the open field of (im)possibility: Within the fragile confines of any socio-Symbolic order, an order of "objective certainty," what is already possible exists *in the capacity of being realized*; viz., there exists only possibilities in the capacity of that which is, and/or *with* what is, already possible, what is "objectively certain," and so on. Here, all meaning abounds as if confined within a large reserve. New

combinations of meaning can emerge (e.g., "non-existing combinations of existing things"), but new forms of meaning and sense are scarce if not virtually absent within this order; and so things that are non-realized remain as such, as non-sense, till otherwise. And it is here where we are, paradoxically, up against real impossibility, a peculiar stasis of sorts in which, amidst all that is possible, nothing radically New obtains (yet, at any given moment, there is the explosive potential that something radically New *can* emerge). On the other hand, in contrast to the socio-Symbolic order and, likewise, "outside" of the correlationist circle (i.e., outside the relation between Being and thought), is an infinite field of unknown (im)possibilities: things that are yet to be possible, things that may "ex-sist" but are yet to be *realized*, yet to be symbolized, yet to enter into inscription within the socio-Symbolic order (for as Pliny once celebrated, *'Quam multa fieri non posse, priusquam sint facta, judicantor?'* ["How many things are considered impossible until they are actually done!"]): The possibility of impossibility—that is the maxim of the Drive! which is the key to Hegel's dialectical approach: i.e., 'what appears at first glance a purely Negative [...] functions as a positive condition of possibility of the entity it impedes.' And so again, this is what Hegel meant by his expression "tarrying the negative": the negation of a negation to arrive at a New development, in which the "old are used to make things new."

Here, one should notice and take advantage of the invaluable framework that Hegel's "tarrying the negative" lends to our practical (ethico-political) dealings with difference *per se*, whether such difference is geopolitical, cultural, ethnic, spiritual, sexual, etc.: To "tarry the negative" is to *engage* with that which opposes, rather than to directly remove that which opposes.

24 E.g., Kant was remarkably bitter over the Church's efforts to enfetter with inflexible orthodoxy a people devoted to the struggle for intellectual and spiritual freedom. In October, 1794, years after openly denouncing Wöllner's repressive edict of 1788 (though never mentioning Wöllner's name), and a couple years after the release of Book Two of the *Religion*, in which he treated biblical doctrines in a radically eccentric way, Kant received the following from the king himself: 'Our most high person has for a long time observed with great displeasure how you misuse your philosophy to undermine and debase many of the most important and fundamental doctrines of the Holy Scriptures and Christianity [...] in your book, *Religion innerhalb der Grenzen der blossen Vernunft*, as well as in other smaller works [...] We demand of you immediately a most conscientious answer and expect that in the future, towards the avoidance of our highest disfavor, you will give no such cause for offense, but rather, in accordance with your duty, employ your talents and authority so that our paternal purpose may be more and more attained. If you continue to resist, you may certainly expect unpleasant consequences to yourself.'

25 If one were to take a moment to give this some further thought, there *is* a way to undermine the most powerful and wealthy exactly through obeying the injunction against "speaking truth to power": as Noam Chomsky writes, 'speaking truth to power makes no sense. There is no point in speaking the truth to [e.g.] Henry Kissinger'; the guy of course already *knows* the truth. That is to say, give up the task of "holding the mirror" to the powerful, such gestures are reflexive of one's own condition: that the enemy is often the precondition of one's own "Beautiful Soul" position; without such a position, writes Žižek, one loses their enemy, the very external point of reference whereby one's 'subjective position acquires its consistency.' Therefore,

many who "speak truth to power" perhaps *don't* want real change, but rather desire for things to remain exactly the way they are; for if there were real change to occur, the entire *raison d'être* of these individuals would dissolve. So the lesson here? If you truly desire to bring about substantial change, perhaps it would be best for you to first identify with, and then go out and speak truth to, the powerless, the disenfranchised, the socially and economically marginalized. Politicize the excess of society — mobilize the revolution through *them*, through today's impoverished masses, the slum dwellers, the ghettoized, the very ghosts of society who go unnoticed everyday.

26 And yet, despite being problematic, there is also a sense in which objectivity *is* necessary: objectivity *not* as *a discrete ideological moment in the ongoing history of ideology per se* — not as *a particular* ideology (i.e., not in the capacity at which it exists today, as in, e.g., the performative we've come to know as "intellectual objectivity") but rather: the necessity of objectivity I'm speaking of here should be considered in the following sense: that objectivity *per se* is none other than the very "constitutive stuff" of the ideological super-structure itself (the Symbolic big Other) — a plexus of social relations undergoing constant deformation and development, involved in a 'long and slow process of transformation and supplementation' following the occurrence of event after event, epoch after epoch, expressing itself through various *particular ideologies* throughout history. In other words, it's a central premise herein that objectivity *per se*, as I've just defined it, is essential to our "(inter-)subjective" lifeworld and that, furthermore, objectivity, insofar as it remains conceptualized as such, gives rise to ideology *per se* — not just to *a particular* ideology. (Here, think the difference between the *diachronic* form of ideology — the structure *itself* — and its *synchronic* expres-

sions over time; or, to put it more simply, think the difference between the structure of the ideological "machine" *itself*, something that is operating continuously and perennially (though always open to new expressions), in contrast to *a discrete ideology*, an ideological function, an expression of the machine itself—a *particular* ideological moment in history as such.) This objectivity-qua-ideology-machine functions *for us*, and *by us*, while also being a Symbolic register *in which, through which* and *by which* our subjectivity is determined. This structure of objectivity-qua-ideology serves as a sort of "caretaker": it is an invisible Symbolic network of categories, conventions, codes, laws, inter-subjectively verified "facts," etc.—sustained as such by its subjects, for its subjects, through a tacit social pact to *believe* that said network (a network in which our lives are inscribed like that of diegetic elements in a narrative) holds and thus forms the very bedrock upon which everything we know, and come to know, is erected. And this function of belief is "programmed" in the human individual during the process of interpellation, by means of the individual's installation into the Symbolic order, the latter being a universal order that, through a given, *particular*, ideology, ultimately serves to instruct the individual *how to be in the world*.

Today's "intellectual objectivity," however, is *a discrete ideology*: a synchronic ideological moment in the long unfurling history of the ideological machine itself. In this sense, we can liken today's *intellectual objectivity* to what Lacan coined the *"point de capiton"* (quilting point), which serves to represent the big Other: it occupies an exceptional place that fixes and maintains the ordered space of a paradigmatic network of knowledge and meaning. In other words, the very paradigmatic structure that governs the relations between its elements exists by dint of this exceptional element as such—*le point de capiton*—insofar as this paradigmatic structure is *embodied by this single exceptional element*, a synchronic "oneness" of ideology as such.

This book aims to explore (and attempts to explain for) the self-division, the *non-coincidence*, of the (diachronic) ideological structure itself; why its diachronic oneness has (always-already) fractured itself into two, into a dyad; its "oneness" always-already "constitutively split" as such (we should think of this ideological oneness as split within itself, involving a gap between its inherent subjective and objective elements), to the extent that the constitutively-split-oneness of ideology as such has both disengaged, and expelled, one of its comprising elements of itself (objectivity) from itself, whereby this exceptional element as such (objectivity) functions as a synchronous, "externalized internalization" of the ideological machine itself—i.e., as a synchronous ideological moment in the diachronous structure of ideology per se. In other words, what we are dealing with here is a very dynamic dialectic: On the one hand, objectivity and ideology share a (non)identity in a unique kind of "fractured oneness"—viz., like the diachronicity of language and its synchronic function of speech, "ideology" and "objectivity" are two incommensurate terms that can, paradoxically speaking, be designated for *same* thing, *that nonetheless differs from its sameness*: i.e., that which we have collectively externalized of our ("historicized and inter-subjectivized" [i.e., collective]) selves as an Other to which we can refer as a means to create, and at the same time, access, both the Symbolic meaning of our lifeworld and, our symbolic place therein. That is to say, there has (always-already) been a self-division, a splitting from within of this monolithic ideological "unary": there has always-already been a separation, *internally*, of its identificatory terms from each other. And as regards the current epoch we are situated in, to speak Nietzschean, "the One has become Two": that is to say, the salient ideological characteristic of (post)modernity is that the (post)modern subject believes and behaves as if objectivity is something separate from ideology, as if it's something that has a higher dignity than ideology itself in terms of dealing with epistemological and ontological matters. And this separation, *the very act of making a distinction between ideology and objectivity*, paradoxically reunites, that is to say, repositions, objectivity back within the oneness of ideology as such: Viz., objectivity becomes a synchronic ideology (precisely in the form of "intellectual objectivity"): objectivity, in these times, is a discrete and synchronic historical moment of the diachronic structure of ideology *itself*. And so, such a separation "reflexively" redoubles objectivity, ultimately transposing it back to the level of the ideological superstructure—though *not* as something seemingly identical with the diachronic form of ideology but rather: as being *a particular ideology* of, and synchronous with, our current epoch. For is it not the case that, e.g., Big Data, a network of informational inputs borne in upon "intellectual objectivity" operates in the precise manner of ideology these days? It shapes and informs the way we experience our lived realities! Hence today's ideology of "intellectual objectivity." In other words, rather than objectivity being solely an interchangeable term for ideology *itself*, it has, in today's modern age, like Jekyll into Hyde, separated a part of itself from itself, and "externalized" this internalized part. That is to say, the modern sense of objectivity is *both* an "external reflection" of ideology per se, and—an ideological moment, i.e., *a moment of ideology itself that functions "outside" of itself*.

What does this all mean? What we should bear in mind here is that, within our ideological space, the reference to objectivity, whether we're talking about objectivity in journalism, or objectivity in the sciences, or in philosophy, and so on, is none other than today's predominant form of ideology in the guise of anti- or non-ideology (i.e., it's ideology *tout court*), its primary injunction being: "Let's put aside our petty ideological struggles, our biases and subjective inclinations, and be as objective as possible here!"

27  Here one should recall the incident in 2000, when Robin Washington of the *Boston Herald* was suspended from his job for writing a series of articles about how customers of FleetBoston Financial Corporation were receiving a higher fee structure after BankBoston and Fleet Financial merged. FleetBoston Financial not only advertised with the *Herald* but had outstanding loans with the paper as well. Or perhaps one would like a more recent account, such as NPR's firing of Baltimore-based freelancer Lisa Simeone for supporting "Occupy DC," or the firing of Brooklyn-Based journalist Caitlin E. Curran from PRI's *The Takeaway*, for rallying in the streets while partaking in an Occupy protest. Or how about the fact that many Chinese journalists who report outside the official party line are being pulled from their positions. Such "divisive" events take place all over the world. There are numerous accounts; one just needs to take the time to do the research.

28  See Frank Smecker, http://archive.truthout.org/how-american-empire-project-trashed-a-planet-profit-while-selling-public-lies-an-interview-with-darh

29  Want more? On 26 October 2002, *Democracy Now!* travelled to Washington, D.C., to report on an anti-war rally that, according to estimates received from both local police and protest organizers, was comprised of anywhere between 100,000 and 200,000 protestors. The following day *The New York Times* reported that 'fewer than expected' showed up, and NPR reported 'fewer than 10,000 people' showed up. A few days later the *Times* ran another story, reporting 'The

demonstration on Saturday in Washington drew 100,000 by police estimates and 200,000 by organizers.' As Amy Goodman of *Democracy Now!* puts it, who do you believe, *The New York Times* or *The New York Times?!* Though this isn't anything new. As former member of British Parliament, Arthur Ponsonby, wrote in his book *Falsehood in War Time* (New York: E. P. Dutton & Co., Inc., 1928): 'There must have been more deliberate lying in the world from 1914 to 1918 than in any other period of the world's history.'

30   Smecker, http://archive.truthout.org/how-american-empire-project-trashed-a-planet-profit-while-selling-public-lies-an-interview-with-darh

31   Universals do not guarantee against their exceptions, "exceptions" being elements of irregularity and excess, which rupture the total unity of a given universal. For example, if I were assigned to come up with a list of vegetables, what am I to do when I arrive at the *tomato*? Whether I'm writing a list of vegetables, or of fruit, the tomato is a remainder, an element of irregular excess that can be placed under either "universal" category. The point is that there is always at least one exception that somehow eludes the universal it indexes (which is "inversely reflexive" of the fact that the universal itself can never coincide with *any* of its particulars; viz., the universal that is *"fruit"* is also its own particular: In the same sense that a kiwi cannot fully coincide with an orange, *fruit per se*, as a mere *category*, cannot fully coincide with any other particular fruit). To complex this even more, to borrow a quote from Claude Levi-Strauss, 'On intuitive grounds alone we might group onions, garlic, turnips, radishes and mustard together even though botany separates liliaceae and crucifers. In confirmation of the evidence of the senses, chemistry shows that these different families are united on another plane: they contain sulfur.' According to this,

sometimes even our intuition, accompliced by our senses, can point toward a different logical categorization other than what is "universally" given. The lesson here is: Universals are not perfectly closed orders; universals can collapse, or, they can develop into, other universals; and, no less important, there is always an exception to the universal which, paradoxically, indexes the universal it's an exception to, while simultaneously rupturing the universal's internal consistency.

32    Terry Eagleton, *Ideology an Introduction*, New York: Verso, 2007, p. xvi.

33    Jürgen Habermas, *Theory and Practice*, Boston: Beacon, 1973, p. 256.

34    See Charles B. Guignon's introduction to Dostoevsky's *The Grand Inquisitor*, Indianapolis: Hackett Publishing Company, 1993, pp. xxvi-vii.

35    Although Lacan himself arrived at this realization, as did Heidegger (evidenced by his later lectures that led up to his "The Question Concerning Technology"), one should also read Derrick Jensen's *The Culture of Make Believe*, Lewis Mumford's *The Myth of the Machine* (volumes I and II), Giorgio Agamben's *Homo Sacer*, and Zygmunt Bauman's *Modernity and the Holocaust*, for more in-depth analyses of industrial society and its modern matriculation towards what Derrick Jensen forewarns as "assembly-line mass murder."

36    ... and to borrow a quote from one of the post-Kantian, Hegel-hating philosophers of the *Vorstellung*, Schopenhauer—whose philosophical thought led him to posit the conjunction of the Kantian thing-in-itself with the will in ourselves (which, unbeknownst to him, brought him closer to Hegel than he would ever admittedly know): 'To truth only a brief celebration is allowed between the two long periods during which it is condemned as paradoxical,

or disparaged as trivial. The author of truth also usually meets with the former fate. But life is short, and truth works far and lives long: let us speak the truth.'

37   G.W.F. Hegel, *The Encyclopaedia Logic*, Indianapolis: Hackett Publishing Company, Inc., 1991, p. 83.

38   Here, what Hegel means to by "matter in-itself" is Kant's definition of "matter": 'that in the appearance which corresponds to sensation.' In other words, what this third significance of objectivity relates to—that which is separate from the "*matter* in-itself"—is the wholly immaterial realm of the Imaginary. Let's flesh this out a little more: If it's indeed the case that, as Kant posited, intuition is related directly to the object-Other—i.e., that which is separate from the cognitive subject though holds a relation to the subject's cognition insofar as the object is "given" to the subject by means of sensibility, intuition—then it must follow that the object is, nonetheless, somehow related to the cognitive subject. What is meant by this, is that the very *idea* of the object—*precisely as that*, as the idea *itself, which is separate from the object itself* (which, in effect, this separation between the idea-of-the-object and the object-itself gives rise to the very notion of the object *in-itself*, precisely as conjecture borne in upon the cognitive subject's mere intuition)—exists only as an immaterial entity of the mind, as an element of the Imaginary, which can only be accessed by the cognitive subject, thus confirming the subjective provenance of objectivity as such—*For is it not the case that one's personal intuition of something is first and foremost, save for all the Symbolic mediation, an individually private phenomenon, and thus not necessarily a universally public one?* That is to say, what is objective according to this third significance is, in fact, first, radically subjective. And no less important, what we're dealing with here is a *thing* of immateriality, a notion, *as* such, a thing of non-physical reality; a product of thought:

that which is separate not only from the object in relation to cognition, but separate from the "matter itself": that which is separate from 'that in appearance which corresponds to sensation': the *purely formal idea* of the object in-itself, an immaterial product of the mind which persists in the virtual world of the Imaginary.

39   Malcolm Bowie, *Lacan*, Cambridge, MA: Harvard University Press, 1991, p. 112.

40   For are we not alienated *first* from ourselves? We know so little about our own manifest character, our own outward appearance, which implies that we know so little about that which is within us that *appears*. We cannot truly experience, in the full meaning of that word, a perspective from outside ourselves; and we surely cannot see ourselves from outside ourselves, the way in which those with whom we are in relation see us, for we cannot see through the eyes, nor think through the mind, of another. This is what it means to posit the claim that "all worldviews (perspectives) are absolute, though *absolutely relative*." Could this possibly have any relation to what Hegel meant when he claimed that the Absolute begins with a radical loss? This particular absence of complete knowledge that is contained within knowledge itself—marked by our own absolute deficiency in terms of truly knowing a wholly other perspective, especially one that is aimed at our own selves—is a blind-spot as such, an enigmatic nothingness, a lack that exists at the very core of our Being and, at the core of our own respective, "absolute" worldviews. This kernel of nothing persists *within* all relations we hold, whether we're talking about our relation to another being, our relation to the world, even our relation to ourselves. Thus the claim that "only Nothing exists outside of relation" should be inverted: what is essentially "outside" is none other than the externalization of this internal void, whereby the object-

Other takes the place of this void, thereby constituting a developing-relation between subject and object.

41    Quotes taken from Lacan's essay "The Mirror Stage as Formative of the Function of the I as Revealed in Psychoanalytic Experience," in *Écrits*, New York: W.W. Norton & Company, 2006, p. 76. To be precise, the mirror stage, technically speaking, marks the moment when the young child first perceives him/herself as an object that can be viewed from "outside" him/herself. At this early period in the child's life (6-18 months), the advent of the mirror stage presents an image of "wholeness" to the child, which conflicts with the child's fragmented body, for the child still lacks coordination at this time despite the child's ability to recognize his/her own image. This, according to Lacan, gives rise to an aggressive duality between the subject and its image. The child begins to identify with his empirical, specular image (though no doubt it's a "false" image) as a means to reconcile this antagonism that results in the creation of the ego, the latter a product, an object, of an "original misconstruction" (*méconnaissance*). According to Lacan, the mirror stage marks the subject's alienation from itself.

42    Stephen Ross, "A Very Brief Introduction to Lacan," http://web.uvic.ca/~saross/lacan.html

43    As the late Otto Fenichel claims, all identifications with an object 'bear an archaic character': they display most if not all the aspects of this primary process. (See Otto Fenichel's essay "Identification", from *The Collected Papers of Otto Fenichel*, New York: W.W. Norton & Company, Inc., 1953, pp. 97-113). By means of the subject's desire to overcome its self-alienation, the subject's ego assumes the very place of the object(s) it identifies with, thereby effectuating a change in the object(s). Is this not an accurate definition for something that is "performative"? Such ideational activity, carried out

by the subject, *changes* its object. That is to say, one's perception of an object undoubtedly has an effect in and on the object: the way one perceives the external world and its entities shapes the way one behaves in the world and thus toward the entities in the world.

44 Rodolphe Gasche, *The Tain of the Mirror*, Cambridge, MA: Harvard University Press, 1987, pp. 201-2.

45 Lacan, *The Seminar of Jacques Lacan, Book XI*, New York: W.W. Norton, 1978, p. 224.

46 Alenka Zupančič, *The Shortest Shadow; Nietzsche's Philosophy of the Two*, Cambridge, MA: MIT Press, 2003, p. 105.

47 As Žižek points out in *The Parallax View*, what Lacan tried to conclude when in 'search of a point at which we enter the dimension of the "inhuman," a point at which "humanity" disintegrates,' is that: all that remains thereafter is a *pure* subject, emptied of all its substance. As Nietzsche claimed, what is "human, all too human" refers to the fact that people can sometimes be "inhuman." And we should not, as Žižek maintains, hesitate to apply this to politics itself; he writes: 'it's only too easy to dismiss the Nazis as inhuman and bestial—what if the problem with the Nazis was precisely that they remained "human, all too human?"' See Žižek, *The Parallax View*, Cambridge, MA: The MIT Press, 2009, p. 42.

48 And for the sake of clarity, in terms of the object-Other that "gives body to" the subject's lack, we are not talking about something other that is, in itself, "wholly" other. We are talking about something *other* that is in the Other, which is more than the Other itself (the *objet petit a*). The subject's notion of Self cannot *really* coincide, in the way that we are currently discussing that it does, with something that is purely other-in-itself, with something that is "wholly" other and purely independent of the subject; in such a case, the relation that subsists between the subject and his Self would

simply not be because it *cannot be as such*, for if the subject's Self were to be posited by and through something "wholly" other, by and through a thing *in-itself* and not by and through an object *for-the-subject*, we would then thereby lose the subject altogether in this fiercely-veritable contradiction—the subject would be retroactively cancelled; for we'd find that there would be no Self to be posited in the "first" place—since this Self would coincide not with the subject's notion, but with some thing in-itself that is wholly other than the subject! By this light, the subject's constitutive relation to an object-Other, by which and through which the subject acquires its notion of Self, is a relation to a "partial object," some *Other* thing that, caught within the gaze of the subject, returns the subject's gaze; it is something Other, as such, which has gone from being a thing *in-itself* to a thing *for-us*, i.e., a thing *for-the-subject*.

Here, one is goaded to wonder if the transformative procedure enacted by the subject's gaze which converts an object from an *in-itself* to a *for-us*—which immediately, and inevitably, results in the construction of what Quentin Meillassoux calls the "correlationist circle" ('the idea to which we only ever have access to the correlation between thinking and being')—is a sort of bulwark against the indelible potential of an obtrusion of the "great outdoors," the raw life-force itself; a flux of chaos comprised of effects isolated from any context whatsoever, which stretches into eternity outside the correlation between thought and Being. In a certain light, correlationism can be seen as a way for us to foreclose ourselves from any direct encounter with the Real. Preventing us from whirling astray into an infinite abyss devoid of necessity and symbolization, and thus destitute of meaning. A field of reality that not only precedes our existence, but that is also contemporaneous with, and succeeds, our existence: an abyssal raw-reality, radically contingent and aleatory, corybantic and chaotic, in which our very Being is revealed for what it may essentially, though remarkably be: unnecessary—*which provides the very wonder behind our lived experiences.*

That the "wholly" other—the noumenal thing in-itself—is, from the standpoint of correlationism, something that is not *for-us, not-given,* but that we can nonetheless *maintain the conceivability* of the wholly other even though we cannot *know* it—that we cannot gain any access to it though we can contemplate it in thought—implies that we can at least think the possibility of a reality that is not *given* to us, a realm of reality that we cannot directly access from within the correlationist circle. As such, it is a reality to which our *direc*t access is not necessary, for if it were necessary then a *direct* access to such a reality would be commonplace… Rather, time is our only access to it; the field of reality outside the relation between thought and Being *unfolds* for us; its infinity revealing itself not *directly,* but gradually, in its finite moments of which we are a part. (E.g., was it not only a matter of time before we were given access to a reality beyond that of the pre-Copernican universe?) And so if a direct access to the "great outdoors" is not necessary— if our relation to an infinitely larger field of reality, one which spans eternally beyond the given parameters of correlationism and thus eternally beyond our knowledge and understanding, is not essential to our lived experiences—then our very existence in reality per se is not necessary, but is rather radically contingent, precisely in the sense that there is absolutely nothing that necessitates our existence. Which is all the more reason to take our lives and the physical world they are situated in seriously.

49  To paraphrase Hegel, it is this cut in reality, the immateriality of pure ideation itself— the empty framework of thought as such that ruptures the inner consistency of the

materiality it mixes with—that engenders all phenomenally perceivable differences; a "tearing apart" of the world into discrete differences that, in effect, gives rise to its reassembly in the concrete universality we refer to as the "conscious Self," whose aim it is to encompass all the differences within this universal oneness as such. Can we not apply this to today's brain sciences? Take for example the function of "mirror neurons": they are responsive to both the subject's action and the object(s) of the subject's action; they provide *for the subject* "action-understanding," which, far from representing the inputs that trigger their firing as such, these neurons represent none other than the Self (qua object)—that being the very locus of the subject around which all activity takes place: a void: the lack of Self which gives rise to the Self as such! Thus the relationship between the subject's actions and the latter's objects is essentially based in a radical non-relationship, one that results in the production of the Self-that-relates/acts. Here, the subject's act of referring/relating to the objects "out there" is merely reflexive of the sense of Self that is created through this very activity, which has its basis in a radical lack of Self, a cut in reality as such! Can we not claim, then, that, For Hegel, the reason why universality is to be seen as a negative is not because concrete universality is some "monism" that encompasses nothing but all differences; but rather: Hegel's "monad" is something that, *within its "total" enclosure, paradoxically contains both nothing (its original loss, the initial "cut" in reality), and the perceived objective differences effectuated by this cut as such.* And it is this exceptional element, the element of a radical lack, a radical negativity that ruptures the wholeness of any and all concrete universality which, from within its own constitution, impedes the universal as such from ever "totally" encompassing anything and everything. Hegel's system is *not* a vicious "monism" but rather a vicious "black hole"—a generative void as such!

50   Judith Butler, *Bodies that Matter: On the Discursive Limits of "Sex,"* New York: Routledge, 1993, p. 152.

51   *Ibid.*

52   Žižek, *For They Know Not What They Do*, p. 59.

53   Lacan, *Book XI*, p. 106.

54   As Vighi calls to mind, one should note that Marx's theories were precipitated by the *idea* that humans 'act in full consciousness of themselves' (determined by material conditions in reality), and that such conscious motivations drive and determine historical progress. Though, as Lacan pointed out, not only was there a good deal of absence regarding psychological factors in Marx's work, but, more importantly, 'the unconscious origin and weight of any knowledge' was missing from Marx's theories as well. And as Vighi claims, one should be mindful of this 'when attempting to resurrect Marx in the XXI century.' Early on, in fact, in *The German Ideology*, Marx writes:

Men can be distinguished from animals by consciousness [...] They begin to distinguish themselves from animals as soon as they begin to *produce* their means of subsistence, a step which is conditioned by their physical organization. By producing their means of subsistence men are indirectly producing their actual material life [...] This mode of production must not be considered simply as being the reproduction of the physical existence of the individuals. Rather it is a definite form of expressing their life, a definite *mode of life* on their part. As individuals express their life, so they are. What they are, therefore, coincides with their production, both with *what* they produce and with *how* they produce. The nature of individuals thus depends on the material conditions determining their production.

What Marx somehow neglects to ask, however, is *why* men produce? And more importantly, *why* do men produce *what* they produce in the manner of *how* they produce it? Marx is correct in claiming that the nature of individuals, on the one hand, *does* depend on the "material conditions" that determine production; but the nature of individuals also depends on *how* one imagines, that is, *thinks of*, what to do with one's material conditions that are laid out in front of him or her. Modes of production are therefore *decided* upon, which means there is a level of conceptualization involved just as well. Not a single materialist categorization and/or postulate can be articulated let alone represented in a field of discourse, in order to formulate divisions of labor, without the immaterial force of human Spirit playing its integral part. If it were not for the immaterial realm of Spirit's *place* (i.e. the realm of the concept, idea, etc.), then the act of *distinguishing* (the latter being the "spiritual" gesture which allows for all this to even take place) would cease to be, and we would be without any idealizing power whatsoever to express ourselves, which would mean that the material life we produce for the sake of expression would come to a standstill, for we would have no *idea* about what to produce out of the materials laid out in front of us. It would be just as naïve to assume that, say, Donatello expressed himself with his production of the *Bronze David* solely through a thoughtless, stupid arrangement of the inert materials he employed, without any idea *beforehand* of how to arrange said materials, and that that would be that; for one would, with much error, be glossing over the important fact that the *idea* behind such a sculpture was an antecedent motivational force behind its production, even if such an idea was merely a crude notion of what to do with the materials at hand.

55   This reading of Deleuze, minus my parenthetical remarks, is

borrowed from Žižek, in *Organs Without Bodies: On Deleuze and Consequences*, New York: Routledge, 2004, p. 29.

56　Perhaps the mystery of consciousness is not hinged on complexity but rather, what if it's a much different beast altogether? The enigmatic aspect of consciousness is its primary function: the simplification of complexity. Of course there is a direct relationship between cognition and the involved neuronal processes in the brain. But the limiting problem still plaguing cognitivism is this: we're not ever conscious of the complexity of non-conscious matter and the mechanical processes involved in their production of consciousness; we're not aware of our own neural activity, we don't experience nerve impulses, and so on. What we do experience is a derivative of these intricacies of matter and forces. And does not consciousness merely serve to simplify such complexity? And *that* is the unsolved mystery of consciousness: How is it that awareness is always aimed at, is always about—for the sake of simplifying, giving reason to—something *other*, as if consciousness is a function of its own accord as something that exists separate from, *as other to*, the inert matter with which it is inextricably involved? As Žižek demands—why awareness? What's its function? Why is it, that, the material processes of neuronal activity are not enough on their own? Why the addendum, why awareness, why not just the simple mechanics of neuronal processes?

57　Žižek, *Organs Without Bodies*, p. 29.

58　*Ibid.*, p. 30, FN 37.

59　Žižek, *The Parallax View*, p. 79.

60　Lacan, *Écrits*, New York: W.W. Norton & Company, 2006, p. 694.

61　Lacan, *Book XI*, p. 141.

62　*Ibid.*, p. 236.

63　Žižek, *For They Know Not What They Do*, p. 50.

64    Bertrand Russell, *A History of Western Philosophy*, New York: Clarion, 1967, p. 830.

65    *Ibid.*

66    This "world-without-us" perspective, however, delineates the fundamental subjective position of fantasy: 'to be reduced to a gaze observing the world in the subject's non-existence.' See, Žižek, *Living in the End Times*, p. 81.

67    Jacques Alain Miller, "Suture: (elements of the logic of the signifier)," http://www.lacan.com/symptom8_articles/miller 8.html

68    Badiou, *Being and Event*, New York: Continuum, 2005, pp. 29-35.

69    *Ibid.*, p. 34.

70    *Ibid.*

71    J.A. Miller, "Suture: (elements of the logic of the signifier)."

72    Žižek writes: 'The picture of the Hegelian system as a closed whole which assigns its proper place to every partial moment is therefore deeply misleading. Every partial moment is, so to speak, "truncated from within," it cannot ever fully become "itself," it cannot ever reach "its own place," it is marked with an inherent impediment, and *it is this impediment which "sets in motion"* [emphasis mine] the dialectical development. The "One" of Hegel's "monism" is thus not the One of an Identity encompassing all differences, but rather a paradoxical "One" of radical negativity which forever blocks the fulfillment of any positive identity.' See, Žižek, *For They Know Not What They Do*, pp. 68-9.

73    McGowan, "Maternity Divided: *Avatar* and the enjoyment of nature," http://www.ejumpcut.org/archive/jc52.2010/mcGo wanAvatar/

74    Bowie, *Lacan*, p. 194.

75    Here, one should recall the scene from Lasse Hallström's film adaptation of John Irving's *The Cider House Rules*, in which Homer (played by Tobey Maguire) projects his gaze

onto Wally Worthington (Paul Rudd) from an upstairs window of the orphanage. Worthington, who is waiting for his girlfriend Candy (Charlize Theron), who is inside receiving an abortion from the orphanage's paternal caretaker, is standing beside his car in the driveway outside the orphanage. Homer watches Worthington from the window above. The camera focuses first on Homer, and then shifts its focus to Worthington in the same shot, as if from the vantage point of Homer's view of Worthington through the window. All that changes is the focus. It is as if the shot is to suggest that Homer, for a moment, is watching through this window his dreams materialize; it is, as if, in this moment, Homer *is* Worthington, as if Homer is watching himself in another reality, not *through* the window but *in the window frame itself*, as if the window is a screen upon which Homer is watching himself in another life, one in which his desire to leave the orphanage is given body and animation in the reality of another who is caught in his gaze. Here, Homer has indeed "elevated" reality to that "magic" level upon which his "dreams are projected."

One should also recall the 1994 film *Sirens*. Set in Australia during the period between WWI and WWII, it is essentially a story about the struggle between desire and inhibition, about exploring the passions, the sensual, and the temptation to lessen one's reservations. At any rate, there is a moment in the film when the artist Norman (played by Sam Neill) and his family watch—along with their guests Tony (a priest played by Hugh Grant) and his wife Estella (Tara Fitzgerald)—Norman's models as they act out a performance art routine on and around a swing-set in Norman's backyard in the middle of the night. Here, the viewer bears witness to the very way in which, effectuated by one's desires as they are staged within the fantasy, reality is elevated, as it were, to that "magic" level of dreams. The models, despite not really floating in mid air, appear to their spectators *as if* they really do! It is not: Those bearing witness to the models' performance are watching real women swing on swings, pretending to be fairies, or sirens—on the contrary: Those watching the performance are literally watching their own desires "play and dance" across their erected fantasy screen: e.g., Sam Neill's character watches on with lustful eyes, and there we see staged the adult fantasy; while his daughter, standing right beside him, giggles at the mere innocent "magic" of it all, portraying the child's fantasy of whimsical enchantment.

76  Kojève, *Introduction to the Reading of Hegel*, p. 37.

77  *Ibid.*

78  While we're tarrying the theme of desire here, it should be made clear that desire never corresponds to a single object; rather, desire denotes a multitude of heterogeneous desires (which are ultimately all cathected into a single object cause of desire, the Lacanian *objet a*), which leaves the subject not only wondering what desire he should choose, but what desire he should desire! Thus desire, as such, is essentially empty, unfulfilled, its satisfaction unknown; it is structured around a fundamental *lack*. The *objet a* is that which fills the place of this void, imbuing object after object with the "mysterious" cause of desire, attempting to fulfill and thereby eradicate the desire as such; for to sustain a desire is to defer its satisfaction. No less important, it is often the case that the subject's desire is not simply *his* or *her* desire, but rather: it is the desire of the Other: That is to say, the subject desires to know what others want from him/her, as in: "What sort of 'object' am I to others?" And fantasy, the tapestry of social narratives, aims to answer these questions. As playwright Peter Shaffer put it: Into these theatrical spaces we contrive, 'flows the communal imagination of audience.'

79   Kojève, *Introduction to the Reading of Hegel*, p. 37.

80   Žižek, "Christ, Hegel, Wagner," *International Journal of Žižek Studies*, see: http://www.lacan.com/zizdigitowag.html

81   E.g., to perceive something as an object is to treat and make oneself as an object: Objectivity is a formal order of our lived experience, and thereby a way to "look into oneself." As such, it is the mode in which we can construct a concept of ourselves in order to access a better understanding of ourselves, and thereby acquire our subjectivity: *Our subjectivity comes from objectivity: The subject creates the objectivity that, in a chiasmic way, gives back to the subject his or her subjectivity. This is why it's important to situate objectivity at the level of ideology: objectivity, too, interpellates the subject.* Do we not find Nietzsche expounding on this when he wrote: 'There is *only* a perspective seeing, *only* a perspective "knowing"; and the *more* affects we allow to speak about one thing, the *more* eyes, different eyes, we can use to observe one thing, the more complete will our "concept" of this thing, our "objectivity" be.' Objectivity is essentially self-reflective of the subject being objective: What is being disclosed through an act of intellectual objectivity is not some "objective truth" about something being looked at "objectively"; on the contrary, such an act of intellectual objectivity discloses a certain truth about the very subject that is being objective—the nature of the subject's desire (to know), and the subject's socio-Symbolic situation, which exerts a certain influence on the subject's perception of—i.e., his "objective" take on—the world.

82   In other words, consciousness entails much more than one's awareness of Self. For Kant (as for Žižek), albeit the conscious Self (as in, e.g., "I think") is able to coexist with the subject's perceptions, this does not mean that the Self itself is a "substantial object." The perceiving subject cannot, in point of fact, see *itself* seeing, Žižek notes, 'any

more than a person can jump over his/her own shadow.' When the subject sees itself in a self-reflective moment, it does not see itself as a subject but as another represented object: what Kant calls the "empirical self," or what Žižek and Lacan refer to as the "Self" (versus the subject). The subject knows that it is something, Žižek and Lacan argue, but it does not, and cannot, ever know what kind of Thing it is "in the Real." And this is why the subject desires its identity within a Symbolic order, within its social and political life. The subject has a desire to know what it is, and it is only in the Symbolic order, in which meaning is established and preserved, that the subject is able to construct its "meaningful" identity, and know itself only *as such*. And ideology functions like a sort of "external organ" of the subject, its purpose is to aid the subject with regard to knowing what to desire and, how to desire, within the subject's given social arrangements, within the very place the subject has come to *be*.

One should also note that there is, in a sense, a sort of enantiomorphic (chiral) shift that occurs in active consciousness itself; a shift that's determinate moment occurs within the locus of the subject's unconscious, to and for the subject; viz., one's awareness of Self is reflected back in an asymmetrical "mirrored" way: Awareness of Self, while rooted in the subject, shifts toward, *and becomes*, awareness of an object of desire, *decentering the subject as such*. It is as if consciousness travels along a path that is congruent with the topology of the Möbius strip (e.g., if a line is drawn starting from the seam, and travels down along the middle of the strip, the line will eventually meet back at the seam but at the other side). By the time consciousness "arrives at its destination" it has been inverted from (un)conscious-awareness-of-one's-Self to conscious-desire-of-an-object: viz., the determination of Self culminates in its self-realization through an inversion in its mirror opposite, in its desired object. Thus Self and desire are mirrored images of each other, but they are not symmetrical with each other. Hence Hegel's claim that, "self-Consciousness *is* Desire."

What one should take away from all this, however, is the fact that the Self is *not* the subject. The proper dimension of the subject is "reflected" in that miniscule blemish, so to speak, on the "mirror" itself, that locus of nothingness which counts for *something*, in which the shift from awareness of Self to awareness of desire occurs: E.g., "I know that I desire such and such objects, but I do not recognize all of myself in these objects of my desire." A pure reflection in this capacity always "fails." As Žižek writes on page 89 in *For they know not what they do*: 'the subject always encounters in a mirror some dark spot, a point which does not return him his mirror-picture'—which is to say, the subject cannot seem to fully recognize itself in its mirror image. And it is precisely this 'point of "absolute strangeness" [when the subject realizes that there is something in the reflection that can never give back to him/her his mirror-picture] that the subject is inscribed into the picture' (*Ibid.*). Perhaps a persuasive example of this is when one sees oneself in a video-recording, or when one hears their voice on a sound-recording; the recording seems to miss some minimal, though fundamental speck of the subject, marked by a moment of disbelief in such a reflection of one's Self: "That's not how I really appear in the world to others, is it?" or, "That's not how I really sound, is it?" This strange distortion, however, is what is *constitutive* of the subject. The subject's mirror image, writes Žižek, 'contains a "pathological" stain—the subject is correlative to this stain.' That is to say, there is, always, a small spot of subjective "residue" that distorts any objective image caught within the range of the subject's perception, which escapes the grasp of the reflection itself; which means that the objective image, the very image to which one cannot fully relate, *is* the objective correlate of the generative void that is none other than the locus of the unconscious of the subject: that which insists on defining the subject.

What we are dealing with here is the way in which, unaware to the subject itself, the subject's desires become transmogrified, "trans-coded", into the very objects of the subject's perception and thoughts, becoming external (Other) points of subjective reference. This is precisely where the unconscious makes its presence felt, though only in the most oblique way. As Freud, and then later Lacan, wrote: the subject is split between a conscious side (where things in the mind are readily accessible) and an unconscious side (a series of persistent drives and forces that are not consciously accessible). The subject itself, however, is in part a collection of memories, desires, and so on; a *subjective set* as such. Some memories and desires do not require any censoring, while others definitely do (e.g., trauma, certain violent and/or sexual desires, any other primal desire requiring censorship, and so on). When Lacan claimed that the unconscious is structured like a language, and to be more on point here, when he claimed that "metaphor" (the substitution of a word for an entirely other word to make an implicit comparison) and "metonymy" (replacing the name of one thing with the name of something else closely associated with it), both correspond to the workings of the unconscious; I believe this should be read quite literally, and, to be joyously unorthodox here, we should read this in an atypical way (while nonetheless retaining Lacan's original formulation, too): Because the subject is in part a collection of desires and memories, and because some of these desires and memories require censorship while others do not, the function of both "metonymy" and "metaphor" are ways for the unconscious to organize and operationalize this entire subjective set as such. Let's say, for example, that person A has a sexual desire that, in a normative sense, may be frowned upon or considered to be unconventional; for example, maybe person A has a desire to have sex with the wife of another man, or with a (of-age) babysitter, or maybe something more uncommon, like "kick-fucking." Whatever activity it is it's not entirely illicit (well…that depends on what US state you may live in), it's just that, this activity is something considered by the social majority as not acceptable for open discussion and/or public performance, not to be disclosed in a public discourse and/or setting. However, through "metonymy," which corresponds to "displacement," person A can seek out things in the world that may be an aspect of, associated with, such a desire, which can substitute for this desire (e.g., a porno movie, or a magazine, and so on). But each object of desire is never enough in itself, since person A is not hitting his or her desire head-on. (Pun not intended for the male side of things here…) Therefore, the subject's desire defers from one object to the next, from one porno film or magazine to another, and on and on. But at least person A's desire is somewhat out of the bag, being recognized as such. On the other hand, with "metaphor" we are dealing with "condensation," a function of repression through which 'the repressed returns in hidden ways': Let's say person A has a primal desire that must be repressed, censored, for if he or she were to attempt to satisfy this desire one would cause much harm to others and potentially to oneself. So, just like the function of metaphor in language, there exist things in the world that reflect this desire, but these correlative things are not related in any immediate direct way, shape, or form to the original "transgressive" desire. And thus this desire is repressed by it being muted by a representation that bears no direct resemblance to it whatsoever, and it therefore remains disavowed as such, (re)appearing only in the capacity of "symptom." One's symptom is thereby "created" in order to bring about, for oneself, certain satisfactions. Freud writes: 'the repressed desire continues to exist in the unconscious; it is on watch constantly for an opportunity to make itself known and it soon comes back into consciousness [for it has traveled along that Möbius path, no?], but in a disguise that makes it impossible to recognize; in other words, the repressed thought is replaced in consciousness by another that acts as its surrogate, its *Ersatz...*' And so it is through the functions of these "axes of language," through "metaphor" and "metonymy," that the entire subjective set becomes operationalized for the sake of ordering its battery of desires and memories for the subject. The compelling question is: who or what is doing the ordering? And there we have the unconscious, what Lacan described as the 'field which, for us, offers itself to the conquest of the subject.' For the subject is never conscious of this 'central mechanism that intervenes' as such, but is only conscious of the results of its work: which are the elements of the subjective set—*as they are "trans-coded" into an objective reality, to be experienced and perceived for the purpose of identifying the subject's Self and the latter's "meaningful" place in the Symbolic order.*

83  See: http://www.bellona.org/articles/articles_2012/Russia _reveals_dumps

84  As Lacan once put it, 'In the beginning, there was not origin. There was the place': that *place we have come to.*

85  Žižek, "Christ, Hegel, Wagner."

86 There's a burgeoning theory that consciousness emerged as the result of a glitch in reality itself, when there was a primordial failure in the standard operating procedure of

things. For example, when I go for a walk outside, if it's a long walk, I'm not fully aware of the movement of my legs, the placement of my feet, swinging of arms, and so on, these things sort of happen automatically. But if I make a mistake, like, e.g., if I trip over something, or if I misstep, or whatever, if there is an unforeseen failure, suddenly my attention, my awareness, is all over this failure: *I become fully conscious of it*. Thus consciousness may be the result of an early, primordial failure, an intervention of some *other* agency whose sole function is to immediately recognize this contingent failure, and to simplify it in order to rectify it.

87  Žižek, *For They Know Not What They Do*, p. 150.

88  *Ibid.*, p. 151.

89  *Ibid.*, pp. 153-4.

90  And to push this idea further, as Žižek writes on page 152 in *For they know not what they do*, the "factual" elements that comprise "objective certainty" form 'self-referring symbolic vicious circles maintaining an unnameable distance from the Real.' Here we should turn to an example that shall fully elucidate that which was just stated. Wittgenstein writes in *Philosophical Investigations*, para. 201: '[N]o course of action can be determined by a rule, because every course of action can be made out to accord with the rule.' And in *For they know not what they do*, on page 152, Žižek summarizes/interprets this claim as: '[E]very course of action that appears to infringe [upon] the established set of rules can retroactively be interpreted as an action in accordance with another set of rules.' In other words, as Žižek illustrates by way of example, drawing from Saul Kripke's analysis of this particular detail in Wittgenstein's *Philosophical Investigations*, we are all familiar with the arithmetical function of addition indicated by the word "plus." But let's say that I interact with someone whom I've never met before, someone who is from an entirely different way of

life than mine. This someone shows me *"Math."* He writes out on a sheet of paper: 4 + 8 = 12. And I immediately reject this, scratching it out, writing beneath it, pointing to it, all the while thinking *No, no, no...* 4 + 8 = 57. After which the other person looks at me with circumflexed eyebrows, exclaiming: "You made a mistake." And then it dawns on me—there was no mistake made. All I did was simply follow *another rule.* For me "plus" has always meant *"quus,"* that's what I've been taught, and 4 + 8 = 57 is the correct way to compute 4 *"quus"* 8.

The crux of this scenario is as follows. What is assumed to constitute a given number ('4' in my world may mean something entirely different than '4' in your world; after all, are not numbers just mere bundles of innumerable qualities?), and, what is designated as an axiom for computing such given numbers via a specific relationship— which, in effect, determines the output (dynamic change) the two numbers will effectuate when placed in such a relation—*obviously may vary from one form of life to another.* Each form of life relies on different respective sets of "objective certainties," rules, which are necessary for maintaining the very internal consistency that each set of "objective certainties," rules, gives rise to—it truly is as Žižek claims: a "self-referring symbolic circle" aimed at preventing an encounter with pure, absolute, raw reality. And it really is as if each rule floats upon "nothing," under-girded by nothing else other than a conjoined socio-historical effort, on behalf of all who partake in the given pertinent "life-form," to *believe* that the given rules make a certain sense out of an original non-sense; which is nonetheless necessary for the very sake of the given "life-form's" consistency. By these lights, mathematics seems to be treated, in a certain sense, as a "last resort": What I mean by this, is that math is often seen as a sort of big Other insurance against an actual loss of some supreme big Other; e.g., "If language were to fail, at least we would still have math, and nothing can fuck with the certainty of numbers…" Which is to say: the manipulation of numbers, mathematics, *is often conceived as the ultimate big Other contingency plan!* (Of course, however, as Lacan once said: 'You cannot teach a course in mathematics using only letters on the board. It is always necessary to speak an ordinary language that is understood').

At the very core of our socio-Symbolic reality there belongs an irreducible and enduring element of fideism to any objective certainty, one that is necessarily disavowed lest the whole thing were to fray apart in consequence to wholesale disbelief. That is to say, within—though concealed by—the illusion of objective certainty, there is only radical contingency and amorphous particularity; a pure multiform flow of raw life, inconsistencies and all. Our endeavors to mathematize and axiomize reality as such, to symbolize reality, indicates that we are not just capable of, but *desire* to, establish patterns within this "multiform flow" of raw reality. And we are thus able to construct (retroactively) presuppositions from these perceived patterns, which thereby serve to establish and maintain the internal consistency, the structural consistency, of a given form of life. And at the most radical level, we do this on faith alone. This is how we are able to structure consistency out of inconsistency. Meaning from non-meaning.

But this perceived frequency of patterns—which gives rise to our ability to mathematize reality, serialize it, structure it, and so on—does not fully insulate the "total" consistency of such patterns from an encounter with an absolute, non-symbolized reality. That is to say, ruptures of inconsistency are not just prone to happen—*ruptures as such happen. All the time.* The Real cuts through because it's always-already there *within* any order of consistency. And consistency is merely a kind of illusion, one that envelops the hard kernel of raw reality that is situated deep within the illusion itself. When we do encounter a moment of inconsistency, after such an encounter we "retroactively posit a presupposition," which serves to put this inconsistency into its "meaningful" and proper Symbolic place within the pre-established set of patterns we all agree to believe exist. (Do we not sense the presence of a "parental" agencies here?!) However, it is because the Real always returns, as an indivisible remainder to any act of ordering—it is *precisely* on account of this paradoxical certainty—that we repeat with so much painstaking effort our fevered insistence for symbolic mediation as such. For the Real, in all of its modalities, as an "abyssal vortex" that disrupts any and all consistency, is, at the same, the "generative void" which precipitates the very *need* for consistency. Without out any symbolic mediation, we would face the "loss of reality": a full-on exposure to the radical contingency of raw reality. It is by dint of this reason alone, that mathematics and language are partly essential to the wellbeing of humanity.

And yet there is another way to read into all this. If we are "programmed," that is, taught, to only recognize "*plus*" as a proper and meaningful expression of a devised axiom, and see "*quus*" as a mistake or as a "slip"—then what happens to the very sense, the very "meaning-to-be-made," behind that which is being expressed by "*quus*," especially if "*quus*" is something that is being expressed repeatedly? We could of course dismiss it as nonsense, but perhaps that would be ignorant. What if "*quus*" applies to an entire set of other rules, a set of rules that can be retroactively posited as being that which determines the very "meaning" of "*quus*"? Is this not a great example of the "temporal-loop" movement through which the expression of necessity arises out of pure contingency? In terms of psychoanalysis, writes Žižek, 'Is not the aim of interpretation precisely to discern a rule followed unknowingly where "common sense" sees nothing but meaningless chaos—*in other words, to discern "quus" where "common sense" sees a simple mistake, a simple failure of our effort to follow "plus"?'* The other question that should then be asked is—what is this hidden rule that is "followed unknowingly," 'the rule that will retroactively confer meaning and consistency upon our slips....'? And lastly, to push the envelope further, who is it, or what is it, that, *from within oneself*, can imply sense that oneself is not fully aware of? As Lacan writes in *Book XI* page 25: 'There, something other demands to be realized—which appears as intentional of course, but of a strange temporality.' Are we not dealing here with the very punctiform nucleus that must be, as Lacan writes, 'designated as belonging to the real—the real in so far as the identity of perception is its rule'? That is to say, when we finally perceive *"quus"* and give to it the recognition it desires, when we realize that the function of *"quus"* can indeed be axiomized, that we can fashion a rule to which we can apply *"quus"* and thereby make sense of the "message" it insists on conveying, that it can be inscribed into our Symbolic order and thereafter *perceived* as something determinate as such, only then can we say that we had come upon, in a very fleeting moment, what Lacan calls *"tuché"*: an encounter with the Real. That is to say, we were given a glimpse of that sea of contingency out of which *"quus"* arose: the very "generative void" from which subjective Spirit emanates and "retroactively posits the presuppositions" that are necessary for structuring symbolic consistency out of an inconsistent and multiform flow of radical fortuity.

In other words, beneath the rarefied strata of "objective certainty," and beneath the very bedrock of our way of life, contained deep within is a beautiful, though dizzying abyss of raw reality. It really is, *as if,* we stand upon thin air. And from this abyss of radical contingency arises necessity—for, if we were not to *find* any stable ground to stand upon, and/or if we were not able to *construct* any stable ground to stand upon, we would thus fall down deeply, back into the caprice of this complete unknowingness and amorphous particularity, submerged into a realm in which our identity would be, as it always-already has been, as certain as the ground upon which we stand. Which is to say, Life per se is aleatory, and therefore it can accord to any set of rules, insofar as there is an illusion of consistency to the rule itself, an illusion that is structured and maintained by the very rule that gives rise to its own consistency. The bedrock beneath our very way of life—that which gives rise to all the ways in which we conceive of and thus perceive the world— is structured like a fantasy. And the structure works, because we take a leap of faith, because we believe it works, because we desire it to work. It must work, we tell ourselves, simply because it must—for here I am, and there you are!

91  This "other space" is what Freud designated as the locus of the unconscious, to which he referred as "another scene," borrowing this term from experimental psychologist Gustav Fechner.

92  Kojève, *Introduction to the Reading of Hegel,* p. 36.

93  Žižek, *The Sublime Object of Ideology,* New York: Verso, 2008, pp. 11-14.

94  Lacan, *Écrits,* p. 458.

95  Žižek, *The Sublime Object of Ideology,* pp. 11-14.

96  Søren Kierkegaard, *Concluding Unscientific Postscript,* Princeton: Princeton University Press, 1968, p. 279. One should keep in mind that the Hegel which Kierkegaard was opposing was the late Hegel, the "Hegel of 1827." Kierkegaard once made the claim that Hegel's philosophy, a

site in which all historical antitheses can be overcome, was a "palace of ideas," that, as such, as Kierkegaard put it, all socio-historical antagonisms, according to Hegel's dialectic, are overcome *only in thought,* and that mere thought is not sufficient on its own to enable one to overcome the contradictions one must deal with. But can we not scratch our heads here and wonder why Kierkegaard decided to gloss over the *motivational* force of ideas—that ideas, thought itself, have real motivating power over its subjects? Hegel even writes to this effect in his preface to *Philosophy of Right,* when he averred that Plato's genius was 'proved by the fact that the principle on which the distinctive character of his Idea of the state turns [see Plato's *The Republic*] is precisely the pivot on which the impending world revolution turned at that time'—this "impending world revolution" is to be referred to as the "Christian revelation": that moral worth pivots not just on the fulfillment of the law, but on the total conscientious acceptance of the law. The point here is that, such an Idea had *real* motivational force in and on the lives of people.

97  *Ibid.,* p. 272.

98  Žižek, *The Parallax View,* p. 78.

99  Here, we should draw attention to the fact that Kierkegaard, unaware to himself, reaffirmed the very Hegelianism he attempted to thwart: In his book *Repetition: An Essay in Experimental Psychology,* he writes: 'the Greek reflection upon the concept of κένωσις which corresponds to the modern category of transition deserves the utmost attention. The dialectic of repetition is easy; for what is repeated has been, otherwise it could not be repeated, but precisely the fact that is has been gives to repetition the character of novelty. When the Greeks said that all knowledge is recollection they affirmed that all that is has been; when one says that life is a repetition one affirms that

existence which has been now becomes. When one does not possess the categories of recollection or of repetition the whole of life is resolved into a void and empty noise [...] repetition is the solution contained in every ethical view, repetition is a *conditio sine qua non* of every dogmatic problem.' (Kierkegaard, *Repetition: An Essay in Experimental Psychology*, New York: Harper Torchbooks, 1964, pp. 52-3.)

100  See Žižek's foreword to Alenka Zupančič's *Ethics of the Real: Kant and Lacan*, New York: Verso, 2011, p. viii.

101  *Ibid.*

102  Here one should recall the line from Oscar Wilde's *Dorian Gray*, in which Sybil Vane tells her mom that she loves Dorian 'because he is like what Love himself should be.' But Sybil isn't in love with Dorian Gray; on the contrary, she's in love with a specific image of Dorian Gray, one that, for her, reflects her heart's desire. That is to say, she doesn't "see" him, Dorian; she is, so to speak, seeing a reflection of herself in his image without recognizing herself in this image. It's as if her desires and passions are distorting reality itself, as if they have transformed Dorian Gray from a self-standing subject and into a representation of her ideal of love, through which Dorian himself takes the backseat while her desire calls all the shots.

103  See, Žižek, "With or Without Passion; What's Wrong with Fundamentalism?": *Lacanian Ink*, http://www.lacan.com /zizpassion.htm

     Also, one should bear all this in mind when Lacan writes that, 'if there is one domain in which, in discourse, deception has some chance of success, it is certainly love that provides its model [...] In persuading the other that he has that which may complement us, we assure ourselves of being able to continue to misunderstand precisely what we lack.' In other words, one's ideal of love serves to replace, in the form of concealment, one's fundamental lack: the preontic void itself.

104 Žižek, *For They Know Not What They Do*, p. 10.

105 Lacan, *Book XX: On Feminine Sexuality, the Limits of Love and Knowledge, 1972-1973*, New York: W.W. Norton & Company, 1998, p. 81.

106 Terry Winograd and Fernando Flores, *Understanding Computers and Cognition*, New York: Addison-Wesley, 1991, p. 113.

107 Žižek, *The Sublime Object of Ideology*, p. 113.

108 *Ibid.*

109 And yes, it can be said that, in a certain sense, any entity under scrutiny gives itself over to its notion in objectivity: the entity qua object reveals its essence in its appearance, revealing its implicit knowledge-to-be-gained explicitly in its notion and then its concept, a concept that develops a network of knowledge commensurate with the unfolding appearance of the object. But eventually, this knowledge becomes *Absolute*, precisely in the sense that, as Žižek puts it, 'in the final moment of this process, when "consciousness" purifies itself of every presupposition of a positive being,' when consciousness ceases to be, knowledge reaches its terminal moment in which it coincides with its radical, original loss, in which it 'coincides with pure nothingness.' See Žižek, *For They Know Not What They Do*, p. 67.

110 Zupančič, *The Shortest Shadow*, pp. 15-16.

111 *Ibid.*, pp. 119-20.

112 Lacan, *The Seminar of Jacques Lacan, Book I*, Cambridge: Cambridge University Press, 1988, pp. 242-3.

113 See Ray Tallis, "Consciousness is not in the Brain": http://www.wakingtimes.com/2012/10/13/consciousness-is-not-in-the-brain/

114 *Ibid.*

115 See: http://www.hungerfreevt.org/learn/what-is-the-issue

116 Hegel, *The Encyclopaedia Logic*, p. 85.

117 To relate objectivity to ideology, here one should note that, on the one hand, like objectivity, all ideological formations serve to mask some sort of lack, some sort of "failure." Though on the other hand, it is this failure, this lack, that is also simultaneously *constitutive of* ideology, of objectivity, since it is none other than the supportive "plinth" upon which all fantasies (ideologies) are erected and rest for their time being. Confront this lack, and one can collapse altogether, for better (*or* for worse), the ideological structure it supports, thereby freeing oneself from its grasp. Though once one finds oneself "outside" of an ideology, one is, if not already situated back within, already inexorably on the move toward another ideology.

118 Lacan, *Speech and Language in Psychoanalysis*, Baltimore: Johns Hopkins University Press, 1991, p. 98, FN 23.

119 Hegel, *The Encyclopaedia Logic*, p. 273.

120 Lacan, *Book XI*, p. 30.

121 Žižek, *Living in the End Times*, p. 231.

122 Lacan, "L'Instance de la letter dans l'inconscient ou La Raison depuis Freud," *La Pschanalyse*, III (May, 1957), pp. 69-70.

123 Desire qua Desire is a 'revealed nothingness, an unreal emptiness' at the base of the subject. This emptiness acquires its positive content by means of the subject focusing his/her awareness upon an object in the external world, thereby transforming the said object into gaze, into a moment of the subject's Self, into a "non-I", an object that is reflexive of the subject's desire as such.

124 Hegel, *Jenaer Realphilosophie*, 1805.

125 As Lacan explained, desire is indestructible insofar as it's sustained as an unsatisfied desire. Representation functions in quite the same way (perhaps because it's borne in upon the *desire* to know): If representation were to be precise, if it

could actually meet the expectations of its very function, if it could "attain itself" in such a capacity that it perfectly represented the very thing being (re)presented, it would, without question, include the original lack of knowledge of this thing—that which hales forth the very need for representation in the first place. But here we have arrived at an impasse: for, is it not the case that such a precise representation would arrive at its own lack of ontological consistency, whereby the very *raison d'être* of representation would obliterate itself in its confrontation with its own radical lack and thereby vanish upon encountering its own non-existence as such? In this case, representation would thus cease to be or perhaps would never have been in the first place. Therefore, representation can exist only as imprecise.

126 Hegel, *The Encyclopaedia Logic*, pp. 131-2. There is a difference between the logic of symbols and the logic of things. Moreover, "paradox", per se, is none other than the inherent limit of symbolic logic: this inherent limit of symbolic logic is that which encumbers total universalization from within; as such, it is the limiting of the logic of the symbol by the absurd logic of the individual. This absurd logic of the individual can be best explained in terms of one's own "inner-logic": that which short-circuits the larger formal universal (Symbolic) logic that one is given access to in, through, and by the process of socialization that inscribes him/her in their socio-Symbolic lifeworld. E.g., there's a scene in Richard Price's *Clockers* in which a guy buys six individual beers rather than a six-pack of beer. His reason is such that he desires to drink six beers, and if he were to buy a six-pack, he knows that there are people in the neighborhood who would flock to him and ask him for a beer (should these folks notice that he would have six beers at one moment should he purchase a six-

pack), thus leaving him with only one beer for himself. By buying one beer at a time, however, he is able to enjoy six beers. Thus his logic is different than that of Rocco's, who sees his purchase of six individual beers as absurd. The point here, of course, is that, even though we are taught how to access an "objectively-certain" universal system of logical reasoning ("If you want six beers, go buy a six-pack!"), the elements comprising these conventional sets of logic and reasoning can be, and often are, manipulated by each and every one of us as a means to make use of our own "inner-logic," which serves to satisfy our private desires.

127  Žižek, *For They Know Not What They Do*, pp. 163-4.

128  Recall Hegel's famous line, 'The secret of the Egyptians were a secret for the Egyptians.' This is more than just a sally of wit on Hegel's part. One should tweak this line and read it as: The secret of the Other is a secret for the Other. The key to decoding the message in this rather cryptic line is simple, just formulate it in its opposite: The secret of oneself is a secret for oneself. Imagine someone asking you the following question: "What is *IT* that compels you to do what you do; what is *IT* that defines "who" you "are""? As you attempt to give a direct answer to this question, you'll come to realize that the mystery behind "who" you "are," and why you do what you do, is a "mystery" to some extent, even for you. What is in one's Self is always something more than oneself; viz., that which makes you tick is never fully given; there is always something about being human that remains somewhat elusive, even at the personal level—i.e., the excess over the human in the human itself. Thus the secret of the Other is always-already a secret for the Other, just as well. And yet there is a more radical way to understand this proposition, found in the inversion of its opposite: There is no secret in one's Self; or rather, the real secret is that there is no secret to be discovered. The belief that there

is some "mystery-secret" exists solely to compel one further, to further develop one's sense of Self or knowledge of an Other, and so on. In this sense, the truth of someone, or some*thing*, changes with the changing knowledge. And vice versa.

129 Kojève, *Introduction to the Reading of Hegel*, p. 4.

130 We can liken this to the experience of going to the movies. One sits down and gives oneself over to the big screen and, once the lights go out, once the images appear on the screen, it is no longer us, the viewer, directing our own eyes where to look, it is rather the camera that directs us where to look. We go from being an active subject to a passive subject. We literally silence our voices in exchange for our gazes.

131 And there are also three modalities as such for the other two dimensions of the *ISR* triad (the Imaginary and Symbolic). This idea is borrowed from Žižek's foreword to *For They Know Not What They Do*, p. xii.

132 *Ibid.*

133 *Ibid.*

134 Žižek, *Organs Without Bodies*, p. xii.

135 See both Žižek, *The Parallax View*, p. 41, and, Karl Marx & Friedrich Engels, *Selected Works*, vol. 1, Moscow: Progress Publishers, 1969, p. 95.

136 Perhaps the most concise formulation of the Real is the one given by Zupančič: 'the Real exists as the internal fracture or split of representation, as its intrinsic edge on account of which representation never fully coincides, not simply with its object, but with itself.' This is why objectivity cannot deliver an authentically complete account of the object it purports to represent: *because representation itself ultimately fails*.

137 McGowan, "The Exceptional Darkness of *The Dark Knight*," *Jump Cut: A Review of Contemporary Media*, http://www.eju mpcut.org/archive/jc51.2009/darkKnightKant/

138  Kant, *Religion within the Boundaries of Mere Reason*, in *Religion within the Boundaries of Mere Reason and Other Writings*, trans. and eds. Allen Wood and George di Giovanni, New York: Cambridge University Press, 1998, p. 59.

139  McGowan, "The Exceptional Darkness of *The Dark Knight*."

140  Žižek, *For They Know Not What They Do*, p. xvi.

141  Brian Greene, *The Elegant Universe: Superstrings, Hidden Dimensions, and the Quest for the Ultimate Theory*, New York: Vintage Books, 2003, pp. 109-110. See also: Richard Feynman, *QED: The Strange Theory of Light and Matter*, Princeton: Princeton University Press, 1988.

142  Bruno Bauer, *Kritik der evangelischen Geschichte des Johannes*, Bremen: Carl Schünemann, 1840, p. 178.

143  Of course, last, but not least, there is also the way in which something is objective in the following sense: Let's say that I'm holding a pen in my hand, and that I drop this pen. Let's also assume that I drop this pen in the presence of others, so that everyone who is privy to this event, me dropping the pen, can confirm that the pen has indeed been dropped. We can thus say it is an objective fact that the pen has been dropped. What this means, however, is that objectivity, as such, is *retrospective*. The pen being dropped is an objective fact only *after the pen has been dropped*. Nonetheless, this objective fact has its roots either in a purely subjective act (I may have dropped the pen to prove a point, *this point*), or, by dint of radical contingency (the pen may not have been dropped otherwise, or, the cause behind the effect of the pen-being-dropped could have been something entirely else than what it certainly was.) What it means to say that objectivity is retrospective is that: objectivity, as such, is to be referred to the fact that objectivity is a "frame" that enframes reality itself (while remaining embedded in reality itself!): *Reality becomes appearance*; viz., through objectivity, things in reality *appear to appear*.

144 Žižek, *For They Know Not What They Do*, p. 229.

145 Hegel, *Lectures on the Philosophy of World History. Introduction: Reason in History*, translated by H.B. Nisbet, Cambridge: Cambridge University Press, 1975, p. 147.

146 Vighi, *On Žižek's Dialectics; Surplus, Subtraction, Sublimation*, New York: Continuum, 2010, pp. 148-9.

147 Zupančič, *The Shortest Shadow*, p. 108.

148 Lukács, *History and Class Consciousness*, p. 6.

149 *Ibid.*

150 *Ibid.*, p. 9.

151 Maurice Merleau-Ponty, *Phenomenology of Perception*, New York: Routlegde, 2012, p. lxxviii.

152 In terms of ideology's "inconsistent" shifting, *protean*, nature, is it not the case that today's bourgeois ideology of the twenty first century appears differently than the bourgeois ideology of the nineteenth century, while nonetheless both remaining *bourgeois* ideologies; or that Laissez-Faire capitalism appeared much differently than today's free-market capitalism, while nonetheless both being per se capitalist ideologies?

153 Vighi provides a decent enough example of this innermost antagonism: 'Thought [...] cannot be treated as an independent entity sundered from the inert thing represented by the skull—nor does it merely originate, as claimed by cognitivism, in a series of neurophysiological processes. Rather, it exists *only* in its indivisible correlation with what is radically incompatible with it, namely inert matter. Just like insemination and urine represent a parallax of the same organ, thought can only become actual as a parallax, i.e. through its relation with its thing-like, unknowable materiality.' Vighi, *On Žižek's Dialectics*, p. 102.

154 Hegel, *The Encyclopaedia Logic*, p. 53.

155 *Ibid.*

156 (Even within the signifying chain itself, the Real, in the

guise of the radically ambiguous signifier *"Is,"* cuts through. It's as if, in the chain of the signifiers, "sense" itself *insists* via the word *"Is"*, and that, in the words of Lacan, 'none of its elements *consists* in the signification of which the sense is capable at that particular moment.')

157 William Rothman, *Hitchcock: The Murderous Gaze*, Cambridge, MA: Harvard University Press, 1982, pp. 10-11.

158 The very movement that persists within this intersubjective network is that of drive: *"repetition automatism,"* expressed best by Lacan's formulation: '*the unconscious is the Other's discourse.*' As such, 'the subjects, owing to their displacement, relay each other in the course of the intersubjective repetition ... their displacement is determined by the place that a pure signifier—[the *objet a*] —comes to occupy in their [network].' Lacan, "Seminar on "The Purloined Letter,"" from *Écrits*, p. 10. Is this not what Derrida was perhaps getting at in his essay, "Différance?" Let's play with a short passage from that essay: '[I]n [the subject's] own (action of) negating, it is related immediately to the other and negates itself by itself...' That 'this relationship is [the] present as a different relationship' marks the very differential/deferential movement of drive as it circulates incessantly around the *objet a*.

159 Žižek, *For They Know Not What They Do*, p. 197.

160 Žižek, *The Parallax View*, p. 61.

161 Žižek, *Living in the End Times*, p. 303.

162 Žižek, *For They Know Not What They Do*, p. 106.

163 As regards the *objet a* qua real obstacle, it's important not to commit the same mistake that Marx himself made: 'ignoring how the [Lacanian *objet a* is] a positive condition of what it enframes, so that, by abolishing it, we paradoxically lose the very productivity it was obstructing.' Žižek, *Living in the End Times*, p. 264.

164 *Ibid.*, p. 334.

165 Vighi, *On Žižek's Dialectics*, p. 11.

166 Žižek, *Living in the End Times*, p. 334.

167 Just like the way an interpretation of a literary production is the result of its socio-historical effectuations over time. Like a litmus test, so to speak, its result reflects the very thing it's "dipped" into. That is to say: the effects of science are not so much a reflection of science per se, but rather a reflection of how science is deployed by the very culture that interprets how it "should" be used.

168 Žižek, "Multiculturalism, or, the Cultural Logic of Multinational Capitalism", *New Left Review* I/225, September-October 1997.

169 Zupančič, *Ethics of the Real*, p. 93.

170 Žižek, "Multiculturalism, or, the Cultural Logic of Multinational Capitalism".

171 *Ibid.*

172 *Ibid.*

173 Viz., the radical (empty) subjectivity inherent in any act is precisely the void at the heart of any act, which corresponds to an act's open potentiality: its potential to unfold in an infinite variety of ways over an indefinite period of time.

174 If you didn't know this, now you do: http://www.toward-freedom.com/home/content/view/1352/1

175 Žižek, *Living in the End Times*, p. 58.

176 Jacque Rancière, *Althusser's Lesson*, New York: Continuum, 2011, p. 83.

177 For more on this, see Chris Harman's, *A People's History of the World*, New York: Verso, 2008.

178 R.D. Laing & D.G. Cooper, *Reason and Violence: A Decade of Sartre's Philosophy, 1950-1960*, New York: Vintage Books, 1971, p. 52.

179 Here, recall Claire Denis' film *White Material*, a visceral and potent post-colonial drama about a white French family in an unnamed country in Africa, attempting to save their

coffee plantation from the destructive tumult of a viciously complicated civil war. This film of course represents the conjunction of many currents of discourse, one of those being the critique of globalization as it exists in the appearance of its opposite: that is to say, today's "all-inclusive" global village obfuscates the fact that the world is comprised of a plurality of subjective positions and relations, culminating in one confused knot of objective existence as everybody struggles to make sense of today's dynamic (read, chaotic) global capitalism. The price we end up paying for this "post-colonial" globalized world is a sustained series of contingent irruptions of sectarian violence, which is often the inevitable explosive response to the repression of trauma and the masking of a history of colonial subjugation, perpetuated and compounded by disavowed acts of neo-colonial Western exploitation. It is no wonder, then, that today such arrant subjectivity overlaps with such utter objectivity: the loss of real diversity and subjective plurality is being supplemented by the promotion of more globalization, with the devastating prospect of establishing what humanity "objectively" is.

180 Eagleton, *The Idea of Culture*, Malden, MA: Blackwell Publishers, 2000, p. 96.

181 Žižek, *The Abyss of Freedom / Ages of the World (The Body, in Theory: Histories of Cultural Materialism)*, Ann Arbor: University of Michigan Press, 1997, pp. 50-1.

182 In the second chapter of *How to Read Lacan*, Žižek explains that Symbolic castration occurs when a subject experiences the 'gap between "what I really am" and the symbolic mask that makes the subject into something. The subject is thus castrated from the "real" "I" by projecting something else. "I am what I am through signifiers that represent me, signifiers constitute my Symbolic order."'

183 Hegel, *The Encyclopaedia Logic*, p. 283.

184 *Ibid.* (Though this does resemble quite starkly an Althusser reference, it is, in fact, Hegel's.)

185 Saskia Sassen, *Globalization and its Discontents: Essays on the New Mobility of People and Money*, New York: The New Press, 1998, pp. xxii-iii.

186 Žižek, *For They Know Not What They Do*, pp. 166-7.

187 Žižek, *Living in the End Times*, p. 285.

188 *Ibid.*

189 Jeff Sharlett, *The Family: The Secret Fundamentalism at the Heart of American Power*, New York: HarperCollins, 2008, pp. 133-134.

190 Laing & D.G. Cooper, *Reason and Violence*, p. 11.

191 Žižek, *For They Know Not What They Do*, p. 160.

192 Žižek, *The Fright of Real Tears; Krzysztof Kieslowski; Between Theory and Post-Theory*, London: British Film Institute, 2001, p. 65.

193 Hegel, *Science of Logic*, London: Allen & Unwin, 1969, p. 402.

194 Marshall McLuhan, *Understanding Media: The Extensions of Man*, New York: McGraw Hill, 1965, pp. 7-9.

195 Lewis Mumford, *The Myth of the Machine Vol. II: The Pentagon of Power*, New York: Harcourt Brace Jovanovich, Inc., 1970, p. 346.

196 I of course cannot speak, and therefore am not speaking, for all. I know many writers, journalists, activists and so on, who believe not in preaching to the choir but rather believe in radicalizing the choir. If one's intent is the latter, then all the more power to you.

197 One may scoff at such a proposal, believing they've stumbled upon some irony in between the lines here—that your author is, nonetheless, merely "preaching to the choir," despite admonishing against such a thing. A crucial premise of this book, however, is that philosophy, the very medium through which your author is operating, should be employed as a means to politicize the intellectual class in

such a way that this class be moved to politicize the disavowed of our society. I'm not a journalist. I simply want to intervene, to make philosophy properly political once again, thereby encouraging it to be that intellectual tool that can and should help direct intellectual class struggle to where it should make a real difference.

Contemporary culture has eliminated both the concept of the public and the figure of the intellectual. Former public spaces – both physical and cultural – are now either derelict or colonized by advertising. A cretinous anti-intellectualism presides, cheerled by expensively educated hacks in the pay of multinational corporations who reassure their bored readers that there is no need to rouse themselves from their interpassive stupor. The informal censorship internalized and propagated by the cultural workers of late capitalism generates a banal conformity that the propaganda chiefs of Stalinism could only ever have dreamt of imposing. Zer0 Books knows that another kind of discourse – intellectual without being academic, popular without being populist – is not only possible: it is already flourishing, in the regions beyond the striplit malls of so-called mass media and the neurotically bureaucratic halls of the academy. Zer0 is committed to the idea of publishing as a making public of the intellectual. It is convinced that in the unthinking, blandly consensual culture in which we live, critical and engaged theoretical reflection is more important than ever before.